Praise for *Death in the Rubble*

"In 1949, a nurse named Elisabeth Kusian murdered two people in Berlin she barely knew on no pretext at all, each killing as cold-blooded as it was banal. Kusian's misdeeds, undertaken so lightly, remind the reader of the easy brutality into which German society slipped in the era of the world wars – and how long it lingered into the tense, twilit years of the post-war."

Monica Black, Distinguished Professor in the Humanities, University of Tennessee, Knoxville

"Richard Bodek's new book combines a story of true crime and a police procedural with the brutal narrative of a serial murder carried out by a serial liar inventing her own reality, which is all placed in the context of a divided post-war Berlin in 1949. While police search for clues to put together the identities and stories of two dismembered bodies, the sites of the city still glow with the horrors of the recent but quickly fading past. Richard Bodek puts a lifetime of research and teaching into delivering this vivid and informative book of history."

Peter C. Caldwell, Samuel G. McCann Professor of History, Rice University

"In *Death in the Rubble*, Richard Bodek tells a fascinating story about a ruthless killer in early Cold War Berlin – a city whose people were wrestling all at once with the legacies of Nazism, the destruction and rebirth of their neighbourhoods, and the coming of the Cold War. Bodek has turned up a lot of intriguing new information and presents it with great narrative skill. It's an absorbing read for any lovers of Cold War history or detective stories."

Benjamin Carter Hett, author of *The Death of Democracy: Hitler's Rise to Power and the Downfall of the Weimar Republic*

"Richard Bodek's book provides an atmospheric reconstruction of a politically divided and rubble strewn Berlin, highlighting the precarious lives of many Germans during the foundation of the Federal Republic of Germany and the German Democratic Republic. Using the case of the murderer Elisabeth Kusian, Richard Bodek provides a tangible sense not just of Berlin's growing bureaucratic and Cold War tensions but of the Third Reich's unacknowledged and unresolved legacies. *Death in the Rubble* is a fascinating read for those interested in Germany's twentieth century history."

Heather Wolffram, Associate Professor of Modern European History, University of Canterbury and author of *Forensic Psychology in Germany: Witnessing Crime, 1880–1939*

GERMAN AND EUROPEAN STUDIES

General Editor: James Retallack

DEATH IN THE RUBBLE

The Female Killer Who Stalked Cold War Berlin

Richard Bodek

UNIVERSITY OF TORONTO PRESS
Toronto Buffalo London

Toronto Buffalo London
utppublishing.com
Printed in the USA

ISBN 978-1-4875-5291-6 (paper)
ISBN 978-1-4875-5294-7 (EPUB)
ISBN 978-1-4875-5292-3 (PDF)

German and European Studies

Library and Archives Canada Cataloguing in Publication

Title: Death in the rubble : the female killer who stalked Cold War Berlin / Richard Bodek.
Names: Bodek, Richard, 1961–, author.
Series: German and European studies.
Description: Series statement: German and European studies | Includes bibliographical references and index.
Identifiers: Canadiana (print) 20250250330 | Canadiana (ebook) 20250250357 | ISBN 9781487552916 (paper) | ISBN 9781487552947 (EPUB) | ISBN 9781487552923 (PDF)
Subjects: LCSH: Kusian, Elisabeth. | LCSH: Women murderers – Germany – Berlin. | LCSH: Murderers – Germany – Berlin. | LCSH: Murder – Germany – Berlin – Case studies. | LCSH: Murder – Investigation – Germany – Berlin – Case studies. | LCGFT: Case studies.
Classification: LCC HV6535.G33 B47 2025 | DDC 364.152/30943155 – dc23

Cover design: Alexa Love
Cover image: Ruins of the Brandenburg Gate, Berlin, 23 March 1950. Photo by Kümpfel. Bundesarchiv, Bild 183-S94818. Alterations by Alexa Love.

The German and European Studies series is funded by the DAAD with funds from the German Federal Foreign Office.

Deutscher Akademischer Austauschdienst
German Academic Exchange Service

We wish to acknowledge the land on which the University of Toronto Press operates. This land is the traditional territory of the Wendat, the Anishnaabeg, the Haudenosaunee, the Métis, and the Mississaugas of the Credit First Nation.

University of Toronto Press acknowledges the financial support of the Government of Canada, the Canada Council for the Arts, and the Ontario Arts Council, an agency of the Government of Ontario, for its publishing activities.

Canada Council for the Arts
Conseil des Arts du Canada

Funded by the Government of Canada
Financé par le gouvernement du Canada

For the four people who made me a scholar

Vernon Lidtke
Katherine Verdery
William Arrowsmith
Michael Geyer

Contents

Maps and Illustrations

Maps

Illustrations

Acknowledgments

One of the great delights of writing a late-career book is the opportunity to thank some of those who have helped sharpen my thoughts and ideas over the years if not decades. *Death in the Rubble* is the product of the institutions, readers, and friends who made it possible. The institutions to which I am unendingly grateful are the College of Charleston, Roehampton University, and the Fulbright Foundation, all of which provided intellectual and financial support. Archivists at the National Archives in London, the Landesarchiv Berlin, and Berlin's Polizeihistorische Sammlung were unendingly helpful. Indeed, the Polizeihistorische Sammlung kindly gave permission for all of the images in this book. My colleague Jason Coy believed that my germ of an idea about violent crime in post-war Germany was worthy of a book. Joe Kelly, my best and most critical reader, is responsible for the book's readability and cogency. Scott Peeples was always game to talk about crime, punishment, and the Gothic. Other College of Charleston friends and colleagues who made a significant impact on this through discussions and by giving sage advice over coffee, as well as by their generous patience, include Lisa Covert, John Cropper, Irina Gigova, Tammy Ingram (fellow historian of murder), Phyllis Jestice, Simon Lewis, and Jacob Steere-Williams. Suzanne Austin and Gibbs Knotts cut through the red tape that let me spend an off-schedule sabbatical/Fulbright year in London for research and writing.

Carie Thomas, the History Department's administrative coordinator and the real brains of the operation, has been indefatigable.

Without her, this book would still be a collection of notes. I'm grateful to her for all the time she took to discuss ideas, organization, and more. Brandon Lewter, Regan Wacker, and Asia Williams of the College of Charleston's Interlibrary Loan Department found sources that I never expected to make their way to Charleston.

Historian and Germanist friends around the country contributed to this book through discussions and by writing their own brilliant works that helped me think through questions. I'm especially grateful to Irit Bloch, Kevin Boyle, Joel Harrington, Todd Herzog, Benjamin Hett, Helmut Smith, and the always kind, always sceptical Elizabeth Wood.

I'm very grateful to Bettine Rau, whose research assistance was invaluable in Berlin. At London's Roehampton University (where I spent one of the most magical years of my career as a Fulbright Scholar), Sebastian Gehrig, Fiona McHardy, Katharina Rowold, Caroline Sharples, Andrew Wareham, and Zbigniew Wojnowski were wonderful colleagues, readers, critics, co-teachers, and beer and coffee companions. Martin Conway and Nick Stargardt of Oxford University's Modern European History Seminar were terrific hosts, and they, along with the audience, gave me both ideas and criticism that made this book far better than it could have been.

Stephen Shapiro, my editor at the University of Toronto Press, was always supportive and curious. His faith and trust meant the world to me.

In my non-academic life, Jessica Hull-Dambaugh (flute teacher extraordinaire) reminded me, even as I was mired in thoughts of murder and violence in a city and era that no longer exists, that the world can be a musical place. Jonathan Donaldson (physician and raconteur) has managed to keep my body going.

Ben and Zachary Bodek provided a welcome distraction from my first book by reminding me of the importance of playing on the floor with blocks and kicking balls in the backyard. For this book, they served as mature and sophisticated sounding boards. Time flies. I love you both.

Berlin Police Ranks

East Berlin – Officers:

Generalinspekteur	Inspector General
Chefinspekteur	Chief Inspector
Inspekteur	Inspector
Kommandeur	Commander
Oberrat	Senior Councillor
Polizeirat	Police Councillor
Kriminalpolizeirat	Criminal Police Councillor
Hauptkommissar	Head Commissar
Oberkommissar	Senior Commissar
Kommissar	Commissar
Unterkommissar	Junior Commissar
Offiziersschüler	Student Officer

East Berlin – Other Ranks:

Obermeister der VP	Senior Master of the VP
Meister der VP	Master of the VP
Hauptwachtmeister der VP	Head Watch Master of the VP
Oberwachtmeister der VP	Senior Watch Master of the VP
Wachtmeister der VP	Watch Master of the VP
Unterwachtmeister der VP	Junior Watch Master of the VP
Anwärter der VP	Candidate of the VP

(Ranks that do not appear in the text are also included here.)

Adapted from "Volkspolizei," Wikipedia, accessed 5 May 2025, https://en.wikipedia.org/wiki/Volkspolizei.

West Berlin – Detective Ranks:

Oberregierungsrat	Assistant Commissioner
Regierungsrat	Government Councillor
Kriminaldirektor	Police Director
Kriminalpolizeirat	Police Councillor
Kriminal-Oberkommissar	Chief Inspector
Kriminalkommissar	Detective Inspector
Kriminal-Bezirkssekretär	Detective Sergeant
Kriminal-Sekretär	Detective
Kriminal-Assistant	Assistant Detective
Kriminal-Anwart	Candidate

Adapted and modified from Liang, *The Berlin Police Force in the Weimar Republic*, xvii–xviii.

Below are the plain-clothed detectives mentioned most often in the book.

West Berlin (in descending order of rank):
Kriminalkommissar Griebsch
Kriminalkommissar Menzel
Kriminalkommissar Schulz
Kriminal-Sekretär Blüme
Kriminal-Sekretär Meiser
Kriminal-Sekretär Oehmke
Kriminal-Sekretär Repenning
Kriminal-Sekretär Wetzel
Kriminal-Assistant Sonntag
Kriminal-Assistant Weisheit
Kriminal-Assistant Zimmermann
Kriminal-Anwart Reichmuth

East Berlin Detectives (in descending order of rank):
VP Kommandeur Rockstroh
VP Polizeirat Pohl
VP Kriminalpolizeirat Schwarz
VP Oberkommissar Plath

VP Kommissar Beutter
VP Kommissar Steffen
VP Hauptwachtmeister Böhlandorf
VP Hauptwachtmeister Rudat
VP Hauptwachtmeister Schiller
VP Hauptwachtmeister Schwalbe
VP Hauptwachtmeister Wriedt
VP Hauptwachtmeister Syllwasschy
VP Wachtmeister Baudasch
VP Wachtmeister Lippert
VP Wachtmeister Rakitovsky

(VP added to clarify that they are officers of the Volkspolizei.)

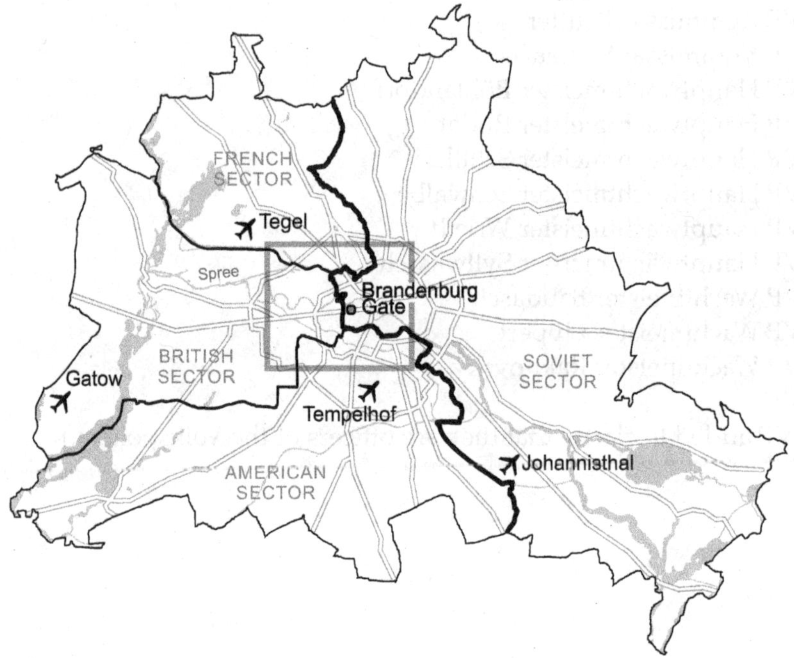

Map 1. Occupied Berlin.

Source: Map by Erin Greb.

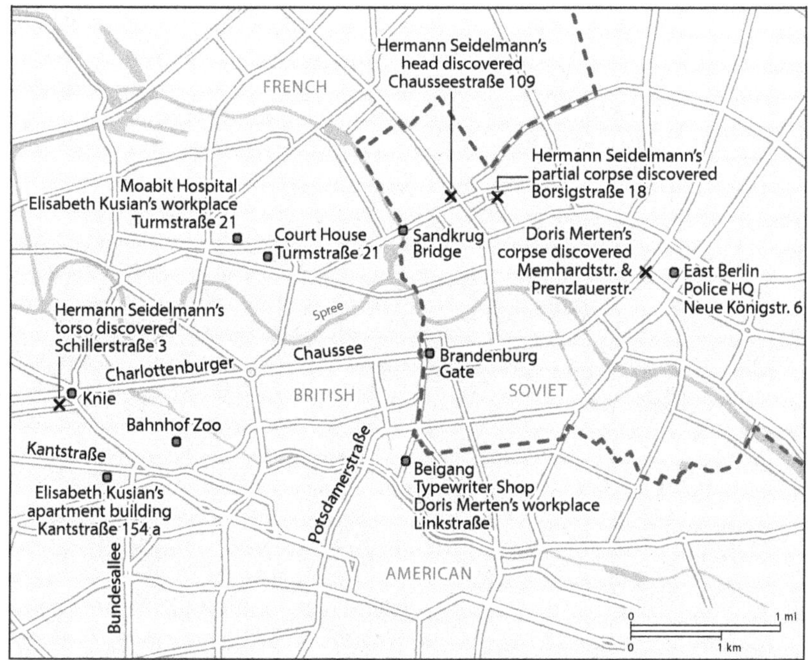

Map 2. Elisabeth Kusian's Area of Activities.

Source: Map by Erin Greb.

Prologue

3 December 1949

Surely things were improving – or at least changing. Braving the mixed rain and snow as he stepped off the tram and headed towards the Charlottenburg district's Kantstraße 154a, Hermann Seidelmann, Communist and one-time victim of the Nazis, may have reflected on the state of his world and looked forward to visiting a warm, intact, inviting apartment.[1] Grey, cold, and cloudy West Berlin looked forward to Christmas and a new decade; the worst seemed to be over. The Berlin Blockade, which started in June 1948 and dragged on for almost a year, was now a memory. And what a memory it was, for Berliners, certainly, but for Germans as a whole. Would the capitalist powers respond? If so, how? Perhaps they would retreat and leave the city unified under Soviet domination. Maybe they would react with a violent confrontation. Instead, the United States and the United Kingdom began a series of round-the-clock flights of American C-54s and British Dakotas. At its peak, one plane per minute took off and landed twenty-four hours a day, seven days a week. Even for a committed Communist such as Hermann Seidelmann, some misgivings had to arise. The West had shown remarkable restraint and cool technological efficiency. But no matter. The episode was over. Peace and stability seemed to be assured.[2]

Better things were in the offing. East Berlin's Soviet War Memorial in Treptow Park had opened six months earlier. This triumphal memorial commemorated the end of the worst chapter in the city's history.[3] Renaming East Berlin's historic Frankfurter Allee "Stalinallee," still two weeks away, would reinforce the Soviet role in the future of the city.

For the time being, though, a more stable Germany, or, to be more accurate, German situation, seemed to be emerging. The Federal Republic of Germany and the German Democratic Republic (GDR) had been founded the previous summer and fall. Perhaps these new countries would bring some stability to a world increasingly coming to grips with George Orwell's aptly named "Cold War."[4] Other encouraging signs boded well. Both halves of the now-divided city celebrated Johann Wolfgang von Goethe's 200th birthday in August. Comedies and crime films played to large crowds in the movie theatres, perhaps taking people's minds off the ever-present rubble still dominating the city's landscape. Although the black market still existed, it was less central to the economy than it was before dual currency reforms replaced the old Reichsmark with the West Mark and later the East Mark. This reform happened, as Friedrich Lutz observed, because trustworthy currency was much more efficient than the very inefficient exchange of goods for goods. "Every firm had several specialists, called 'compensators,' on its staff. If, for example, cardboard for packing was needed, the compensator might be obliged to barter the plant's own products for typewriters, the typewriters for shoes, and the shoes for cardboard. All this was not only illegal but involved tremendous costs. In one case known to the present writer, five long trips by a compensator were required to obtain a case of special varnish, whereas formerly a postcard dropped into the post box would have been sufficient."[5]

Hermann Seidelmann had these or similar skills. Even with the black market's fading into the background, he was able to scuffle, to make a living. Life was always challenging and demanded Germans develop new abilities and attitudes, but the coming year promised to be better than the last few had been.

Amid this change, Hermann Seidelmann had taken the streetcar to Charlottenburg that evening to meet with Elisabeth Kusian, a well-liked nurse who worked on Robert Koch Hospital's gynaecology ward. The two first met at about 2:30 p.m. that afternoon in the Bahnhof Zoo (the Zoo Train Station), where Seidelmann operated as an unofficial currency trader. He exchanged a few of Kusian's West Marks for 150 East Marks.[6] Kusian seemed happy with the trade, told him she had additional cash at home, and invited him to her room to trade more. Seidelmann readily agreed, jotted down her address, and promised to visit at the latest at 8:00 p.m.[7]

Charlottenburg carried more than a few connotations for Berliners and other Germans. The district's prehistory traces to 1695 when Friedrich III of Prussia started the construction of Charlottenburg Castle. It would be the summer residence of his wife, Sophie Charlotte.[8] Charlottenburg itself was founded in 1705. Its residents were to enjoy a range of privileges, including exemption from the need to quarter soldiers. Frederick the Great made the town his "Residenz" in 1740, but after a few years, he found Potsdam more to his liking.[9] It soon became one of Berlin's most prosperous districts and home to many of the city's better-off Jewish citizens. More Jewish students, dentists, journalists, engineers, professors, and artists were there than in "old Berlin," even though Charlottenburg's Jewish population was 30,553 and "old Berlin's" was over 87,000.[10] Possibly giving Seidelmann pause was the knowledge that, during the now-long-dead Weimar Republic, Charlottenburg had been home to the Nazi SA's Sturm 33, one of the city's most violent troops, established in 1928. The Communist newspaper *Welt am Abend* had called it a Storm of Murderers, and 90 per cent of its members lived in the district. Might some of them still be there? They were known for their hatred of Communists, as well as of Jews and the "effeminate" bourgeois elites.[11] This is not surprising for a district known for its wildly varied populace. Everybody from the wealthiest, chicest Berliners to some of its poorest workers lived there.[12] Indeed, Charlottenburg was home both to Siemens and fashionable shopping.[13]

One, however, could only dwell on the past for so long. The present of 1949 was quite different. At the war's end, Charlottenburg evaded much of the destruction of the rest of the city. Street vendors plied their wares for passersby – sometimes shielded from the elements by colourful umbrellas, sometimes open to the elements.[14] To the naked eye, its city hall and Academy of the Arts appeared to be unscathed. Admittedly, though, the Knie Corner and the Kaiser Wilhelm Memorial Church were bombed-out wrecks. The church still has the same, eerie, bombed-out look eighty years later.[15]

Who indeed was Hermann Seidelmann? He was a survivor, one of many who operated on the black market and the legitimate economy's margins, developing the business acumen and skills necessary to live and maybe even thrive. Recent German history shaped Seidelmann's life. It certainly dictated some of his choices in this unsettled post-war era. Seidelmann was an itinerant trader in Silesia before the Second World War.[16] By its end, he was one of the millions of Germans expelled from Silesia when it was transferred to the newly reconstituted Poland. Surely he felt the minus 20 degree Celsius temperatures, heard the cries of children, saw families who had to abandon everything but hand luggage. As he walked west, he had to pass with some kind of contemplation the piles of belongings abandoned in the trek: "sewing machines, barrels of cured meat, radios, comforters, boxes of valuable porcelain and family silver."[17] Perhaps this vision of accumulated, and abandoned, possessions inspired him to continue his life as a trader when he finally washed up in the town of Plauen in Thuringia's Flöhe region in what would become the German Democratic Republic, aka East Germany.[18]

Plauen is the kind of town where somebody like Hermann Seidelmann would end up. It both had potential and a need for somebody with his skills. In the years before the Second World War, the economy of this city of about 100,000 centred on the production of nylon and printing presses. The industry, though, shifted to military production in the years leading up to 1939.[19] Its 1933 Jewish population of 519 shrank to 116 in 1939. Few survived the camps. Of those who did, 15 returned to the region. One of these, Manfred Herzfeld, took over the leadership of the Betreuungsstelle für Opfer des Faschismus.[20] Perhaps the two men knew one another.

Like so many manufacturing towns, Plauen suffered a great deal of war damage. In September 1944, the Eighth US Army Air Force bombed the city because it was a centre of production for Panzer IV tanks. In April 1945, in an attempt to "dehouse" its inhabitants, the Royal Air Force dropped 248 two-ton bombs on Plauen.[21] Indeed, throughout the war, somewhere between 45,000 to 50,000 bombs were dropped on the town, killing more than 2,300 inhabitants. Four of every five houses were damaged or destroyed, and the population at the war's end had dropped to just under 81,000.[22]

There was much recovery work to do: 1.8 million cubic metres of rubble (about 15 to 20 cubic metres per inhabitant) would need to be cleared. The black market flourished. Materials and tools of all sorts were needed to rebuild.[23]. Hermann Seidelmann was the right man in the right place.

Hermann Seidelmann used his trading skills to start a new venture: he took orders for metal goods from the local, rural population; found them in Berlin; and shipped them back. He had travelled to the former Reich capital five to six times that year alone, both for business and pleasure. Indeed, his wife, Gertrud, recalled a Berlin motorcycle trip they took.[24] Like so many others, Seidelmann did this and that to keep afloat in the turbulent post-fascist moment. The Reich had collapsed; stabilizing the two Germanies under Allied occupation was just beginning.

It is possible that, for Hermann Seidelmann, the expulsion from the East took on a gravity that outweighed the horrors committed by the Third Reich. It certainly did for many if not most Germans.[25] For him, though, that is unlikely. In this post-war moment, Hermann Seidelmann was politically active, belonging to the VVN (Vereinigung der Verfolgten des Naziregimes or Association of

Figure 0.1. Elisabeth Kusian lived in Kantstraße 154a. The arrow shows her room's two windows.

the Persecuted of the Nazi Regime) and the SED (Sozialistische Einheitspartei Deutschlands or Socialist Unity Party of Germany). The former was an organization of the Third Reich's political, "racial," and religious opponents.[26] In its early years, it was committed to working in both East and West and being "above" party strife.[27] That would not last. The latter was the ruling party of the GDR, essentially a reconstituted German Communist Party.[28] The trip that ultimately led him to Kusian's door differed from the others that had brought him to Berlin. It was neither political nor economic. He was in Berlin for his mother's funeral. At some point, he decided to remain for a while, stay at his brother's flat, and earn some money before returning to Flöhe. Unfortunately, locating goods for his customers went slowly. Perhaps because Seidelmann had made no business purchases by 3 December, he saw Kusian's invitation as a lucky turn that would result in a quick, easy profit.

After alighting from the tram, Hermann Seidelmann confronted Elisabeth Kusian's bourgeois apartment building, which, like the district surrounding it, survived the war relatively unscathed, except for the façade's few bullet-inflicted pockmarks. The building's ground-floor shops sold tobacco, fruit, and vegetables. A Berliner Kindl pub welcomed passersby who might want a beer or a bite to eat. Like many other structures in this former capital, this residence's façade both hid and revealed its past.

Eleven years earlier, on Kristallnacht, residents saw the Fasanenstraße Synagogue going up in flames, heard its windows shatter. This was the synagogue to which, for its 1912 construction, Kaiser Wilhelm had donated glazed tiles from the royal factory.[29] Joseph Goebbels, Nazi minister of propaganda, had specifically called for its destruction.[30] Certainly its destruction left an impression with other witnesses. According to Ernst Günther Fontheim, "the place of worship was one of the most beautiful synagogues that I had ever seen, both from the outside and the inside." As Fontheim took the S-Bahn home from school, he looked out the window: "Between the Zoo and Savignyplatz stations, I could see the synagogue on Fasanenstraße, right next to the S-Bahn overpass … As the train passed the synagogue, I could see a cloud of smoke rising like a column from the central dome – the synagogue had three domes … At the next stop I leapt from the train and ran back as fast as I could to see what was happening. On a pavement opposite the synagogue there was a crowd of people being held back by the police. There was a lot of anti-Semitic … shouting. I stood there in the middle, oblivious to the danger, completely hypnotized by the sight of the burning synagogue – that was all I could think about."[31] When Isaac Behar, a former resident of the building that Seidelmann was visiting, thought of that day, his memories were similar. "I went to the window. Opposite, on Fasanenstraße, not fifty yards away, a huge fire raged. The synagogue burned! My eyes fell on the entrance to the mighty house of God, whose domes now drowned in flames. I could not believe my eyes: SA men ran again into the synagogue and came out with stacks of prayer books, the parochet, the curtain of the Torah shrine, some Torah scrolls, and bundles of prayer shawls. They threw everything into a pile, then ran in again. What was that? The SA rescued our Jewish ritual objects?" To his horror, Behar realized that the Stormtroopers only "rescued" the ritual objects to make it easier for them to pile up and burn.[32]

During happier times, Kurt Tucholsky, famed Weimar political satirist, dubbed the building "the patriotic synagogue."[33] Living in exile in 1935, Tucholsky would commit suicide out of horror of the world that the Nazis had built. His tragic obituary stated for the record: "The general depression embittered his last years as he saw his worst fears realized. In letters to friends he often returned to the idea of suicide, and his few intimate friends knew that he always carried poison."[34]

Four years later, in the middle of the night, neighbours might have heard Gestapo agents round up one of the building's families, the Turkish-Jewish Behars, the family of Isaac quoted above, to send them to Auschwitz on 13 or 14 December 1942. Isaac was the only survivor, going underground in Berlin for the duration of the regime.[35] Now Berlin's Jewish community, whose future looked so bright a generation earlier, was gone, murdered.

Elisabeth Kusian had not yet moved into the building, but at least some of her neighbours would remember. Kusian, who was elsewhere in Berlin, surely knew of other deportations to concentration camps. Perhaps it is fitting that the stay in Kantstraße 154a of Elisabeth Kusian, the building's most notorious resident, is forgotten, but a stumbling stone remains to memorialize the Behars.

Upon entering the building, Hermann Seidelmann climbed the stairs to the fifth floor and saw its aura of middle-class respectability, admittedly somewhat down on its heels. This former one-family apartment was now divided between tenants and subtenants. To reach Kusian's room, Seidelmann walked 9 metres along a carpet runner, passing lamps and doilies perched on the dark, heavy furniture that, when added to the other accoutrements, bespoke solidity. Nevertheless, such stuff harkened to an era seemingly gone forever, with its placement in the shared hallway reminding visitors and tenants of a much more uncertain and certainly poorer present.

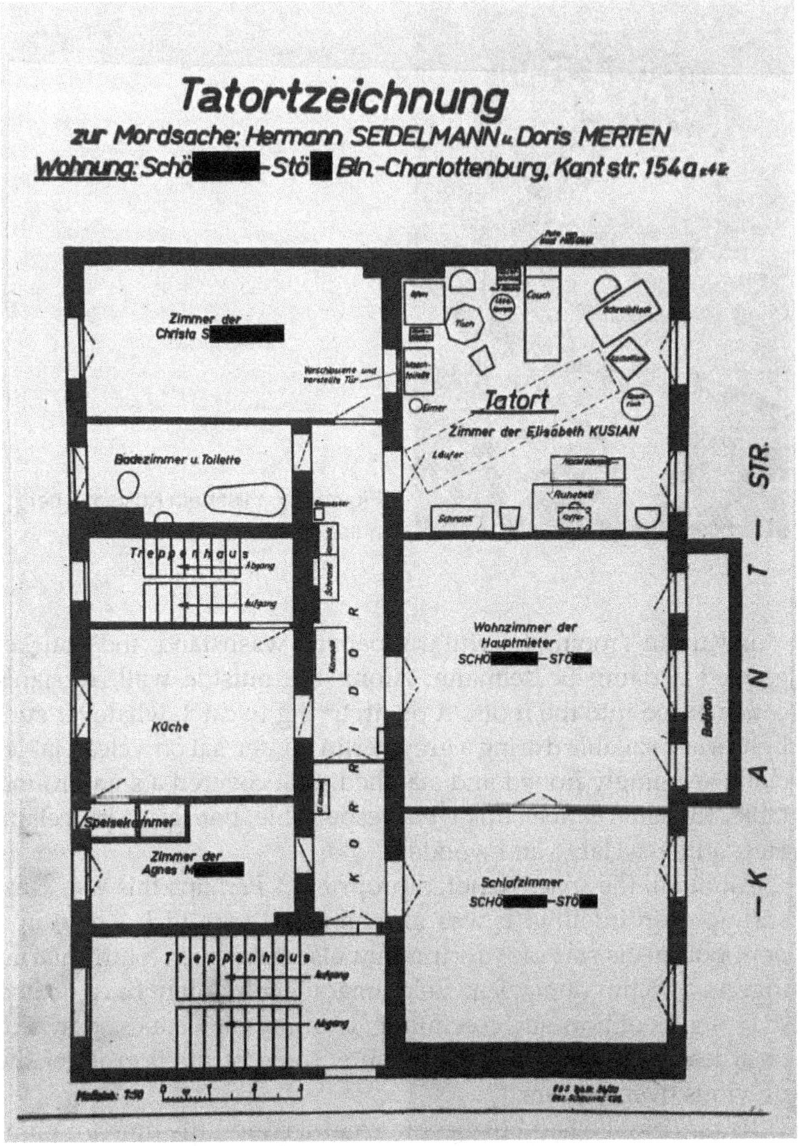

Tatortzeichnung

zur Mordsache: Hermann SEIDELMANN u. Doris MERTEN

Wohnung: Schö■-Stö■ Bln.-Charlottenburg, Kant str. 154a

Zimmer der Christa S■

Badezimmer u. Toilette

Treppenhaus

Küche

Speisekammer

Zimmer der Agnes M■

Treppenhaus

Tatort

Zimmer der Elisabeth KUSIAN

Wohnzimmer der Hauptmieter SCHÖ■-STÖ■

Balkon

Schlafzimmer SCHÖ■-STÖ■

KORRIDOR

KANT - STR.

Figure 0.2. Police schematic of the apartment building floor on which Elisabeth Kusian lived. The right rear details her room and the placement of all of her furniture.

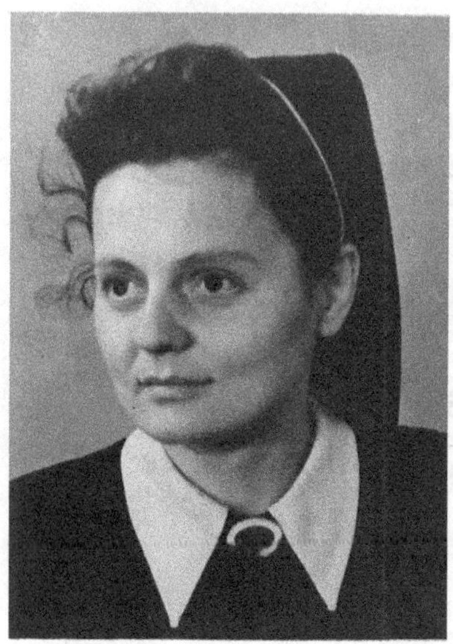

Figure 0.3. Elisabeth Kusian in her nurse's uniform.

In Kusian's room, cheerful wallpaper, a washstand, and a bucket greeted a damp Seidelmann. Along the outside wall, Kusian's couch jutted into the room. A plant, trying to catch whatever sunlight was available during a grey Berlin winter, sat on a clean tablecloth, seemingly ironed and starched, that covered a small round table. Kusian's coffee cups were respectable, bourgeois porcelain. Her radio was large and wooden.

All in all, the space denoted propriety.[36] Perhaps this was reassuring, even inviting. It was undoubtedly gemütlich (cozy) in a petit-bourgeois sort of way. It might also have been a little alarming. As a victim of Nazism, Seidelmann's mind may have drifted to thoughts of how such seemingly comfortable venues spawned, or at least accepted with equanimity, some of the horrors of the previous twenty years.

Regardless, he had business to conduct and little time for painful memories. Elisabeth Kusian greeted him at the door, wearing the traditional German nursing uniform that closely resembled a nun's habit. Nurses in Germany had a reputation for caring, sympathy, and honesty.

Hermann Seidelmann did not know that on 26 October, fewer than two months earlier, Kusian had resigned from her position at the Robert Koch Hospital, effective 31 December. Although she would try to withdraw the resignation on 28 December, just a few weeks after Seidelmann's visit, her immediate supervisor would have no interest in Kusian remaining longer than necessary.[37] The matron suspected Kusian of involvement in illegal abortions.[38] Though she could not prove this crime, she knew Kusian was a liar. How she resented having to handle patient complaints about Sister Elisabeth's borrowing money that she never repaid. What a damage to the profession's reputation.[39] Elisabeth Kusian understood that her finances would be in poor shape very soon and was cagey enough to use nursing's reputation for solidity to her advantage.[40]

Did Hermann Seidelmann think that "Sister Elisabeth" just finished a shift and had no time to change into "civilian" clothes? Regardless of any rush she might have felt, Kusian was the model of hospitality. After helping him with his coat and hat, she made coffee for them both, coffee to which she denied adding Dolantin or Phanodorm, sleeping pills she had in her room.[41] Seidelmann's visit lasted two hours or more, a surprisingly long time, although Kusian later stridently insisted that the two of them had no sex.[42] Having concluded their business, Seidelmann asked permission to look at some of Kusian's illustrated magazines because, as he told her, the GDR had none. While he sat on her couch paging through one or another periodical, wholly absorbed in the pictures, Kusian opened her vanity, removed a clothesline, formed it into a noose, dropped it over his head, and drew it tight about his throat. In seconds he lost consciousness; Kusian moved to her armchair to watch him die.[43]

Elisabeth Kusian's state of mind during the killing is a mystery. Her radio was tuned to the station RIAS – the radio in the American sector – and played "beautiful music" in the background, quieting any frightful sounds that might waft from her room.[44] The year had its fair share of hits, any one of which could have been playing. Rita Paul's popular big-band swing tune "Barbara, Barbara, komm' fahr mit mir nach Afrika" would allow her some respite.

Figure 0.4. Elisabeth Kusian's room as it would appear from the window. In the foreground is the couch on which Hermann Seidelmann was killed. In the background is the vanity in which she stored her clothesline.

The lyrics painted a picture of the new world that American culture promised to usher in when the present moment – no longer Nazi, not yet democratic or Soviet – had passed. At the least, this song reminded listeners of the world beyond the bombed-out, impoverished, occupied Germany surrounding them, a Germany so different from what Berliners imagined only a few years earlier. Perhaps Jupp Schmitz's "Wer soll das bezahlen?" was on. Ironically appropriate for Winter 1949, its lyrics told of a husband's lament that the year's currency reform left no money for the things he wanted for and from his wife.[45]

Elisabeth Kusian might have been thinking about nothing at all; that evening, a potent drug cocktail coursed through her system. She had injected her thigh with 4 cc of morphine before the trader's arrival.[46] When Hermann Seidelmann remarked that she seemed tired, she topped off this opiate with the once-popular German methamphetamine, Pervitin.[47] The stimulant would undoubtedly aid the tasks she had planned for the rest of the night.

What happened next is murky. Kusian was either stunned by the enormity of her actions, trying to contemplate what she had just done, or acted the cold-blooded killer and con artist looking to move on as quickly and efficiently as possible. The second seems more likely. Throughout her adult life, Kusian manipulated others into doing and providing what she wanted as she conned and robbed family, friends, co-workers, institutions, and patients. Ultimately, she murdered strangers in hopes of living her dream life.

Perhaps, as she confessed to the West Berlin police after murdering Hermann Seidelmann, Kusian sat in her desk chair until 3:00 a.m., lost in thought, understanding the need to prepare the body for disposal while too horror-stricken to look at the man's identification book. It was too awful to learn anything about whom she had killed.[48] Her interrogator, Kriminalkommissar Menzel, rejected this idea. He believed that she robbed the still-warm body of 200 DM and 135 DM East, took the coin purse Seidelmann kept in his pocket, covered him with a blanket, then immediately took the #2 streetcar to visit her friend and former neighbour, Anni Glißmann, from whom she hoped to borrow a suitcase to transport Hermann Seidelmann's corpse. Glißmann, a thirty-five-year-old housewife and mother, lived at Turmstraße 39, the same building where Kusian had sublet a room until the previous June. The friends visited each other often. Elisabeth Kusian was comfortable asking Glißmann for help with small business dealings, like borrowing money, dealing with the families of former lovers, and pawning some of Kusian's things for her. Glißmann always seemed eager to do favours for Kusian. She most likely received some of the profits from Kusian's various dealings. Perhaps Kusian's personality made her requests irresistible.

When Anni Glißmann regretted not having a suitcase to lend, the pair went to one of her neighbours who did and who loaned it to them.[49] Kusian then asked Glißmann to deliver 50 DM to a creditor while she, Kusian, babysat Glißmann's children.[50] In short, Sister Elisabeth showed neither regret nor horror, merely the desire to get on with her self-assigned task and use others to make it possible.

Suitcase in hand, Elisabeth Kusian rode the streetcar back to her building at about 11:30 p.m.[51] She must have understood the enormity of her actions. She later claimed that she did not have the stomach to return to her apartment house and needed to walk up and down the street to steel her courage. Kusian had seen many bodies before, whole and shattered. She had tended the wounded and viewed the dead in the final Battle of Berlin. That horror – those visions – was scarring, indeed life-changing. What were Elisabeth Kusian's experiences during the Battle? They are impossible to recover but were undoubtedly awful. By 1945, British and American bombers had dropped more than 68,000 bombs on the city.[52] The urban fighting was street to street – often floor to floor. Avenues were littered with bodies, many of them German soldiers executed by SS and Field Police units for abandoning their posts or for desertion.[53] As a nurse walking Berlin's thoroughfares, helping whomever she could, she surely saw some if not many such sights. Estimates are that Soviet soldiers raped between 95,000 and 130,000 German women. Approximately 22,000 civilians were killed or went missing.[54] Gerda Drews, another young woman trapped in the city, lived through the same nightmare that surrounded Elisabeth:

> There was no escape. I prefer not to talk about what happened when the Russians arrived at our house and discovered us, because it is too painful.
>
> The front-line Russian troops who did the fighting – as a woman, you didn't have to be afraid of them. They shot every man they saw, even old men and young boys, but they left the women alone.
>
> It was the ones who came afterwards, the second echelon, who were the worst. They did all the raping and plundering. They went through all the houses and took whatever they wanted. They stripped homes of every single possession, right down to the toilets.[55]

We cannot know whether this was Elisabeth's fate. We can be sure that she knew of it. For her, though, 1949's moment was worse.

Kusian had murdered a man in cold blood. Could she return to her room? Ultimately, she knew she had no choice but to climb the stairs and walk down the hallway to the nightmare that awaited her, the nightmare she herself had caused. She crossed the threshold, turned on the light, set down the suitcase, removed her coat, and saw Hermann Seidelmann lying there, covered by the blanket she had laid upon him.[56] First, she grabbed a hypodermic to inject herself with a pair of 1 cc morphine ampules that she had on hand. Shooting up helped with the next task.[57] In her most professional manner, she adjusted Seidelmann's corpse to create room to work. Kusian then went to the floor's shared bathroom to fill a bucket with water for any mess she might make. Disrobing Seidelmann was not too tricky. Rigor mortis had not yet set in. After removing his wristwatch, Kusian realized that her knife was too dull for the task ahead.[58] In the shared kitchen was her landlady's much sharper kitchen knife. It paired nicely with a scalpel stolen from the hospital.

The scalpel loosened the joints while the kitchen knife made deeper, dismembering cuts possible. Blood streamed, but the washbasin caught it. Kusian removed Seidelmann's arms to lay them flat on a hefty rag. She repeated this procedure with his legs because they would have to be removed from the torso to fit into the newly borrowed suitcase as well as into the rucksacks she had borrowed earlier. The nurse would butcher most professionally that night, rinsing her ever-bloodier rag in the bucket. As the water reddened, she hauled the bucket to the toilet, flushing its contents into the sewer system. Surprisingly, despite the number of trips it demanded, nobody in the building heard the noise she must have made. Kusian finished her final gruesome task by removing Hermann Seidelmann's head from his trunk.[59]

Elisabeth Kusian then focused on her next step. After tossing her clothesline and Hermann Seidelmann's coin purse into the stove for later incineration, she wrapped Seidelmann's limbs in newspaper and his torso in a blanket. The wrapping was supposed to prevent their leaking blood into the borrowed bags. Kusian then carried them to the door, mopped the floor as best she could, cleaned up the bits of flesh that remained, and flushed the contents of the bloody bucket down the toilet. Her cleaning complete, Kusian turned her attention to Seidelmann's clothing. After some thought, she decided to keep it in her room to deal with later.[60]

Domestic chores complete, Elisabeth Kusian thought about catching a streetcar for the next round of tasks. Would Pervitin give her the energy she needed? Maybe, but as she reached for her box, her nerves made her spill its contents onto the floor. She glanced at the clock as she picked the pills off the floor. It was 3:15 a.m.[61] Now, with both morphine and Pervitin in her system, she heard a streetcar's clanking. She quickly dressed, grabbed a rucksack and suitcase (with their contents of extremities and head), stepped out, and locked the door. She was fortunate not to meet any neighbours as she strode towards the Zoo Station.

Elisabeth Kusian bought a ticket with little thought to its direction. As the first train departed towards the Lehrter Station and Friedrichstraße, so did she. It determined her direction. While riding the train, she remembered that the area around the Friedrichstraße Station, an area she did not know particularly well, was still littered with rubble. Her next decision practically made itself.[62]

With no particular disposal destination in mind, Elisabeth Kusian ambled along Friedrichstraße, then across the Weidendammer Bridge towards Stettiner Station. Perhaps a likely site would suggest itself. The combination of uncertainty and the scurrying pedestrians must have played on her nerves. The fear of looking furtive and suspicious prevented her from entering some otherwise promising-looking places. Finally, as she crossed the Invalidenstraße, she stumbled upon a suitable location, a house entrance surrounded by debris leading into a courtyard. After Kusian entered along an already cleared path, she walked across rubble and stones into a ruined room hidden from view. She put down the suitcase, took off the rucksack, and dumped their contents without ceremony. Quickly gathering her bags, she returned to Invalidenstraße and boarded a streetcar for home. The next trip took her to a ruin at Chausseestraße 109, where she walked into the building's side wing, found a room, dumped Seidelmann's gruesome remains, and departed as she had come.[63]

Figure 0.5. Chausseestraße 109. Arrow #1 indicates where the police entered the building. Arrow #2 indicates where Hermann Seidelmann's partial remains were found.

For her final journey, Nurse Elisabeth took the torso, packed in a rucksack, and walked along Kantstraße towards Knie. She was familiar with this area near the Robert Koch Hospital. Finding yet another ruin, she descended into a basement, removed the torso from the bag, and laid it on a cement slab. She then repacked the blanket in which the torso had been wrapped and went home.

Elisabeth Kusian had finished the most dangerously exposed part of her self-appointed task. She did not notice the time but was so exhausted that she collapsed into a chair when she returned to her room. After this rest, Kusian tossed the newspaper she used to wrap Seidelmann into her heating stove, then half-heartedly cleaned the rucksacks and suitcase. Perhaps the drugs made it difficult to understand that this bloody mess would be problematic when she returned the bags to their owners. Her crime netted her currency worth 268.50 DM and Hermann Seidelmann's clothing, which she would later give away and sell. This was a small sum indeed.[64] Was she finished and safe? She thought so.

Berlin had experienced Kristallnacht, the deportation of its Jewish population, Allied air raids, street-fighting, mass rape, near starvation, occupation, division, blockade, and more. Still, there was something peculiarly horrific about the deliberate murder, dismemberment, and dispersal of victims. Perhaps the violence that echoed the city's fate struck Berliners as uncanny, at once familiar and monstrous.[65] The murder (later murders), the police investigations, and the subsequent trial would hold the interest of residents even as foreign powers determined both the city's and Germany's fate. Like the body, then bodies, Berlin and Germany were dismembered. The case and its resolution would mark the passing of one Germany and the beginning of another. As for Elisabeth Kusian, she assumed that her potential problems ended when she dumped Hermann Seidelmann's corpse, believing it would remain hidden for a long time. The next day proved her wrong.

chapter one

Who Was Elisabeth Kusian?

Murderers, certainly multiple murderers, don't spring full-grown out of the ground. At least Waldemar Weimann, the famed pathologist/psychiatrist who was central to the Kusian case, believed that. Elisabeth Kusian's lifetime of experiences, disappointments, and disasters helped pave the path to her Christmas 1949 crimes. World historical events also shaped many of her choices, or at least flowed through Elisabeth Kusian's life, sculpting it as they did the lives of countless other Germans. Her choices were certainly extreme, but recognizable, maybe even understandable.

Elisabeth Kusian was born Elisabeth Richter on 8 May 1914, just three months before the outbreak of the First World War. She was the sixth and final child born to a poor, rural family in Thuringia, a steadily industrializing part of the Reich.[1] Her mother, a Hungarian immigrant, married her father, an "Oberviehmeister" in charge of the domestic animals on a large estate in the hinterlands. Even at this early stage, Elisabeth was caught between two worlds.

Of the over 167,000 parcels of Thuringian land given to agriculture in 1927, fewer than 800 were large enough to employ a Viehmeister (livestock manager). In Thuringia, these animals largely consisted of sheep, cattle, pigs, horses, and goats. Sheep dominated the landscape, averaging 111.2 per hectare. This was more than double the number of cattle, which was almost double the number of pigs.[2] Yet, in the generation before Elisabeth's birth, the Thuringian region slowly but surely evolved from a hub of traditional production to one of Germany's most densely packed industrial regions. By the turn of the century though, the textile industry (in which her mother worked) had stagnated.[3]

Elisabeth never knew her father; like so many millions of others, he fell in the war. What she learned of him was not particularly remarkable, savoury, or reassuring. Elisabeth grew up with the knowledge that, though he was not an especially heavy drinker, he was easily angered and did not take his marital vows seriously. As she understood it, her parents' relationship was not very harmonious. Another disconcerting item for her to consider was that her paternal grandfather died in an insane asylum.[4] Did this knowledge haunt her as she grew up? To take care of her children, the Widow Richter worked in a local button factory, earning barely enough to feed her family. She would come home so exhausted that the children had to do most of the housework.[5]

Elisabeth Richter's childhood was challenging but not particularly unusual. The politics of the volatile Weimar Republic made such a little impression on this young girl. Revolution, counterrevolution, inflation, and a failed coup meant less to her than school, sickness, and other family matters. Elisabeth attended the Volksschule, the lowest type of public school, and survived the then-normal childhood diseases, including measles and scarlet fever.[6] Several of her siblings, on the other hand, suffered from a series of small tragedies. One brother died of tuberculosis. Another was killed in an unsolved 1929 murder in a trainyard in Schleswig-Holstein. Sisters disappeared from her life as she grew into a young woman, perhaps moving to cities in search of better opportunities.

In what must have been a stinging rebuke, Elisabeth's mother told this unfortunate daughter that she was the only child who had ever caused her grief.[7] Elisabeth remembered her childhood more fondly than did her mother. When she was still a girl, she played with friends, dogs, and other animals. Indeed, Elisabeth emphasized that she never tortured them (a regular activity for young psychopaths). Still, in what might have been a foreshadowing of her adult years, she told police that, as a youth, she enjoyed snacking and lying. "If I was going to be whipped, I, of course, swindled."[8]

Perhaps Elisabeth's dishonesty was at the root of Frau Richter's unhappiness. Also troubling might have been the difficulties of single parenthood or of raising Elisabeth. Regardless, when Elisabeth was about ten years old, her mother embarked on a "wild marriage" with a man five years her junior. The pair seem to have been deeply in love, staying together for more than ten years until he died. According to Elisabeth, after her partner's death, Frau Richter would use all her spare money to purchase flowers to place on his grave.[9] Elisabeth's recollections of this "husband" were less warm. To her mind, he stole her mother away. There is also some evidence that he abused Elisabeth. Kusian recalled that this stepfather surrogate demanded that she undress and wash in his presence. When she would enter his bedroom, he would uncover himself in front of her, something that she found shocking. She told psychiatrists that their relationship moved from tension into enmity.[10]

There is thus little wonder that Elisabeth's mother sought another place for her then eleven-year-old daughter to live, landing upon a farm in Saarbrücken.

> Saarbrücken, in the west of Germany, became a border region with France after the end of the First World War. For reasons of reparations and security, the French government largely controlled the region's economy. Indeed, France had hoped to annex the area, but American President Woodrow Wilson vetoed the possibility. Although the population was largely split between supporters of political Catholicism and Socialism, residents had no lack of resentment towards France. This atmosphere may have made Elisabeth's subsequent acceptance of Nazism a little easier.[11]

Elisabeth found the owners to be strict. Still, they provided her with a life she much preferred. At thirteen, when she reached puberty, her mother placed her in a combination school/estate in

Crimmitschau, Saxony, known for its textile production, where she spent almost two years working in the fields from 5:00 a.m. until 11:00 a.m. Elisabeth Kusian saw these years as formative, reminiscing, "at the age of thirteen I got my malaise. Subsequently, I also attended the household school in Schmölln for one year. My mother could always rely on me to do my work, which is why she got me this education."[12]

After this, the then seventeen-year-old Elisabeth went into domestic service in the villa of the director of the Bombastus-Werke.[13] Bombas, a firm specializing in natural medicines and cures derived from plants grown nearby, was founded in Freital, near Dresden, in 1904. Named after the Renaissance physician Theophrastus Bombast, better known as Paracelsus, this placement might have been the ideal place to land for a young girl with romantic visions of the world. Perhaps it was here that Elisabeth became interested in a health-care career. It certainly was here that Elisabeth developed her taste for a life with money and opportunity, as her employers would take her along for walks, theatre visits, and more.[14] She next moved to service in a spa, the "Weisen Hirsch."[15] Though a wallflower at this point in her life, she began to develop feelings for men. The first of these was a composer who lived on the premises. In her own words, for Elisabeth, it was "a serious thing. I was stuck. You rave and know no bounds!"[16] It did, though, know some bounds. Elisabeth Richter was still a virgin, something she had to tell her mother whenever she visited home.[17]

From the spa, Elisabeth moved back into domestic service in the home of a lieutenant colonel in Ludwigsruhe (Landsberg). She remained there for about nine months until the then twenty-year-old developed a suppuration of the bursa, which necessitated her going to the nearby hospital for treatment. Here, in 1932, she met the then thirty-three-year-old Walter Kusian, whom she would later marry. When the two met, Walter Kusian was an operating room assistant.[18] He was also an "Old Fighter" or alte Kämpfer. To quote Patrick Tobin, an Old Fighter was "someone attracted to the party early on when it was little more than a thuggish movement of anti-Semitism, racism, and Versailles revisionism."[19] Still a waiter when he joined the Nazi Party on 13 July 1926, Kusian had the low party card number of 40272.[20] Kusian may not have been committed enough to pay his party dues consistently. He was, though, willing to get into street fights with political opponents. In April 1932, Marxists beat him seriously enough for Kusian to require hospital admission.[21] When he joined the Nazis, there was little reason to believe that this association would bring him much social capital. By 1932, when the pair met and the Weimar Republic was on its last legs, it would have been foolish to think such an association might not prove advantageous.

At their meeting, Elisabeth believed Walter Kusian was the man of her dreams.[22] The colonel, though, disapproved of the match. He fired her shortly after they became a couple, presumably due to Elisabeth's relationship with Walter.[23] The firing was a blessing in disguise, as it allowed Elisabeth to pursue a career that interested her as a caretaker in a hospital. It also let her go to autopsies with some regularity.[24] They celebrated their engagement in 1935. In 1936, they moved into a Berlin apartment after Walter landed a job with the Nationalsozialistische Volkswohlfahrt, a Nazi social welfare bureaucracy that quickly grew during the regime's early years.[25] When Walter began to develop cold feet about the relationship, Elisabeth perfected tricks she would use for the rest of her life. Among these was her ability to faint when conversation became inconvenient. At the same time, she developed lies about her and her family that made them appear to be of a much higher class status. After their March 1936 wedding, the Kusians moved into a 3½ room apartment in Berlin.[26] At the beginning of her marriage, she was happy. This, though, was short lived. The marriage quickly moved from harmony to tension and unhappiness.

Among the reasons for Elisabeth's misery was the discovery that Walter had little to no interest in going to films or theatre. The couple did not even go into nature. She discovered that he was, in the words of Waldemar Weimann, "a primitive and narrow-hearted, pedantic and petty, opaque man." Her marriage to him "was a complete mistake for her and only possible due to her youth, inexperience, and lack of determination." Weimann added that Walter tried, "in her opinion, to intimidate her, to dominate her, and to inhibit her development where he could, but he succeeded only in part."[27]

At least, Elisabeth thought, he was at work most of the day. She would not have to deal with him for hours at a time. Even this discovery, though, brought unhappiness. She found that she could not run the household to his satisfaction. Walter gave her no money as, he claimed, he was saving to buy a hotel. In short, Elisabeth could only get what she wanted "with cunning and smooching." According to Walter, she would also break into cabinets to steal his things.[28]

Between 1937 and 1940, Elisabeth Kusian gave birth to three children. Parenthood only worsened her marriage. Fights became nastier as Walter's jealousy increased. Elisabeth thought that he was jealous of the affection that she gave to their daughters and son rather than to him.[29] Life got so bad that she made many suicide attempts, sometimes with gas, sometimes with pills, and at least once by attempting to slit her wrists. In Nazi Germany's last days of peace, she did not try to hide her hatred for her husband from him.[30]

When Germany invaded Poland to begin the Second World War, things began to look up for Elisabeth. At this moment, her fantastic lies began, some of which were useful and some of which simply improved her social standing.[31] Walter was inducted into the army. Though he was initially stationed nearby, she did not have to see him during the week.[32] As she saw it, "while my husband was a soldier, I received the usual Wehrmacht support, which increased after the birth of another child. Now I could freely dispose of my money and felt quite comfortable in this state."[33] Elisabeth used his absence to begin an affair with a three-years-younger, working-class air force assistant bandmaster from Weimar who was studying in Berlin. The romance ended when he got another woman pregnant. In a gesture that must have struck Kusian as magnanimous, though, she gave him her wedding ring to give to the other woman as, in her mind, the Kusian marriage was already a ruin.[34]

After the affair's end, Elisabeth Kusian rented a piano, told Walter that she was piano sitting for another family, and began to take lessons. She was not the slightest bit contrite about this. "If my husband further stated that he had suddenly found a piano in our apartment during another vacation; and (if he added) that I told him it had been placed with me by bombed-out people in the neighbourhood. (And if he then said) that he later had to find out that it was a rented piano, then I do not deny having lied to him about this."[35] At about the same time, she began another affair, this time with a paymaster (Zahlmeister). He made a deep impression on her, as he showed Elisabeth that she was, in her own words, "a woman and that one can also be treated differently by a man." She added, "I must correct myself. He was killed in a bombing raid on the suburb of Velten near Berlin, that is, I was out there that day. When I came out of the air-raid shelter, the disaster had happened. Of course, I then tried to make life relatively pleasant for myself by dealing with colleagues who also knew soldiers, that is, colleagues who visited me with their acquaintances. So I did not escape this life and the hustle and bustle."[36] As Robert Moeller reminds us, "the destruction of housing – or 'dehousing' as the British called it – achieved by using incendiary bombs, was, they reasoned, potentially as disruptive to industrial production as the levelling of factories." By spring 1945, Allied bombs had killed over 400,000 Germans.[37]

Especially after 1943, Elisabeth Kusian became known for the dance- and music-driven parties she threw at her apartment. Guests included men from all military ranks, spanning enlisted to high-ranking physicians. These parties would continue until the next morning, sometimes even into noon of the next day. Neighbours spoke of "orgies" and remarked on how Elisabeth was known for drinking and merriment. Her former shyness, timidity, and reputation as a wallflower were all gone. She was now a woman, unrestrained by inhibitions, who thoroughly enjoyed her life. Unhappy as these parties made the neighbours, they refrained from complaining because of Walter's status as a long-term, committed Nazi.[38] The wife of an Old Fighter was not to be trifled with.

Were such fears justified? Klaus-Michael Mallmann and Gerhard Paul argue that the climate of fear in the Third Reich was greatly exaggerated. The Gestapo, they claim, was not everywhere. Rather its strength lay in the general population's willingness and even desire to rat out one another for personal gain. Udo Grashoff, though, reminds readers that resisting or criticizing the regime was a real danger. About 20,000 German Communists died in concentration camps or were executed, and the Gestapo was known to recruit people to spy on others.[39]

As the war continued, Elisabeth Kusian worked as a caretaker in various field hospitals around the city and at the children's home in Hermsdorf. "As far as I remember, I started about three-quarters of a year before the collapse in the Städt. Kinderheim Hermsdorf, which belonged to the Dominikus Hospital. This was partly because I brought my own children there. At the time of the collapse, however, when the S-Bahn stopped running, I stayed in Eulerstraße and worked as a volunteer helper after bombing raids. I did this because the home in question provided us with appropriate clothing. In short, I had clothing as long as I worked in Hermsdorf."[40]

Elisabeth was caught in the thick of the war's last days. "When Berlin was occupied, I was wounded while helping wounded soldiers – I wanted to bring coffee – and from the same day on, I had to be admitted to the collective hospital Grünthaler Straße myself." She would spend eight weeks recovering from her wounds.[41] The war's end and the occupation's beginning brought both possibilities and problems.

Kusian would need to transition from patient to nurse. Her first stop was the Virchow Hospital, where she was a student nurse from August 1945 until April 1946, then worked as a nurse until October.[42] The Virchow Hospital was looking for nurses who had worked for and with the Red Cross. Virchow had a great reputation in Berlin. It was a trailblazer – the first in the city to be divided according to specialties and the last to be built in the one-floor, pavilion style.[43] Promising as this opportunity was, Elisabeth Kusian realized that, at some point, she would have to fill out one of the Allies' endless questionnaires about her background. How to do this? After all, she'd told her colleagues, with whom she was quite popular, about her late husband, the medical student, who had died tragically young.[44] On or about 1 December 1946, she decided to fill out such a questionnaire for a nursing position at the Robert Koch Hospital.

The Robert Koch Hospital was a venerable institution on Berlin's medical scene. Opened in 1872, it housed its own Pathology Institute and the Werner-Siemens Institute for X-ray Research. During the war, it was used as a military Lazarett. Although it suffered war damage, it was operational again soon after; it changed its name to the Moabit Hospital and would have provided a wonderful professional opportunity for a young nurse.[45] Elisabeth saw the possibilities, so lied on her application. She declared that she had studied at a Lyzeum in Altenburg, Thuringia, and that her husband disappeared in the war in 1943, never to return.[46] Study at a Lyzeum would give her life story a bit of polish. As one nineteenth-century critic put it, such schooling was designed for "purification of the will, refinement of taste, [and] enlightenment of the soul."[47]

Perhaps the relief afforded by telling these two lies provided the release Elisabeth needed to begin her peculiar nursing career at Moabit. Though she was very popular with her patients and "especially zealous in her care of the sick," colleagues suspected she stole a watch from a patient with cancer.[48] She was said to have shown an odd interest in autopsies, even though they had nothing to do with her duties.[49] One neighbour passed on a rumour to police that "Kusian apparently did not take her care of patients very seriously, as she had mentioned … that, if patients made too much work, she would help them with a few drops." This neighbour also shared the rumour that Kusian was a morphine addict. If this were not damning enough, the neighbour shared the gossip that Sister Elisabeth "hastened the demise of a patient in the Moabit Hospital with the help of an overdose of an injection and by lowering her head."[50]

In this post-war moment, Walter returned to Berlin from an American POW camp, a return that made Elisabeth's life miserable in so many ways.

He always had to do something to the children. When they did their schoolwork, he erased what they wrote. They then had to rewrite it. Of course, he and I had disagreements. These usually ended with him reproaching me for living alone during the war, using the most insulting language for a woman. Among other things, he accused me of having had an affair not only with the already mentioned paymaster but also with other men. Board money? I still did not receive it. On top of that, we were expelled from our apartment because my husband was a Pg. [Party Member]. So we moved to Sternstraße 11a on 1 November 1946.[51]

Elisabeth blamed Walter for her increasing drug use.

I had the idea of injecting myself with morphine. I stole the ampules from Virchow Hospital and kept them at home. Then, I injected in the evening when I had arguments that made the drugs necessary. The highest doses were when I'd had it. 5 cc. I only reached doses of 8 cc in Kantstraße 154. I injected myself in different body parts, mainly thighs and arms – partly because it was not noticeable. If I did not have enough, intravenously. After that, I had a quiet, carefree night. I was not so tormented by my worries then. When I was tired and sleepy in the morning and had to go on duty, I would take Pervetin tablets – which I always had – to freshen up. Depending on my needs, I took up to six of them. (Sometimes I obtained doses in) the Virchow-Hospital. I also got the morphine through nurses who still had packages from the Wehrmacht. I bought the morphine for East and West money. For an ampule of 0.02 cc, I paid 3, also 4 Westmark … I bought Pervitin partly from black marketeers and partly from pharmacies when I explained that I was a night nurse. In the time before the crime, I injected up to 8 cc. I only used Pervitin when I wanted to be fresh.[52]

Elisabeth Kusian's situation was indeed grim, but after 1 November 1946, it took a turn for the better.

One day, I heard from a lawyer that my husband had filed for divorce. At that time, I was in the Robert Koch Hospital because of my leg.

> This news came as a surprise to me. I had already been thinking that something had to happen to change my circumstances; I even considered filing for divorce on my own initiative.[53]

At long last, she was free of the drag of Walter Kusian. For 75 Reichsmarks per month, she could lodge her children with a religious institution. By May 1947, she had put her eight- and ten-year-old daughters into the care of a Catholic home for children (the Heim Maria-Frieden in Berlin Niederschönhausen). She sent her six-year-old son the next month. Walter knew nothing of the arrangement. He assumed that their children were with Elisabeth's mother in Thuringia.[54]

After the children's departure, Sister Elisabeth moved to a series of rooms sublet in others' apartments and into a much more active romantic life. By February 1948, she was living in a room on the Bundesratsufer that cost her 50 DM per month. She left because her landlady disapproved of Kusian's growing relationship with the twenty-six-year-old burglar Hans Boguslawski. The landlady would not let him into the apartment.[55] Boguslawski was a rather suspicious character and a thief. At first, Elisabeth claimed to have known very little about him. They met through a friend of his, a physician at the hospital where Elisabeth worked. She did not know his profession, only that he worked at night. That mattered little to her, though, as the couple would do many things Elisabeth had missed in her marriage to Walter. They often went to movies and the theatre, albeit to matinees. He, in turn, would sleep over at her place. It was probably during one of these nights that Elisabeth became pregnant.[56]

Elisabeth changed addresses, though, as her relationship with Boguslawski blossomed. Boguslawski maintained his own set of rooms where Kusian would sometimes stay when she was between abodes and rooming at the hospital where she worked.[57] By March 1948, Elisabeth Kusian was living as a subletter in Elise Nee.'s apartment. Here she paid 35 DM per month for space in a two-room apartment consisting of a kitchen and a side room. Kusian told Frau Nee. that she was a widow, the stepmother of her "late" husband's three children, who sometimes lived with her. Nee. would often care for the children in Kusian's absence.

Her husband, Elisabeth claimed, was a physician who died in a plane crash during the war. The general aspects of the story she would tell others seem to have taken shape during this tenancy. In the months between March 1948 and June 1949, Kusian added the details of her mother's nobility, her uncle who owned a clinic and paid for the children's upkeep, and two brothers who died in the war.[58]

On the morning of 11 May 1948, probably much to Frau Nee.'s chagrin, police came by the apartment to arrest Boguslawski, whom the court sentenced to a year in jail for complicity in a burglary.[59] Only when he was in prison did Elisabeth tell Boguslawski that she was pregnant, an angle that interested the police. When they spoke with Hans Boguslawski, interrogators asked, "What special incidents are known to you from when you had a relationship with Ms. Kusian?" Boguslawski responded, "As far as I remember, this question can only mean Kusian's pregnancy. It was in April or May 1948 when she came to see me in custody and told me that she was in other circumstances. I answered that nothing could be done and that she should carry the child to term."[60] Elisabeth now faced the problem of dealing with her pregnancy alone and decided to get an abortion, for which she had to pay 700 Reichsmarks. Boguslawski insisted that Elisabeth never told him about her abortion.[61] Perhaps that is true. Perhaps not. Although she visited him in jail and paid his defence attorney, there was a price to be paid.[62]

Hans Boguslawski had plenty of time to consider the end of his relationship with Elisabeth. He visited her one last time to get the storage ticket necessary to retrieve the goods he had stored while sitting in prison.[63]

> On 10 December 1948, I was provisionally released from prison, and my first trip was to Kusian's apartment at Turmstraße 39. Here, I realized that she had ended our previous relationship. I only got to know her new boyfriend in passing. She said he was a criminal investigator. Because we had lived together, I had gradually brought my property into her apartment, that is, underwear, suits, three coats, one armchair, smaller utensils, and a bicycle. When I demanded these objects back, she informed me that she had brought everything to the storage facilities at

> Zoo Station. She wanted to have nothing more to do with my things. She handed me the storage vouchers, and when I got my things back, I found that a man's suit, a pair of shoes, some underwear, three shirts, and some other articles of daily use were missing. I wanted to confront her about this, but I didn't. First of all, I didn't find them. Secondly, she had given me a coat and appointed me a lawyer, so I considered the matter settled.[64]

Elisabeth Kusian sold many of the articles Boguslawski entrusted to her. The bicycle went for 600 Reichsmarks. She sold the suit, shoes, coat, and more for an additional 2,000 Reichsmarks.[65]

Even before her final interactions with Hans Boguslawski, which one might view as either theft or simply repayment, Elisabeth Kusian was involved in stealing and setting up others to take the blame for her actions. During Christmas 1948, Johanna Dei., a student nurse and colleague of Elisabeth Kusian's, brought a suitor (Hans Schu., who had told her that he was divorced although he was married to his third wife) along on a visit to Kusian. The somewhat naive Johanna must have shared her suspicions and disappointment with Kusian. In early January 1949, in a rather clumsy move, Kusian told Johanna that Frau Nee.'s leather case with gold and jewels was missing. Kusian added that Nee. suspected Johanna and Hans of the theft.[66] It seems that Elisabeth Kusian had allowed Johanna and her lover to use the Kusian room for a tryst.[67] Perhaps she always intended to use this favour to implicate her colleague in a theft that Kusian herself had perpetrated. Kusian presented her with documentation stating that Frau Nee. would press charges if Johanna did not agree to a repayment scheme. Johanna told the detectives that, fortunately for her, she had not paid Frau Nee. any money.[68] Indeed, Elisabeth Kusian later confessed to having stolen the jewellery, taken it to Zoo Station, and sold the entirety for 400 DM.[69]

By the end of May 1949, Elisabeth Kusian vacated the building to sublet a room from Marja Sobe. Frau Sobe. had asked the Moabit Hospital's caretaker (Pfortner) if he knew of a single person looking for a room. The caretaker recommended an admitting nurse, Elisabeth Kusian. Kusian told her that she was interested in a new, larger space than the one she had been leasing from Frau Nee., which was too small for her needs. She moved to Birkenstraße 13 on 3 June 1949.[70]

There were some advantages to this new space. It was "'an empty room,' a larger room with a separate entrance." Kusian claimed, "I had already, at the time of my separation from my husband, some pieces of furniture such as a wardrobe, table, four chairs, one bedside table, and one bed in my possession, and these I used to decorate my room at Frau Sobe.'s."[71]

Her former neighbour, Anni Glißmann, helped her to move into this new space over August 1949.[72] Among her new neighbours were the Schrö. family. Elisabeth Kusian and the Schrö. family developed a good relationship, partly because they had children of the same age. Kusian used this relationship to ask for a series of favours, including a loan of 150 DM sometime between June and November 1949, which she told them she needed because she had decided to board her children outside of Berlin at an expensive place.[73] Not surprisingly, when the time came for repayment, she explained that she had lost all of her money at the hospital where she worked. Until then, though, the children stayed with her in her room. Indeed, in June 1949, she informed Walter that she would pull the girls out of the home where they lived and he should stop sending them money.[74] He would, though, often come to the apartment, both to bring firewood and to check on the children. Elisabeth told her neighbours that he was her brother-in-law. Although she had the children call him "Uncle," Elisabeth claimed to believe that he visited the children to control them.[75]

In the summer and fall of 1949, Elisabeth Kusian continued many activities that would pile up problems for her. On 1 July, she borrowed 500 DM from a patient of hers, a haulage contractor who may have hoped she could help him secure a disability payment. She told him and his wife that she needed the cash for her children but that her father-in-law would be good for the debt. She never repaid the money.[76] It is unlikely that she then needed such a sum for the children's care. Walter was spending a great deal of time with them, even taking them to the Wannsee for swimming.[77]

For more than a century, the Wannsee, an easy ride on the S1 from the city, has been a classic recreation place for Berliners to get away from it all for a few hours. This beautiful lake, surrounded by woods, offers swimming, hiking, cafés, and more. Billy Wilder and Robert and Curt Siodmak set their classic Weimar-era film, *People on Sunday*, there to show Berliners at play. All three of them would go on to become important Hollywood directors, known – respectively – for comedy, noir, and horror. All three left Germany because of the rise of Nazism.

During the Third Reich, the KdF (Kraft durch Freude or Strength through Joy) – Nazi Germany's organization dedicated to recreation and its contribution to the building of a strong Volk – held mass exercise events there.[78] Its picturesque North German landscape and vistas ought to have contributed to a sense of unity. Historian Julia Timpe comments on how much fun the participants seem to have been having.[79]

Ultimately, though, Wannsee is probably best known to most as the site of the infamous Wannsee Conference, the 1942 meeting at which high-ranking Nazi officials decided on the details for the extermination of European Jewry.[80]

Walter's visits must have been a cause for concern as much as they were a pleasant diversion. Elisabeth told her landlady that this "uncle" dropped by to help with schoolwork. She never varied from the story that she was a widow. Tragically, she explained, her husband died in a Soviet camp. She then faced the indignity of the Allies confiscating her father-in-law's comfortable apartment where she lived. Frau Sobe. often served lunch to Elisabeth Kusian, perhaps out of pity for her circumstances. Elisabeth, though, instead of helping or responding in kind, would, when she had funds, throw parties to which she invited police detective Kurt Muschan. This lack of reciprocity caused some friction between the two women.[81] Perhaps Frau Sobe. was bothered by the fact that Walter and Elisabeth Kusian had resumed their sexual relationship, meeting twice weekly in both his room and hers.[82]

It was also at the same time, between June and November 1949, that Elisabeth began to use Anni Glißmann to do a series of business-related favours for her. Kusian sent Glißmann to the area around Tauroggener Straße to meet with Hans Boguslawski's sister to ask for a table, bicycle, and chair. If the sister refused, Kusian told Glißmann that she would take further steps.[83] Elisabeth also began to set her sights on stealing from Frau Sobe. and Sobe.'s mother, Frau Ja. To earn some extra cash, Frau Ja. collected all the rent for the building where she lived (Stephanstraße 60), totalling a not inconsiderable 560 DM per month.

One day in August 1949, while visiting Frau Ja., Elisabeth learned how the rent was collected. With this knowledge, it is little surprise that the rent money and the collection book disappeared after her visit.[84] A few days later, Frau Ja. told Kusian she still had some cash, 275 DM, from the previous month's rent in her kitchen. Kusian advised her to bring the money to Frau Sobe.'s apartment and hide it in the baby's crib. When Frau Ja. returned to the crib for the cash on 6 August, 150 DM was missing. As nobody else had access, Frau Sobe. believed that Elisabeth was the thief. However, Kusian claimed that she never stole the funds, flatly stating to the police, "If I had committed the thefts I mentioned earlier, I would have admitted them because they are of no more importance in the whole complex."[85] Still, the whole affair was in keeping with her general behaviour, and Frau Sobe., who was then in the hospital, later accused Sister Elisabeth of the theft. At this point, Elisabeth Kusian bridled and shut the door in her face. Frau Sobe. terminated Elisabeth Kusian's lease effective 11 November 1949.[86] In September 1949, only a month after Elisabeth Kusian began to engage in ever more criminal behaviour, Gertrud and Hermann Seidelmann enjoyed a motorcycle trip together to Berlin, the last time the two would travel together to the former capital. At about the same time, Doris Merten began her job at Friedrich Beigang's typewriter shop, and Anni Glißmann visited Elisabeth more frequently.[87]

Unsurprisingly, Elisabeth Kusian gave Anni Glißmann a different reason for vacating her room, explaining that she had to move out of Frau Sobe.'s place because the landlady bothered her nights and weekends. At one point, Elisabeth explained that she owed 40 DM in rent and that the Housing Authority told her she had to leave because she was disturbing Frau Sobe.'s peaceful life.[88] To a different audience, she claimed she left because "Frau Sobe. asked for too much rent." Even this simple move, though, was not without its drama, which revolved around money and shady dealings. According to one report, Frau Sobe. brought a civil suit against Elisabeth Kusian as she vacated her room on 15 November. More likely, the claim was because Kusian left still owing 18 DM for rent and 14 DM for electricity. At the time, Kusian had cash in hand. She had sold her furniture to the Schrö. family, her neighbours, netting 60 DM each for two seats and an additional 150 DM for the couch. The Schrö. family, who assumed that they were taking part in a simple transaction, were surprised when agents from the Hopp Furniture Company came by after visiting Frau Sobe. Elisabeth Kusian had paid a 100 DM down payment on the set but still owed the company 350 DM. The Schrö. family were ultimately able to recoup 150 DM from Kusian. They lost less money than they might have, but Elisabeth Kusian's behaviour left a bad taste in their mouths.[89] As events would show, Elisabeth Kusian may only latterly have become a killer, but she was a long-time thief and con artist.[90]

Defrauding the Schrö. family was little more than background noise to Elisabeth Kusian. Elisabeth tendered her resignation effective December at the Moabit Hospital as Hans Boguslawski left Tegel Prison in October.[91]

Elisabeth probably thought little about the place where her former lover had been held. Tegel Prison is a storied location in the history of Berlin and German crime. Originally built in 1898, it held Wilhelm Voigt, the Captain of Cöpenick – immortalized on the stage and in film for buying a military uniform in a suburb of Berlin and then using his supposed authority to take over a town hall in one of Berlin's surrounding towns, emptying the treasury in the process. Franz Biberkopf, the anti-hero of Alfred Döblin's modernist classic, *Berlin Alexanderplatz*, began his journey into supposed freedom by walking past its red-brick walls and through its gates into the city. Carl von Ossietzky, 1935 Nobel Peace Prize winner and editor of *Die Weltbühne* – Weimar Germany's pre-eminent left-wing political journal – was imprisoned here during the Third Reich before being sent to a concentration camp where the regime would murder him. It is also where many of the plotters against Hitler were held before their executions.[92]

Boguslawski's imprisonment was much less significant and far less unpleasant than were the imprisonments of Tegel's more famous inmates. His time in prison was most likely of no concern to Elisabeth Kusian.

The financial ramifications of Kusian's resignation had to occupy her thoughts. Also of interest was the new love in her life. Elisabeth met Kurt Muschan, one of the detectives in charge of the Boguslawski burglary case.[93] Muschan's first interaction with Kusian had been little more than a clumsy flirtation. While interviewing her, Muschan started a conversation that soon became much more. He told Kusian that he had hurt his toe; she invited him to her apartment where she could give him some Rheumasan, a topical cream, for some relief. "In the course of this affair, we became better acquainted. Later, a friendship developed."[94] Soon the children would integrate "Uncle Kurt" into their lives, as he would take them out on jaunts to the city zoo.[95] By November 1949, much of Elisabeth Kusian's life began to lose focus and seemed ever more desperate. She and Anni Glißmann visited each other more frequently, presumably to do more deals to keep Kusian financially afloat.[96] Her drug use increased even as her financial decisions became even more erratic. At one point, Kusian cut her finger so severely while chopping wood for the oven that she needed treatment at the hospital. She tried not to tell the detectives how her injury occurred, which baffled them. Indeed, they thought it came during a crime. She finally said, "If I am to tell the full truth, I must say I was high when this happened to me: when a person is in his right mind, this cannot happen. I should have told everyone I was shooting up with narcotics."[97]

In early December 1949, she purchased an expensive radio, then traded it to Muschan for his much cheaper set. "The radio set was on the instalment plan. The device cost 295 DM. I bought it from the radio dealer Schwenke, Lübecker Straße 37 … I made a down payment of 20 DM. Later I traded this radio with Muschan, that is, he brought me his radio and took mine. However, I emphasize that Muschan did not want this at first and that it only happened at my express wish."[98] She would need to do something, perhaps something even more desperate than her previous actions, to keep her finances afloat. On 3 December 1949, Hermann Seidelmann left his brother's apartment to exchange currency with a woman he had only recently met. His family never saw him alive again.

chapter two

The Seidelmann Case

Monday, 5 December 1949

When she arose, Elisabeth Kusian must have thought that her problems were over. Was she thinking about the beautiful life that awaited her? She had, after all, acted in the name of love, love for Kurt Muschan.[1] Hermann Seidelmann's murder should provide her with the cash she needed to buy Muschan a Christmas gift that he would remember and treasure – a typewriter so that he would no longer need to fill out his reports by hand. This gift would certainly cement their relationship. Later, she decided that a gift of cutlery for Muschan's wife would make the holiday even more special.

In short, Elisabeth Kusian's disquieting weekend was behind her. In a stroke of personal luck, an 80 mph windstorm had ripped through Northern Germany the night before. Buildings shook, ruins collapsed, and chimneys and walls toppled across Berlin. The divided city's fire brigades responded to more than 130 calls for help. The unnamed storm killed ten people across the country; five died in Berlin alone. A further fourteen were severely injured. For Elisabeth Kusian, though, such a storm and its resulting destruction might just ensure that Hermann Seidelmann would remain buried for a while, perhaps forever.[2]

With these or similar thoughts in mind, Elisabeth Kusian left her apartment at 7:00 a.m. and rode the tram once again to visit Anni Glißmann.[3] If she were lucky, she might even avoid the Schrö.

family. Her debt to them, though, was relatively minor. Too much else was at stake. In the first of what would prove to be a series of clumsy mistakes, when Kusian returned to Anni's that dark morning, she carried the now blood-caked suitcase she had earlier borrowed. Glißmann, more than a little taken aback by the gore, only came to terms with the stains when Kusian lied that she and her lover had used the bag to transport slaughtered rabbits whose carcasses must have bled. After Kusian left, Glißmann cleaned the bag as best she could, dried it on the stove, and then tried to return it to her neighbour. Frau W. refused to accept it in that condition, saying that her husband, a police officer, would complain about the stains. Glißmann understood and took the bag home for yet another cleaning. Her second delivery passed without complaint.[4] A stroke of luck! This incident set a pattern that Elisabeth Kusian would follow for the next few weeks. She convinced others to do what she wanted while making startlingly short-sighted moves and disregarding the possibility that police could catch her. When they finally did, detectives would spend weeks trying to understand the paradox of a murderer with the peculiar combination of technical surgical competence and fatally flawed decision-making.

Such questions, though, lay in the future. For the moment, Elisabeth needed Anni Glißmann's services. Within a few days of returning the bloody suitcase, Elisabeth reappeared at Glißmann's apartment bearing a somewhat worn, grey men's winter coat flecked with a black pattern, a pair of men's brown shoes, and 50 DM for the Schrö. family's furniture. Given Elisabeth's relationship with the Schrö. family, of course, she would want an agent for the transaction. After a chat, the two women took the #2 streetcar to Zoo Station and sold the coat for 30 DM to a man whom Glißmann believed to be an Italian. He quickly donned it and faded into the crowd, never to be seen again. A chocolate dealer from the station's underpass bought the shoes for 8 DM.

The sales went so well that, three days later, Elisabeth returned to her friend's with a man's wristwatch. She feigned regret. It had been hers for a very long time; she could barely bring herself to part with it. Glißmann took it to a Wilmersdorf pawnshop with instructions to accept an offer as low as 5 DM. Not believing her good fortune, Anni took 30 DM.[5] Why was Anni Glißmann so helpful to Elisabeth Kusian? In all likelihood, she received some commission for her services. In a city where life was still close to the bone, any edge, any angle that helped with survival, counted.

Anni must also have felt some sympathy for Elisabeth's tales of woe. The nurse told her about so many tragedies, almost like a film noir, a melodrama. One day, when Anni noticed a bloody wound on Elisabeth Elisabeth's left hand, she "learned of" a fight with a violent brother-in-law who had long been in the habit of giving her money. Things, though, had worsened. Elisabeth wailed about his jealousy. He insisted that she belonged only to him. In a rage, he threw her onto the sofa and hurt her hand as she tried to choke him. Between her tears, Elisabeth cried that she should commit suicide.[6] Of course, Kusian had no brother-in-law. This tale, like so many others, was probably fabricated on the spot.

On this December day, though, after a night and day of violence, skill, cunning, and carelessness, Elisabeth must have believed that her most significant difficulties were over. Hermann Seidelmann had been permanently buried in the rubble! Just this morning her friend had cleaned the remaining forensic evidence that advertised his murder. Even better, neither personal nor known business connections linked her to Hermann Seidelmann. In short, as the morning ended, all seemed well in her world.

When he ran into the collapsed building's ruins and rubble, twelve-year-old Günther A. only expected to find the ball he and his friends had been kicking in the street. Sometime between 1:00 and 1:30 p.m., it bounced into the remains of Borsigstraße 18, a hulking ruin looming over the Invalidenstraße near the Stettin Train Station in Berlin's Soviet sector. The behemoth was barely a structure. Only a few outer walls and a blasted ground floor remained to indicate what it had been. The other ruined buildings that surrounded the site also stood eerily. No passerby could tell when or whether they would be rebuilt or cleared.

To Günther's left as he entered stood a gate visible from the Invalidenstraße. Its bricks were collapsed into heaps, while the remaining debris's shadow darkened the street. Still, he skirted the flotsam and jetsam lying across the damp mortar dusting the

Figure 2.1. The building in which Günther A. found a partial corpse. The arrow shows where the partial corpse was left.

area. Picking his way among broken bricks, wall fragments, and the rest of the detritus, he likely shifted objects in his search. Perhaps he squinted in the shadows and dust. Soon after he made his way inside, his eyes adjusting to the gloom, Günther forgot about the lost ball. A man's left arm, two legs amputated at the knees, and a thigh lay about 10 metres into the ruin.[7]

Elisabeth Kusian should have known that Berlin's children enjoyed ruins and rubble. An American newspaper columnist noted that they even played in the rubble-strewn remains of Hitler's chancellery.[8] Rubble was everywhere. By one estimate, at the war's end, Berlin alone was covered by 55,000,000 cubic metres of it.[9] The 1950 edition of *Berlin in Zahlen*, West Berlin's official statistical publication, claimed that, by the end of 1949, the city's western sectors had removed 8,843,564 cubic metres.[10] For adults who had lived through Berlin's halcyon days, this was a Hellscape, a latter-day Götterdämmerung. The stone and cement cadavers both recalled Nazi promises of a glorious future and mocked them.

For children, though, ruins were wonderlands, magical playgrounds. Decades later, when Silvia Koerner thought back to her youth in late 1940s Berlin, she remembered bombed-out buildings as being among the best places to play. What could be more appealing to children than an area rarely visited by many adults? It was almost inevitable that Seidelmann's corpse would be located sooner rather than later, and probably by children.[11] Finding an unexpected, dismembered, partial corpse broke the spell of Günther's wonderland and changed his castle into a slaughterhouse.

Scrambling into the daylight, Günther quickly found and informed a local patrolling officer, VP Wachtmeister Rakitovsky, who entered the site, unsuccessfully searched for more of the body, cordoned off the area, and telephoned East Berlin's police headquarters to report the gruesome discovery. He requested that the Volkspolizei murder squad begin an investigation.[12] Within an hour, VP Kommandeur Rockstroh, head of East Berlin's murder squad, accompanied by six other Volkspolizei officers (including a draftsman and photographer), began the investigation. Proceeding slowly and methodically, they searched, diagrammed, and photographed the site and corpse.[13] At about 2:45 p.m. that afternoon, a canine search handler brought "Lux K 22" to sniff around the scene. Because they were starting from nothing, any details might help the investigators.

Finding no more of the anonymous corpse, Lux left the site at about 4:00 p.m. Detectives remained, looking for all possible clues.[14] The spectacle's peculiarity must have struck VP Kommandeur Rockstroh. The corpse's limbs were artlessly piled, stacked atop shattered bricks and metal piping. The left arm lodged on the bottom against the remains of a wall between two gaping arches that had once been doors. Half-clenched fingers, not quite a fist, not fully open, looked like they were grasping a broken brick. Piled unceremoniously on top of the arm were a right thigh (with the arm's hand seemingly emerging from the knee) and two legs, both severed just above their knees, toes pointing upwards in the opposite direction from the arm. Whoever had done this made little to no effort to hide these limbs; any observer entering the structure would find the remains with minimal delay.[15]

In seeming contrast to the remains' random piling, their dismemberment was professional, even artistic. Rockstroh noted how fresh the cuts were. The murder had probably happened the previous day or night, as somebody had likely transported the remains the night before. Scrutinizing the partial cadaver, Rockstroh scanned for anything that might help. Perhaps the elbow and foot scars would help identify the victim. His colleague, VP Kriminalpolizeirat Schwarz, pondered the still wet remains, probably from the previous night's storm. Refocusing on the many piles of human excrement near the body, he mused that this ruin served those who had nowhere else to relieve themselves.[16] The detectives understood something the unknown murderer did not. Constant traffic in these ruins, whether by scavengers, the homeless, or children, doomed any hope that the partial corpse would remain undiscovered for long. Had a child not happened upon the remains, somebody else would have. What kind of criminal would so carefully and professionally dismember a corpse and so carelessly discard it? VP Kommandeur Rockstroh ordered that the unidentified remains be transported to East Berlin's morgue at Hannoversche Straße 6.

The partial corpse needed to be available for comparison with any other body parts that might later turn up. Rockstroh hoped that some detail or abnormality would lead to the victim's identification.[17] Laconic optimism marked Rockstroh's first report: "The murder squad has begun the investigation. It will provide the results when it is finished with the process."[18]

Once the remains arrived at the Hannoversche Straße morgue, East Berlin authorities invited West Berlin pathologist Waldemar Weimann of the Institute for Legal Medicine to autopsy it. This invitation painfully reminded local authorities that every East

Berlin pathologist had fled the newly declared German Democratic Republic for better prospects in the West. The haemorrhaging of talent that was to afflict the GDR had only just begun. It would lead to the construction of the infamous Berlin Wall twelve years later.[19] A minor consequence of this loss of talent was Eastern authorities' dependence on Waldemar Weimann, a specialist in "Gerichtsmedizin" (legal medicine). Even in 1949, this field was beginning to dissolve into the very different fields of forensic pathology and psychiatry. The thinking behind this kind of dual training was that "Gerichtsmediziners" could approach both victims and perpetrators with expertise.

Certainly the Institute for Legal Medicine's work gained it an international reputation for forensic medicine, but, nevertheless, as a field, "forensic medicine had been fighting for acceptance as an independent academic subject for decades." Even its work with the police did not make that acceptance a given. Happily for its practitioners, this situation would change after 1930 under Victor Müller Heß, the director of what grew into the University Institute of Legal Medicine, which would promote both the study of traditional forensic medicine and forensic psychiatry.[20] In the wake of this university acceptance, in 1937 the State Institute for Forensic and Social Medicine Berlin came into being under the direction of Waldemar Weimann. Early in its "career," the institute was known as the Berlin Corpse Viewing House (Leichenschauhaus). Before 1930, Berliners in search of sensation would visit to watch autopsies. By the time that Weimann had taken over, those days were done. The fully respectable institute had taken over other, smaller offices to give the discipline a new, state-sanctioned home.[21] Except for bullet pockmarks, the institute was repaired and back in use by the time of the Kusian murders.[22]

As one contemporary practitioner explains, legal medicine is a complicated field, certainly broader than pathology, that includes both autopsies of the dead and studies of the living, and "assessments and reconstructions of legally relevant bodily injuries, damage to health, and analyses of medical malpractice"[23] The field was established in

Berlin in January 1833 when Wilhelm Wagner proposed the formation of a "Teaching Institution for State Pharmacology," which formed the basis for Berlin's Institute of Legal Medicine. This institute was meant to further the study of "living individuals, bodies, and inanimate substances."[24] The construction of a new morgue, built in 1884 and opened in 1886, was, at the time, a state-of-the-art, modern horseshoe-shaped building. Its basement had facilities to store thirty-six corpses. Aerial bombardment left it severely damaged at the Second World War's end.

In 1949, fifty-six-year-old Waldemar Weimann was a well-known specialist who had served as both an expert psychiatric and pathology witness in a series of trials.[25] Weimann showed great regard for himself and a need to cultivate the sympathy of others. His published memoirs are full of attempts to wring sympathy from his readers. He claimed that his profession weighed heavily on his mind. He explained that most of his patients were murder victims, suicides, people killed in automobile accidents, or victims of other dubious cases. Even his live patients generally did not see him of their own free will.[26] As Weimann put it, "it takes only about ten minutes to walk from the morgue to the Alt-Moabit remand prison. Here I dissect the bodies of dead people, there the souls of perpetrators – often it's about the same case."[27]

Waldemar Weimann styled himself as a latter-day Sigmund Freud. His psychiatric perspective leaned heavily on psychoanalysis. Even his hobbies aped Freud's. Weimann collected figures of the Buddha and Indian gods and goddesses, figures for which he was proud to have paid astronomical prices and which he believed stirred the envy of collectors worldwide. Stone and bronze figurines, reminiscent of Freud's similar collection of classical statuettes, stuffed the bookshelves, tables, cupboards, and more of his home office.[28] Weimann would come to see the Kusian case as an opportunity to display his forensic and psychiatric skills. East Berlin detectives were very curious to learn all that his autopsy could tell them.[29]

Having gotten Weimann's preliminary report, Volkspolizei detectives could concentrate their effort on more immediate strategies to solve the murder. After returning to police headquarters,

VP Kriminalpolizeirat Schwarz typed up a press release, "Breaking News," full of morbid detail to help identify the victim. Among the release's points were that the deceased appeared to be somewhere between thirty and forty years old, had a surgical scar on the left arm, and wore a bandage on the sole of his right foot. Hopefully this minimal description would alert family or friends to the discovery of a missing person.[30]

Perhaps even as Waldemar Weimann autopsied the body, VP Wachtmeister Lippert canvassed the area around the Stettin Train Station and Borsigstraße. He interviewed people who lived and worked nearby about anybody or anything suspicious that they might have seen. Several described unusual activities that took on retrospective significance. Approximately four weeks earlier, a fifty-year-old woman saw a group of men gathered in the area at about 11:00 p.m. Another potential witness, a fifty-six-year-old man, claimed to have seen a hatless, fifty-year-old male in a dark jacket, carrying a rucksack and wearing a sandbag around his neck, at about 8:45 p.m. on 4 December. Most of the conversations, though, proved fruitless. Stettin Station's taxi drivers, baggage carriers, and railroad employees knew little. Lippert then visited nearby pubs, restaurants, a house, and a hotel, again with no success.

After detectives digested this first round of interviews, they turned to Waldemar Weimann's initial autopsy report that concluded the deceased had a lame left arm. This potential identifier promised enough to return VP Kriminalpolizeirat Schwarz to the scene in the failed hope that the additional detail might ring some bells with locals.[31] This slim hope collapsed when a reanalysis of the limbs showed that the left arm's purported scars and seeming lameness occurred post-mortem.[32] Every turn stymied investigators as they worked to produce more evidence. Even the fingerprints provided by the morgue were useless.[33] When nothing noteworthy happened the next day, progress slowed to a crawl.

Wednesday, 7 December 1949

Progress appeared the next day. At about 11:00 a.m, VP Wachtmeister Rakitovsky, the first officer on the scene two days earlier, telephoned headquarters. A young boy claimed to have found a man's head in the Borsigstraße 18 ruins. The ten-year-old Günther J. told Rakitovsky that, at about 3:00 p.m. the day before, he and his friend Klaus S. discovered a human head lying on a tin plate resting on a destroyed oven in one of the ruin's basement rooms.[34] Günther J. described a head of dark brown hair wearing silver-coloured glasses. Günther continued that, when he first told his mother, she chided him that he was crazy (daß der Junge "spinne"). Not to be put off, the next day he told the story to his teacher, who sent him to the police. Five Volkspolizisten then escorted the boy and VP Wachtmeister Rakitovsky to the site to await the murder squad. Once they arrived, the team fruitlessly combed through the ruin. An undoubtedly disappointed VP Kriminalpolizeirat Schwarz reported that "the head was not found, and since the rubble was constantly collapsing near the site, the rubble was cleared away because it was assumed that the head had fallen and was buried."[35]

Günther's story became even more dramatic over the next few days as he added detail upon detail. First, he claimed that the head belonged to Maximilian T., who lived in a room in his grandmother's building at Borsigstraße 7. The "shady Maximilian T." frequently brought strange people home from the Stettin Train Station and robbed them while they slept. Günther added that Maximilian T. went missing on 1 December; perhaps, the boy mused, a robbery victim murdered him.

This development sent police to Maximilian T.'s filthy, neglected room, bare but for the most necessary furniture; its only adornment was a grimy duvet lying atop the mattress on an iron bedstead. They found no evidence that the lodger was a murder victim, only that he had suddenly left.[36] Still, this was a lead, more than detectives had earlier. T.'s details fit the picture of a criminal typical of a city down on its heels. An impoverished man robbing unsuspecting visitors to survive was in keeping with occupied Berlin. West Berlin had 345 arrests for robbery in 1949. The previous year, the city as a whole had 1,066.[37]

That night, before officers could expend much energy on this new development, two more people visited Volkspolizei headquarters in response to Schwarz's press release. At about 9:00 p.m.,

Ernst Seidelmann, a travelling salesman, and his sister Anna Granzow walked into the Neue Königstraße building to view the dismembered remains described in the newspapers. Slim as the details about the partial corpse were, the siblings were afraid that they might belong to their missing brother, Hermann.[38] Before being led back to the police morgue, Seidelmann and Granzow told officers about their brother and their suspicions. Hermann had come to Berlin on 19 November 1949 to attend their mother's funeral, remaining for a short while to conduct some business. Anna explained that Hermann had approximately 1,800 DM East (and 60 DM) for purchases on Chausseestraße, a major thoroughfare in the city centre.

Chausseestraße had once been an important location for Berlin's industry. In 3½ years, it would be one of the sites of the city's workers' uprising on 17 June 1951, when demonstrators took to the street to protest rising production quotas and worsening conditions. It is also where sixteen-year-old Werner Sendsitzky would be shot and killed by East Berlin police on his way home on that fateful June day, simply walking past the demonstration to go home and celebrate his birthday with his family.[39]

Unfortunately, in 1949, Anna Granzow could not tell detectives which firm or firms Hermann meant to visit.[40] Seidelmann left his brother's lodgings midday on Saturday, 3 December, heading for the Silesian Station, planning to buy a train ticket home for the next day, but never returned. The newspaper's mention of the corpse's bandaged foot sent the pair to Volkspolizei headquarters; it seems that Hermann Seidelmann had a painful corn that had kept him bedridden for two days. Ernst had bought him a bandage at an apothecary to allow Hermann some mobility.[41] Police, hearing this detail, allowed Ernst and Anna to view the remains. Once the grief-stricken siblings made their identification, Ernst Seidelmann telegraphed the tragic news to Hermann's wife in Plauen, their hometown.[42]

8 December 1949

Before moving to the investigation's next phase, which would concentrate all resources on learning as much as possible about Hermann Seidelmann, the Volkspolizei returned to the non-existent head. When several detectives visited Günther J.'s neighbourhood for some follow-up questioning, he and Klaus muddled their stories. Günther J. not only stuck to but expanded his claim by adding such details as the head's grey stubble and explaining how he told both his grandmother and teacher about the find the day after he had stumbled on it. In the first telling, Günther stated that he had told his mother. His friend Klaus quickly retracted his eyewitness account. Klaus's new story for the detectives was that Günther had told him everything; he saw nothing. As the officers' conversation with Günther progressed, VP Wachtmeister Lippert asked Günther's grandmother why she had not informed the police of her grandson's claimed discovery. Because, she explained, her grandson often told fibs and loved to spin "fairy tales." She never gave his story much credence.[43]

Horst S., one of Günther's playmates, confirmed this. Even as police talked to Horst, two passing street sweepers told them that Günther had spoken of the body parts that the police had collected. Klaus's mother added that Klaus had related the story to her of the head that Günther claimed to have discovered. She, however, did not take the tale very seriously. In the end, VP Wachtmeister Lippert and his colleagues concluded that Günther's family saw through this untrustworthy boy's vivid imagination and continued to search for Maximilian T.[44] Investigators found him alive, if not well, in the hospital. He had been admitted the previous 30 November with a lung infection.[45]

Having sorted out Günther's false leads, VP Wachtmeister Lippert visited the area where Hermann Seidelmann's body lay, wandering about, speaking with residents, hoping to learn something valuable about the crime. Eva K. was among the people with whom he chatted. This young woman from Novalisstraße, a street that lay only a few minutes from where children had discovered the body, told Lippert a long, unbelievable story. She claimed that, at about 11:00 p.m. on 3 December, her fiancé saw two men standing near a corpse sprawled on the ground. Odder still, it lay beside a taxi parked in front of the Café Metro. Might this body be related to the Seidelmann case? Lippert hit yet another dead end. Local police had no reports of a body, nobody in the vicinity had seen one, and the taxi company had no missing drivers.[46]

VP Wachtmeister Lippert next looked into the appearance of a mysterious bundle of clothing discovered by a local married couple (Adolf and Anna S., ages sixty-five and fifty-nine) in front of their building at Borsigstraße 1, also close to the discovery site. The building's concierge, Frau G., explained that, although she had found the bundle, she left it in front of her house, whence it disappeared. When asked why she had not alerted the police, Frau G. responded that she had found laundry on the stairs twice already that year. Each time, Frau G. tossed it into the street. She added that somebody must have deposited the clothes during the day.

It only took a glance into Frau G.'s clean, orderly apartment to convince Lippert that she was trustworthy, solid, and respectable. Perhaps to add to this impression, Lippert's report noted that she lived alone because her husband, a soldier, had disappeared into the maelstrom of 1945. For these reasons, Lippert could not imagine Frau G. keeping or disposing of the items for gain.[47] Cleanliness, order, and a husband gone missing during the war enhanced her standing in his eyes. Taken together, these signs of trustworthiness speak volumes about this moment. Frau G.'s stereotypical solidity provided a comforting link to the stable society that Germany seemed to be before the occupation and would seem to become in the 1950s.

As early as 1946, the four occupying powers enacted new marriage laws designed to eliminate Nazi racism while avoiding Germany's earlier, patriarchal systems. Many contemporary Germans, alarmed by increases in divorce, illegitimacy, marital strife, and "non-traditional" families, embraced the move. To quote Alexandria Ruble, "West Germans proclaimed that women's 'freedom of choice' in the West stood for 'liberty, democracy, and capitalism,'" which allowed women, and especially mothers, to stay at home. Meanwhile, "women's emancipation" in the East represented the "progress of socialism," which liberated women, made them equal to men, and enabled mothers to do full-time work.[48] By 1948–49, some Christian conservatives embraced the opportunity to return to more traditional behavioural norms.[49]

Robert Moeller also writes of the return to tradition: "Equal with men and worth no less, women's difference nonetheless fully justified their special protection in marriage law, family allowances, and maternity legislation."[50] Frau G.'s ultra-traditional appearance and activities fit very nicely into this renewed interest in tradition.

Hewing to traditional ideas certainly helps explain why the police would initially imagine that the killer or killers were socially disruptive outsiders (foreigners, long-term criminals, black marketers, and the like) outside the bounds of the "normal" to which they wanted to return.[51]

In the day's most productive conversation, VP Wachtmeister Lippert spoke with Ernst Seidelmann, learning details that would help the investigation progress. On 2 December, Hermann had a currency trade go badly wrong. A couple of Poles had approached him to exchange currency. Later, after Hermann had traded his eastern Marks for their western ones, he looked into his wallet to discover that he was short 200 DM. Hermann told Ernst that he would certainly recognize the pair if he saw them again. Unfortunately, he never said where the trade took place.[52] The two currency swindlers would take on fundamental importance as the investigation progressed.

VP Kriminalpolizeirat Schwarz worked a different angle, trying to piece together a picture of Hermann Seidelmann. He began by interviewing Seidelmann's brother-in-law, Albert Granzow, at headquarters. After Granzow handed Schwarz a photograph of Seidelmann, the two discussed Hermann's trip to Berlin for his mother's funeral, his business, and some personal details that the police might find helpful in their investigation. A portrait emerged of a quiet man, a married father who drank very little but smoked a great deal. Hermann enjoyed seeing films by himself or with one of his brothers but never went dancing. In short, the man was the very image of a devoted husband and father.[53] Armed with new information, the Volkspolizei had every reason to expect that standard police procedure would succeed. Initial false leads could be dispensed with, allowing detectives to investigate any links that Hermann Seidelmann's life and connections might have had to his death. There was no reason to assume that their investigation would not proceed apace.

9 December 1949

Subsequent developments quickly added unexpected wrinkles both to the investigation and the city's tense, complicated political situation. At about 2:35 p.m. on 9 December, two days after Seidelmann's siblings identified their brother's remains, twenty-two-year-old Wachtmeister Werner Klemm stood at his post at the Knie subway stop in West Berlin's Charlottenburg district. Bombing had turned this area, once a prosperous, bourgeois shopping district, into a patchwork of buildings of different heights and character, resembling a once beautiful smile now showing broken teeth.[54] As Klemm surveyed the scene, a stranger approached him complaining about people combing through nearby Schillerstraße's ruined buildings collecting scrap. Knie, meaning knee, bore a name it had had for centuries. It "marked the bend of the axial connection between the two palaces in Berlin and Charlottenburg."[55] For the moment, it was just another grey area, surrounded by ruins and scavenged for anything valuable.

The stranger, whose name Klemm never noted, may have had an antiquated sense of urban order. He might have been bothered by outsiders treating his neighbourhood as a potential treasure site. Then again, perhaps he wanted a cop to roust them so that he could scrounge, unbothered, for treasure. The Wachtmeister ascribed him no particular importance; later, he could not even provide a detailed description. The most that the embarrassed Klemm told his superiors was that he would recognize the stranger were he to reappear.[56]

Combing ruins for useful or valuable items was illegal but not unusual. Only the day before, the *Berliner Zeitung* had published a three-column article about the illicit collecting of non-ferrous scrap metal from ruins. This politically charged exposé emphasized the social costs of such activities. Its anonymous author stressed that tons of rubbish shipped from the East to the West every month. Not only did this scrap leave Germany and weaken its reconstruction. Smugglers shipped it to the United States and the United Kingdom. This East German newspaper was horrified that Western imperial powers would grow stronger at Germany's expense. More immediately, it noted, such collecting was hazardous. A few weeks earlier, on 27 November, two youths searched in a Nollendorfstraße ruin for scrap. A collapsing wall killed them.[57] Neither the Cold War nor death were far from the surface in 1949 Berlin.

Klemm, on duty to keep the peace and protect order, understood that he had to follow up on this seemingly minor complaint. After another Wachtmeister relieved him half an hour later, he strolled to Schillerstraße, expecting to uphold the norms needed to allow his city to rise to its feet.[58] Arriving at Schillerstraße 3, he saw several women, a man, and a child poking around for scrap in a ruined building flanked by two wings. Most of them quickly disappeared when they spotted him, leaving Klemm to tell the two who remained that collecting things from ruins was punishable as theft.[59] As they had not yet taken anything and moved along when ordered, Klemm could not be bothered to take down any of their details.

Curiosity or a sense of order prompted the policeman to explore the cellar's poorly-lit left wing. He expected to chase away others rooting about inside. Shuffling about, Wachtmeister Klemm kicked something soft that aroused his curiosity; everything was helter-skelter in the dark, but he had no flashlight. Whatever he had kicked would remain hidden for a while. Frustrated and curious, he resumed patrolling his beat for the next several hours but knew he would return later.

When his rounds returned him at about 7:00 p.m., Klemm had a flashlight that helped to quickly find what he had accidentally kicked earlier – a human torso. After immediately calling another officer, the pair promptly took charge of the scene. While Klemm secured the scene, the second officer went to the nearest police station. Within about thirty minutes, Kriminal-Sekretär Meiser arrived at the scene, took Klemm's statement, and inspected the ruins at Schillerstraße 3. Meiser described the scene:

> The house at Schillerstraße 3 lies in total ruins. The cellars are mostly buried. The ruin consists of a front house and two side wings. The walls are mostly standing. The rear part of the property, closest to Knie, is also a ruined area ... on which there are some cinder stones. The discovery site lies in the mostly buried cellar entrance of the first-floor side wing.
>
> The body is lying with its back pointed upwards and shoulders pointing towards the entrance.[60]

After further searches turned up nothing, Meisner contacted the Charlottenburg criminal police. The "Kripo" in turn telephoned West Berlin's murder squad.[61] Kriminalkommissar Menzel, head of the murder squad who took over the investigation from Meiser, added that the careful dismemberment suggested very skilled perpetrators, and Menzel remembered the body parts that East Berlin newspapers had reported on near the Stettin Station. He then ordered the torso to be sent to the morgue so that Dr. Weimann could determine its probable age and perform an autopsy. Menzel assumed that he would soon release the torso (presumably to the East Berlin investigators).[62] This spirit of cooperation soon dissipated.

At about 7:30 a.m. the following day, Dr. Weimann bent over a torso lying on the sixth of twenty dissection tables in the Robert Koch Hospital's morgue.[63] Although it was still little used, the Robert Koch Hospital had a new name in 1949, or, to be more precise, it had returned to its pre–Third Reich name of Krankenhaus Moabit. In 1935, the Nazi government bestowed Koch's name on the facility to foreground the regime's interest in the intersection of science and racial cleansing. Perhaps this was a cruel joke. It was at least ironic. The hospital had enjoyed a reputation as a place welcoming to Jewish faculty and practitioners during the Weimar Republic.[64]

By the time of Waldemar Weimann's preliminary autopsy, though, the new powers in West Berlin were trying to move beyond the Third Reich. Administrators, nurses, and physicians strove to present an image of caring, decency, and normality. Weimann is the first medical professional to have an impact on this case. Nevertheless, the remains on the table reminded the physicians and staff present of the horrors still possible in this post-fascist moment. Weimann was a veteran of over 10,000 autopsies. Yet even he was taken aback by the horror of the sight. So was his twenty-seven-year-old secretary. When she walked in with a cigarette, she quickly handed it to Weimann, allowing her to press a perfumed handkerchief to her mouth and take a few breaths. Green as she turned, the Lysol-infused atmosphere combined with the perfume enabled her to continue taking Weimann's dictation as he proceeded with his work.[65]

While describing the torso on the table in front of him as belonging to a middle-aged man, Dr. Weimann remarked that a surgeon could not have done better. His assistant, Dr. Spengler, added that a butcher would do equally well. Curious about this turn, the other, unnamed official, present as an official witness, asked if they believed a physician was responsible. If that were the case, police could shorten their list of possible suspects. Weimann, too careful to make such an assumption, replied that somebody with a good knowledge of anatomy had performed the deed. The pathologists knew something that they thought the West Berlin police did not. Four days earlier, the Volkspolizei had sent a left arm and pair of legs to the morgue on Hannoversche Straße in Berlin's Soviet sector.

Waldemar Weimann later claimed to have telephoned Kriminalkommissar Menzel immediately to tell him that the body parts from different city sectors, divided by borders and politics, belonged to the same victim.[66] Weimann's memory of the conversation differs significantly from Menzel's contemporary notes. With his flair for the dramatic, the pathologist's tale emphasized Menzel's confusion and trepidation while showing the effect of the city's recent history on criminal investigation.

> But are you absolutely sure, Herr Obermedizinalrat?
> I would have to have the parts from over there, I say.
> They won't give us anything over there …

Then I'll go over there …
But not with our torso![67]

Waldemar Weimann meditated on Menzel's thoughts and bureaucratic issues; the Kriminalkommissar approached the case as a Cold War issue. Weimann, though, reflected on Berlin's dismemberment even as he worked on a much more literal dismemberment on the cold table in front of him. Both the detective and the pathologist understood the prohibition that forbade police from one sector visiting the other. Perhaps Menzel was frustrated that the western department obeyed a rule violated with impunity by the eastern force.

It should come as no surprise that Berlin's police department, like Berlin – like Germany as a whole – was split and doubled by 1949. Soviet occupiers reestablished the department in May 1945 under the leadership of a former army captain and Soviet POW named Paul Markgraf. In captivity, he studied with Wilhelm Pieck, Hermann Matern, and Walter Ulbricht, all future East German luminaries. Markgraf was not particularly competent but unquestionably loyal to Moscow. His second in command was Dr. Johannes Stumm, a skilled, Weimar-era police officer who was best known for cracking down on Nazi activities before the onset of the Third Reich. As political difficulties arose among Berlin's occupying powers, the police department became a site of contention. By 1948, each occupying power had named an assistant police chief for its sector. These assistant chiefs, in turn, paid little to no attention to Markgraf, resulting in the de facto splitting of the department. In July 1948, the Western Allies declared Johannes Stumm to be the new chief of police – which meant he would be chief of the West Berlin department, a position he held until 1962.[68] The departments would lose no time blaming and accusing each other for as many problems as possible.

Georg Schießer, a member of the early department, remembered the difficulties of the police department's initial days. "The working conditions in the office were catastrophic. There was no paper and no forms. Reports were often written on the backs of old wanted posters. It was only much later that the then president of the Central Administration for the Fuel Industry in the Soviet Zone and later deputy mayor of Berlin, Ferdinand Friedensburg, obtained twenty typewriters for the criminal police, which he had got hold of from somewhere in the magistrate's office."[69] Certainly, the shortage of typewriters would have pride of place in Elisabeth Kusian's story.

Waldemar Weimann knew, though, that he had freedom of movement, as the East Berlin system needed him because of East Berlin's legal-medicine state of emergency. He formulated a plan to which Menzel agreed. Weimann called East Berlin's prosecutor general and explained things to him in the strict materialist terms that Weimann believed that the prosecutor, a Communist, would understand. Western police had the most significant part: the torso. Eastern police only had some limbs. In short, the West had the "body." He was sure that the East Berliners would accept this logic. The "Comrade Prosecutor General" agreed. "In half an hour, our people will be over there." Menzel, stunned by this generosity, agreed to jump into his car to meet them.[70]

Carrying the dismembered limbs, VP Hauptwachtmeister Schwalbe and Wachtmeister Lippert crossed the city's border on their way to the morgue at the Robert Koch Hospital. Now having more to work with, Weimann told the assembled detectives that he believed Hermann Seidelmann's date of death lay between 1 and 3 December. When he lay the body parts together, Dr. Weimann quickly confirmed police suspicions: all probably belonged to the still-incompletely reconstructed cadaver. The Eastern detectives quickly noted in their report that the body parts fitted together. Kriminalkommissar Menzel, in turn, determined that it was much likelier that Hermann Seidelmann had been murdered and dismembered closer to the Zoo Station, which was relatively close to Knie, than in East Berlin. Menzel and his team knew that the torso was the heaviest part of the corpse. Its size and weight made it the least likely to be hauled far from the scene of the murder.[71] Perhaps this is one reason West Berlin authorities quickly notified their East Berlin counterparts about the torso's discovery. Regardless of the reason for their notification, the latter immediately joined the West Berlin investigation.

After viewing the more complete remains, the two East Berlin detectives went to the West Berlin discovery site, where they noted the cleared debris on the Schillerstraße side of the site. Still, though, rubble heaps dominated the Bismarckstraße side. They peered into the cellar vault beside a decayed stairway where the torso once lay. There seems to have been little more to say except that West Berlin authorities had not disturbed the area as they were still waiting for the forensics team to arrive and do its job.[72]

10 to 14 December 1949

On 10 December, Waldemar Weimann established that strangulation or choking caused Hermann Seidelmann's death. Weimann again emphasized that the unknown assailant had removed the arms and legs with a knife and considerable professional skill.[73] Meanwhile, detectives from the two squads met to combine and compare notes, and Hermann Seidelmann's wife and daughter travelled to Berlin, visited the morgue, and positively identified Seidelmann's remains. These steps ended the investigation's first phase.[74] As the case took firmer shape, newspapers from across the city paid it more attention.

Both *Telegraf am Abend* and *Der Abend* reported on the finding of the torso. *Der Tag* added that somebody had stolen Seidelmann's currency, watch, and clothes.[75] However, the seeming progress and added publicity hid a painful truth. The investigation had stopped moving forward. East Berlin detectives understood this. On 12 December, VP Kriminalpolizeirat Schwarz noted that his squad had hit a dead end. Regardless of their feelings about the matter, he wrote, his department might have to cede the entire investigation to the western force.[76]

Luck again helped the Volkspolizei detectives two days later. Sometime between 3:30 and 4:00 p.m. on 14 December, two teenagers, fourteen-year-old Horst J. and fifteen-year-old Hans-Joachim Z., heading home from the Lehrter Train Station, ducked into a house ruin so that Hans-Joachim could relieve himself. He quickly called his friend over. He had found something curious – a

Figure 2.2. The police offered a 500 DM reward for information that would help their investigation into Hermann Seidelmann's murder.

right arm, right leg, and head of what looked like a clothing store mannequin. They examined the find more carefully and, to their horror, saw that the dismembered "dummy" was sitting in blood. The youths quickly ran to the nearby Precinct Station #4 to report their finding to one of the station's officers, VP Wachtmeister Molkenthin, who called the East Berlin murder squad to the location, situated less than a mile away from the Friedrichstraße Train Station, one of the city's most important transport hubs.[77] VP Kriminalpolizeirat Schwarz and his team arrived at the scene at about 4:00 p.m. to restart an investigation that had seemingly stalled.[78]

It was cold, cloudy, and dry as seven officers and a police dog descended, for the second time, into a cordoned-off site to view parts of a dismembered corpse. Now the site of a luxury apartment complex, in December 1949, Chausseestraße 109 was yet another bombed-out ruin. Detectives negotiated a 1.5-metre wide, 10-metre long pathway across a rubble-strewn outer courtyard surrounded by walls whose buildings had disappeared. Only then could they reach the fragmented parts of a corpse. They picked their way to the inner courtyard's cleared entrance that was only passable for about 2 metres. Yet more rubble confronted them. The squad then turned left to face former doorways leading into bombed-out rooms.

To reach the body, they waded through debris, ducked under collapsed doorways, and jumped about a metre into an approximately 10 × 4.9 square metre room filled with rubble and corroded metal. In a corner, half-hidden behind a rusty stovepipe near heaps of garbage and discarded coal, lay a partially decomposed right arm, thigh, and man's head. The expertly severed head's nose and forehead pressed against one of the ruin's walls. Rain-washed grime indicated that the remains had been there for days. VP Kriminalpolizeirat Schwarz noted that one leg found at Borsigstraße was similarly grimy. He deduced from this that the still-unknown perpetrator initially might have brought the limbs to Chausseestraße, then later moved them to another location to confuse the police.[79] This discovery reignited the investigation. Schwarz informed the East Berlin Public Prosecutor that the murder squad would remain on the case even though they still had no clues to the perpetrator's identity.[80]

Having sent his report to the prosecutor, VP Kriminalpolizeirat Schwarz issued another press release to elicit public help. After briefly recapitulating the crime, the description of Seidelmann's clothing, the 1,800 DM East he had been carrying (all presumed stolen), and the sites where children had found his dismembered corpse, the release detailed Seidelmann's possibly running afoul of "wild" money traders. Schwarz made the following public plea:

> Who saw a person with clothing fitting this description on 3 and 4 December 1949? Who noticed persons with striking luggage at the announced places of discovery? Were there any cries for help or traces of blood in any part of the city (especially around the railroad stations) around the time indicated? Where have the stolen items been seen or offered for sale?[81]

Figure 2.3. Chausseestraße 109.

The notice concluded with the request that anybody who wanted to make a confidential report could go to the murder squad at police headquarters on Neue Königstraße 27/37, a former department store, Karstadt, that had been repurposed into a foreboding state office building.

Like many other sites attached to the case, this Neue Königstraße address resonates with pre-war and post-war German history. The building that stood there and would serve as East Berlin's police headquarters until 1990 had earlier housed the corporate offices of Karstadt, a department store chain. After its construction in 1931–32 as Berlin's largest office building, it proved too large for the firm, so the government purchased it in 1934 for 15 million Reichsmarks. Karstadt remained for two years but was replaced in 1936 by the Statistischen Reichsamtes, a bureau that, among other tasks, gathered censuses of German Jews. In 1945, after the Third Reich's collapse, the police moved in.[82]

As VP Kriminalpolizeirat Schwarz sat in his headquarters thinking about wild money traders and their likely attacks on Hermann Seidelmann, Kriminalkommissar Menzel's West Berlin squad reached roughly the same conclusions. Menzel understood the shady and dangerous nature of Hermann Seidelmann's business and the kinds of characters with whom it brought him into contact. Menzel found two such, who agreed to snoop around the train station to find anybody linked to Seidelmann. Kriminalkommissar Menzel's terminology for informant was V-Person, the singular of V-Leute.[83] They must have hoped that such informants would break the case open.

As December reached its midpoint, police thought they were on the verge of solving the case. Elisabeth Kusian, believing that she was beyond suspicion, began to plan her next move. Newspaper articles convinced her that police were on the wrong track. Because her friend Anni Glißmann had been so helpful in finding a suitcase, Kusian approached her for a second favour. Elisabeth Kusian wanted to borrow a comforter cover that could wrap another corpse.[84] As her hopes and plans began to take shape, she understood that she would need another victim. While police looked ever deeper into the black market, Elisabeth Kusian started to visit the Friedrich Beigang typewriter shop on Potsdamer Straße. Kusian held a series of conversations with Beigang and his sales associate, Dorothea (aka Doris) Merten, about purchasing a portable typewriter. She and Beigang negotiated the details and settled on a 250 DM machine, for which Kusian would make an initial 50 DM down payment. As with the furniture that she had acquired, then sold, earlier, she agreed to pay the rest of the debt in instalments. Kusian showed Beigang her employee identification from the Moabit Hospital, and the two of them readily agreed that a nurse was a trustworthy, indeed a risk-free, client. Concluding their discussions, Kusian and Beigang decided that she would pick up the machine on Christmas Eve.[85]

At about the same time that Elisabeth Kusian carried on her negotiations with Friedrich Beigang, she met Hedwig U. In late 1949, the sixty-one-year-old Hedwig U. owned a firm that did laundry for the Moabit Hospital. Because this entailed her going from floor to floor collecting sheets and other bedclothes, Hedwig U. came to know many of the hospital's nurses, and knowing them helped her develop a side business. Starting in the second half of 1949, Hedwig U. had become a distributor for the "Stahl-und Silberwarenfirma Fritz Müllhoff Solingen/Ohligs." In this capacity, she offered cutlery to potential clients. On 15 December, Hedwig U. showed Kusian her wares, enthusing her so much that the nurse placed a 122 DM delivery order for 22 December.[86] In short, only two and a half weeks after killing Hermann Seidelmann for less than 270 DM, she already committed herself to two expensive purchases that exceeded her takings.

Perhaps at the same time on 15 December that Elisabeth Kusian and Hedwig U. finalized their deal, West Berlin police arrested Herbert H., a twenty-three-year-old currency trader, on suspicion of murder. Two of Kriminalkommissar Menzel's informants informed the police that Herbert H. had swindled Seidelmann out of a good deal of money during a currency exchange. Officers arrested Herbert H. as he left a butcher's shop in Marburger Straße, where, only the night before, he and twenty-eight-year-old Czech citizen Josef J. had slaughtered an East German pig to sell for West German cash.[87] Police later picked up Josef J. at his rented room at Luitpoldstraße 48. At the end of a lengthy interrogation, Josef J. admitted that he had exchanged currency with Seidelmann and cheated him out of roughly 200 DM. Menzel and his squad saw Josef J. as the most likely murder suspect. He fit the common German stereotype of the foreigner as violent and dishonest – the opposite of the good German.

Such suspicion, indeed, racism, is to be expected at this moment. Nazi propaganda in the Third Reich successfully encouraged German youth to think in terms of "National Community." Of course, such ideas would still have currency a mere four years after the regime's collapse. Young adults, including many police officers, would have grown up in this world of ideas.[88] Social Darwinian notions of races' evolution were part of the previous school curriculum.[89] As John Connelly noted, "before 1939, a vague notion thus seems to have existed in leading Nazis' minds that Slavs constituted an inferior group, but just how inferior was an issue to be decided later."[90] Only ten years before the investigation of Hermann Seidelmann's murder, Albert Brackmann of the University of Berlin wrote in a pamphlet that "the German people were the only bearers of culture in the East and, in their role as the main power of Europe, protected Western culture and carried it into uncultivated regions. For centuries, they constituted a barrier in the East against lack of culture (Unkultur) and protected the West against barbarity."[91] Thus it is no surprise that, although Germans primarily controlled the black market, "for the East Berlin press, foreign black marketeers were parasitic nuisances who should be energetically dealt with by the police." Phrases like "parasites on the racial body" were tossed about. The combination of Nazi racism with Communist prejudice against DPs made such ideas almost inescapable.[92]

On 17 December, police brought Josef J. in front of an interrogating judge on suspicion. Furthermore, they asked the judge for permission to jail him.[93] Menzel then telephoned VP Kriminalpolizeirat Schwarz to inform him of the arrests and gloat about solving the case. He added and simultaneously dismissed Josef J.'s claim that he was not in Berlin at the time of the murder. Of course, he interjected, the West Berlin force would check the alibi.[94] In a surprise to Menzel, both Josef J. and Herbert H. proved that, on the night of 3 December, they travelled from Zoo Station to their home in Germany's Soviet-Occupied Zone.[95] Yet again, the investigation returned to square one.

For a brief moment, after police had freed Josef J. and Herbert H., neighbours tried to direct the officials' attention to Seidelmann's brother Ernst. At least a few of them (unnamed in police files) explained to the police how odd it seemed that, in the aftermath of Hermann's death, Ernst suddenly had the resources to open a fruit and vegetable stand in the neighbourhood. Suggestive as was

Menzel's use of the Gestapo term for an informant, such snitching is equally reminiscent of the Third Reich. The success of the secret police rested on the German public's voluntary, even enthusiastic, cooperation.[96] This behaviour would not change overnight.

Kriminalkommissar Menzel raised and dismissed the possibility of Ernst Seidelmann's involvement in one sentence buried in a paragraph about Josef J. and Herbert H., never giving it serious consideration.[97] Several days after the detectives saw their hopes about the larcenous currency traders dashed, both departments began to rethink their strategies.[98]

Perhaps detectives began to wonder whether Hermann Seidelmann had really led a blameless life. In the wake of a series of dead ends, they began to expand the focus of their conversations with witnesses and possible witnesses. The Volkspolizei continued its painstaking work by talking with ticket sellers at the Friedrichstraße and Silesian train stations. Had station clerks sold any suspicious train tickets to Flöhe?[99] What clues might Seidelmann's life provide to his murder?

VP Hauptwachtmeister Syllwasschy began to paint a more rounded portrait of the victim. A clerk at one shop that sold the kind of agricultural equipment Hermann Seidelmann sent back to his customers in Thuringia remembered him well. Seidelmann, memorable for his purchases of harrows and other such goods, was the sort of person who would trade in illegal goods at the Zoo Station. A sideline in black-market stockings would not surprise her. After all, did he not often appear at the shop in a drunken state? Who was Hermann Seidelmann? This is a far cry from the teetotaller described by his brother-in-law. Such details helped round out the authorities' picture of the victim. It seemed like a good time for new lines of inquiry that assumed a different understanding of Hermann Seidelmann.[100]

Servers and other personnel at train stations' pubs and cafés did not remember Seidelmann. Prostitutes working nearby, though, thought they did. One woman who worked at the Café Schauspielhaus on Max-Reinhardt-Straße insisted that she recognized his coat; she had recently seen a theatre agent wearing it. Volkspolizei thought this hot lead might take detectives to the killer. When they located the agent, though, he produced a receipt that proved he had owned his coat since the late 1930s. A nearby bar owner was confident that he recognized Seidelmann as a well-known, shady local character. Excitement melted into disappointment when police determined that "Hermann the Sprat" was an unrelated fishmonger with shops in Moabit and the market hall on the Turmstraße.[101]

As the Volkspolizei worked to rethink their image of Hermann Seidelmann's life and personality, the West Berlin squad performed a forensic analysis of the room where he stayed when visiting his brother Ernst in Berlin. Among the objects they found were a woman's brown hat, which shifted their suspicion to Gertraud A. Gertraud A., a recently divorced thirty-two-year-old woman who lived in Wittstocker Straße 2, had known Seidelmann for some time and owed him money. Menzel was intrigued and suspicious. "Investigations of A.," he believed, "revealed that she was consorting with an undetermined number of men."[102] His squad searched her apartment for evidence, like traces of blood that might have flowed between the floorboards. They found nothing. Still, she had recently painted the floor. Kriminalkommissar Menzel pondered this but had to conclude that she had no connection to the crime. He let her go.[103] Once again, out of frustration, he reminded the press of the investigation. Police also printed pictures of Seidelmann for the Litfaßsaüle in Charlottenburg, Tiergarten, and Schöneberg, which advertised a 500 DM reward.[104] Litfaßsaüle, large cement columns that dotted Berlin, are still a common sight in the city. They advertise theatre, opera, and other items of interest to contemporary passersby. In the immediate post-war era, the occupying powers used them to make announcements.[105] Police notices would fit right in.

As Christmas loomed, both of Berlin's police departments continued to widen their net for Seidelmann's murderer. One line of inquiry led them to compare Seidelmann's murder with other, at least superficially similar, murders from the previous nine months. Hermann Seidelmann's connection to Gertraud A. may have prompted Volkspolizei detectives to think about sex-linked crimes. They thus revisited the case of Hertha Ei., a forty-one-year-old prostitute whom somebody had strangled and hanged on a girder at about 2:00 a.m. in the ruins of Artilleriestraße near the Spree River on 30 March 1949. Seven months later, on 17 October, the naked body of thirty-seven-year-old Agnes Sz., also a prostitute, strangled with a stocking, clothes, and handbag missing, was discovered in her Krausnickstraße apartment.[106] These connections that had seemed promising came to nothing.

As police investigations into the life of Hermann Seidelmann seemed to turn up ever less helpful information, Elisabeth Kusian's life proceeded apace. Her preparations for the Christmas holiday grew ever bigger but forced her to balance her very different lives. Her ex-husband, Walter Kusian, dropped by her room a few days before the holiday with food and toys for the children. Although she had accused this former Nazi, high-ranking stormtrooper, German soldier, and inmate in an American POW camp of brutality to her and their children, he often helped her with day-to-day concerns such as procuring firewood and coal for her stove. On this visit, Elisabeth told Walter that a truck-driver friend would deliver to the children their cornucopia of puppets, building set complete with a wooden locomotive, Christmas Stollen, apples, oranges, nuts, chocolate bars, Pfeffernüsse, and various baked goods. He, in turn, was happy that these would arrive at her mother's home in Thuringia, where Walter thought the children now lived.[107] Walter was wrong. Finding their presence inconvenient, Elisabeth had again placed them in local orphanages. The presents, though, would prove useful when she regifted them to her lover's children.

As the holiday neared, Elisabeth Kusian tried to clear up some complications and details, and make plans to bring her life into better order. Radio and Elektrohändler Schwenke, the shop from which she had purchased her radio, tried to reach her about missing instalment payments on yet another of her ill-conceived instalment purchases. Kusian invited Herr Schwenke to visit on Christmas Eve or Christmas Day to sort out the payments, but he already had plans, plans that he later thought saved his life.[108] She did make the time to take Hermann Seidelmann's stolen hat to the C. Waenke hat shop at Kirchstraße 1a for a cleaning and blocking. Should she sell it? Might it make a good gift for somebody? She insisted it be ready for the holiday but never bothered to retrieve it.[109]

In another snag, Elisabeth Kusian believed she might have to deal with the reappearance into her life of one of her former lovers, the burglar Hans Hubert Boguslawski, newly released from jail on 19 December.[110]

On 22 December, Elisabeth Kusian still had not received the cutlery she ordered from Frau Hedwig U., cutlery that she wanted to form part of a collection of gifts for Kurt Muschan. Kusian telephoned to complain.[111] Admittedly, not yet having the silverware in hand had financial advantages. Until she received it, she would not have to make any payments. This seemingly minor detail would matter to a woman deep in debt for a typewriter and an ongoing drug habit.[112] Such calculations, though, seem to have been beyond her. The following morning, probably while Elisabeth still brooded over the missing silverware, Kurt came by to visit but had to wait for about half an hour. Elisabeth was out, ostensibly running errands.

When she finally arrived, Elisabeth prattled on about her visit to the hospital to help with two complex cases. Kurt gave her an assortment of Christmas gifts, including a coffee service for two, a red scarf, a carton of soap, a box of candy, and a flowerpot. Combining the practical and pleasant, the presents were anything but extravagant. In Muschan's telling, as the couple chatted, an older woman arrived with some silverware. Muschan claims to have stepped into the hall so as not to overhear their conversation. When he stepped back inside, Elisabeth Kusian showed him the cutlery to ask his opinion. During this piece of theatre, her elderly visitor seemed to be impatient to finish the business arrangements and be off. Nevertheless, the old woman, hoping to turn an even greater profit, asked whether they had any interest in dress shirts. Kusian, having no cash on hand, declined. The women agreed on terms for the silver. Half listening, Muschan heard Kusian tell her that if nobody were home to take delivery, the landlady could. Muschan never heard any discussion of the price. He also never caught the old woman's name.[113]

The "old woman" of Muschan's memory, Hedwig U., recalled the details differently. She claimed to have arrived at about 2:30 p.m., then waited for ten or so minutes before anybody arrived. She remembered this vividly. Why would Kusian be so impatient to get the silverware and then not be there to finish the deal? Nevertheless, Kusian was more than pleased when she saw it.

Hedwig U. saw Kusian convince Kurt Muschan that her sister viewed the same set in the hospital and wanted one for herself. Kusian, turning to Hedwig U., asked if she could buy a second, identical set. Hedwig, of course, immediately agreed to an instalment plan. Now Kusian owed 248.80 DM for silverware.[114] Did Kusian double the amount of silverware for Muschan because of the gifts that he had given her? Possibly. Just as likely, though, Kusian hoped to pawn it for quick cash.

The following morning, Christmas Eve, Elisabeth Kusian cast the die for her next series of actions. With yet more debt burdening her, Kusian showed up at Anni Glißmann's door with four grey boxes filled with silverware. Kusian explained that they belonged to colleagues, that the silverware had to be worth a lot of money, and asked Glißmann to act as her agent and pawn it. Kusian must have thought of this in advance and seems to have been on edge to have the transaction done quickly.

Anni Glimann had not yet dressed when Elisabeth Kusian asked her to walk to the Moabit Hospital. She demurred, hurriedly threw on some clothes, and met Elisabeth a bit later at her nurses' station. As Kusian handed her the utensils, she told Anni that they "probably" cost about 280 DM and should bring at least 180 DM from the pawnshop. But the pawnbroker only offered 40 DM. What to do? When Anni telephoned with the disappointing news, a likely frantic Kusian told her to return to Moabit with the silverware. The failure to turn the cutlery into cash dealt her an unexpected blow. It guaranteed that there would be no money for Beigang's down payment. Elisabeth was both cash-strapped and stuck with two sets of expensive silverware.[115] Then things worsened. One of Hedwig U.'s employees visited Kusian at the hospital for a signature.[116] Kusian began to adjust her plans.

When Anni Glißmann returned that afternoon to the hospital, she and Kusian took the #2 streetcar to Steinplatz, about midway between Knie and the Zoo Station. Kusian waited there and sent Glißmann to Kantstraße 154a with a note for her landlady, Frau Stö., scrawled with the words: "Please give the bearer 90 DM from the desk on the left. If Herr Muschan is in the room, please do not go to the desk, but please give her 70 to 80 DM of your money. At noon I will be at home, where you will get it back immediately." Because Frau Stö. was not there, Anni Glißmann handed the note to Frau Schön., Stö.'s eighty-six-year-old mother, with whom she lived.[117] Schön. gave Glißmann 80 DM, assuming it was for Kusian's Christmas presents. Unsurprisingly, she later had to remind Kusian, in writing, to repay the loan.[118]

Elisabeth Kusian had both more money and more debt. What a burden. As Anni Glißmann handed her the money, the nurse wept. Between tears, she told Anni that Kurt Muschan was married with children. His happy family life meant that poor Elisabeth would have to spend Christmas Eve alone, heartbroken. When Anni invited the murderess to spend the evening with her family, Kusian accepted but would not be able to come until 9:00 p.m. They then went their separate ways, Anni watching as Kusian wandered towards Zoo Station.[119]

After leaving Anni, Elisabeth stopped at a public telephone to call the Beigang shop. She apologized to Herr Beigang; something had come up. A new admission at her station made it impossible to leave work. Could, perhaps, Beigang's sales clerk, "Fräulein" Merten, as she mistakenly called her, deliver the machine on 26 December instead? Beigang explained that he had no control over his employee's free time but would put Merten on the line to discuss a possible delivery. Not a problem, Merten told her. By happy coincidence, she would be travelling past Kusian's home on the way from her sister's to visit family. These plans made Elisabeth Kusian's request no bother. Kusian thanked Merten for her help and promised her some lunch in return. When told that she would have to provide a 50 DM down payment, Elisabeth readily agreed.

Friedrich Beigang and Doris Merten closed the shop at about 2:00 p.m. on Christmas Eve. Beigang was leaving early for a short ski vacation in Oberhof, Thuringia. Merten packed up the typewriter, an "Erika," and took it to her sister's with whom she was staying. Erikas were a storied typewriter model. Introduced in 1910 by Seidel and Neuman in Dresden, they would continue to be manufactured in the GDR and have some popularity in the East Bloc.[120] Beigang and his wife had known Merten for years; he had no reservations about leaving the Erika's delivery and the shop in her capable hands.

When Doris Merten arrived at her sister Charlotte Strach's house that afternoon, they had much to discuss. Merten complained that Herr Beigang left too little cash in the shop. It would be hard for her to buy and sell independently to make extra money. But then she dismissed this with a wave of her hand. Somehow she would do some business together with Herr Steg. Who was this man? Strach knew next to nothing about him. Could, she mused, the two of them have some kind of romantic relationship? No time for this musing as the conversation turned to Kusian. In her recollection, Strach said that "when she mentioned the name of the nurse, that it was a funny name, Merton replied, 'Yes, she is also a funny woman.'"[121]

Having finished setting the stage for what would be her second murder, Elisabeth Kusian turned her thoughts to her Christmas Eve plans. At about 6:00 p.m. that evening, after Kusian had finished her shift, Frau Schön. brought her a fruit plate (Bunten Teller) to help celebrate the season. Schön. was struck by Kusian's rather downcast mood:

> She sat at the desk in her coat, somewhat dejected, propped her head up in her hand, and said to me: "I have to collect myself first, please not today, rather tomorrow." She did not want to accept the fruit plate, but I left it in her room. I did not talk to her about her depression because I assumed that it was because she had to celebrate Christmas without her children.[122]

At about 7:00 p.m., Elisabeth Kusian decided to leave her apartment, telling Frau Schön. that she had to tend to a very sick woman.[123] Rather than heading to the hospital, though, she visited her ex-husband, Walter, and stayed with him from about 8:00 to 10:30 p.m.[124] Walter then accompanied her on the S-Bahn, bringing the two rucksacks she had asked to borrow. One was full of coal. The other was either empty or filled with firewood.[125] He did not expect to see Elisabeth the next day as she had told him about hospital shifts on Christmas Day and 26 December.[126] When Kusian arrived at her room sometime around midnight, she again ran into Frau Schön. A sad night had passed, she said; the woman she cared for in the hospital died at about 10:00 p.m.[127]

For Berlin's police, the Seidelmann murder case stalled again by Christmas. Likely leads pointing towards currency traders, black marketers, and dwellers in the demi-monde went nowhere. Detectives had run out of options. Forensic and eyewitness evidence took them in no particular direction. Investigations were likely bound to fail with Christmas, the New Year, and the new decade just a few days away. At best, the police departments and their homicide squads could console themselves that they had worked well together. Perhaps, some thought, this might herald ever-growing cooperation as the new cities and countries took on a more coherent shape. They could not know that Elisabeth Kusian's borrowing of rucksacks meant that she was preparing for at least one more murder.

Doris Merten and her sister Charlotte Strach, Friedrich Beigang, and Kurt Muschan each spent a quiet Christmas Day with their respective families. As Merten and Strach passed the holiday together at home and Beigang skied with his wife in Thuringia, Kurt Muschan was with his family. For Christmas, Kurt Muschan gave his wife an imitation gold necklace. Sadly, Frau Muschan could not wear it often; the cheap metal's tarnish stained her clothing.[128]

Walter and Elisabeth Kusian's day was rather tense, pointing to coming horrors. On Christmas Day morning, Walter Kusian wandered into his apartment's shared kitchen, exchanging pleasantries with the landlord's family members as they made coffee. Their conversation turned to Christmas trees. When the others talked about theirs, Kusian sadly explained that his children lived so far away, it was pointless for him to hang holiday decorations.[129] Reflections on Christmas, children, and the time on his hands turned Walter Kusian's thoughts to his ex-wife. Maybe Elisabeth wanted to avoid him for the holidays. Did she really have a shift? Walter determined that he would look into this on 26 December.[130]

Elisabeth Kusian had told him a partial truth about working a Christmas shift. Once home, she spoke with Frau Schön. and Frau Stö. sometime between 7:00 and 7:30 p.m. Kusian explained to the two women that the large case full of toys she had brought home "from the hospital" was for her children. Frau Stö. helped her carry it, neatly wrapped in a blanket, upstairs. When Frau Schön. remarked upon a Stollen that Kusian had packed with the toys, Kusian claimed it was a gift from another nurse. She then told a story about a death in the hospital that morning, one she claimed was due to a physician's forgetting to remove a tampon from a patient. As is the case with so many of her stories, it is impossible to untangle the truth from the lies; it does, though, show that death was on her mind.[131]

chapter three

The Murder of Doris Merten

Sunday, 25 December 1949–Friday, 6 January 1950

Both Berlin and Doris Merten enjoyed a relatively quiet Christmas in 1949. Another year passed without snow, but, as the *Neue Zeit* reminded its readers, Berliners had become used to that. Churches were so packed that extra services were held for all those who wanted to celebrate. Huge numbers of eager travellers overwhelmed the public transport system. Thieves stole metal wherever they could find it. Some daring criminals even managed to steal a 50-metre long telephone cable, which they cut and removed with professional tools.[1] There were few major news stories to occupy Doris Merten's thoughts. Perhaps she reflected on the city's post-war holiday cheer and woes on the cold, rainy early afternoon of 26 December when she left her sister's home to deliver the promised typewriter.[2] Maybe she was grateful for her loving family. She had a sister to stay with and extended family to visit for lunch and gift exchanges. Why bother to take the house key that her sister Charlotte Strach offered? It simply was not necessary. She would be home early. When Doris did not return on time, Charlotte did not worry. Her sister must have decided to spend the night with the Glaubitz family whom she planned to visit after the delivery[3]

Doris Merten arrived on time at Kantstraße 154a and was let in by Frau Schön., staying about fifteen minutes.[4] The speed was not because her transaction was easy; it was frustrating. Elisabeth Kusian did not have the promised down payment ready. Could

Figure 3.1. Doris Merten, date unknown.

Merten, perhaps, leave the typewriter and accept silverware as a guarantee of payment? Doris, of course, could not know that Kusian had acquired the set only a few days before or that it was barely worth pawning. The women agreed that, when Merten returned at about 8:00 p.m., Kusian would have the cash on hand, exchange it for the silverware, and finish the transaction. Kusian also gave Merten a house key to let herself in. She presumably told Merten that the key was for her convenience. Doris Merten's convenience, though, was far from Kusian's mind. Having a house key would encourage Doris Merten to trust Kusian and, even more importantly, allow her to return without alerting Kusian's neighbours that she had a visitor.[5]

Doris Merten, certainly annoyed, continued on her way to her family visit. Knowing that she would have to return to Kusian's later that day, she nevertheless was delighted to see her nieces who were visiting the city to celebrate the holiday. There they were at the bus stop to greet her at about 4:00 p.m. and escort her to Charlotte and Paul Glaubitz's home. Paul Glaubitz quickly noticed how nice she looked in her matching brown fur coat, hat, and shoes. He was struck, though, by the bag of silverware. Holidays are good for stories, and Doris had a peculiar tale of a nurse who wanted a typewriter for her boyfriend, "a member of the press." "Sister Elisabeth" tried to satisfy her with an IOU. Merten regaled her family with this piece of nonsense. Of course she needed collateral that had intrinsic value.[6] Silverware? It was something.

Charlotte Glaubitz found the whole transaction very peculiar and warned Doris to back out of it. Nobody would want to conduct such business the day after Christmas. The sheer weirdness of using silverware as a bond was alarming. Merten just scoffed. Sister Elisabeth was fine. Wasn't she the mother of three children who went to boarding school? Was there a surer sign of respectability? Frau Glaubitz retorted that Kusian had to have enough cash for a typewriter. Boarding schools were expensive. Merten remained unmoved. Frau Glaubitz's objection that a mother should spend the holidays with her children neither swayed Merten nor unnerved her. The sad part of this story, she told them, was that she could not stay long.[7] The evening ended at 9:00 p.m. when the children accompanied Merten to the bus stop to finish the odd transaction. Her family never saw her alive again.[8]

At the same time that Doris Merten planned to leave or was already going, Kurt Muschan, Walter Kusian, and Elisabeth Kusian were laying their own plans. Muschan told his wife that one of his colleagues had fallen ill. He was sorry, but he would have to take night duty that evening and leave the house early enough to be at the police station by 7:00 p.m.[9] Walter, feeling lonely, telephoned Elisabeth Kusian's hospital floor to see if she had duty that evening.[10] When he found out that she did not, he also went to her place, both for some company and to collect 20 DM that Elisabeth owed him.[11] Frau Stö. greeted him at about 7:00 p.m. Then he climbed the stairs to find Elisabeth wearing her blue nursing uniform. She must have looked much the same as she did when she wanted to calm any anxiety Hermann Seidelmann might have had. This visit, though, was both different and unwanted. Elisabeth did not let him in, claiming that Muschan was there. After they had spoken for about fifteen minutes, and as Walter turned to leave, Elisabeth did something so unusual that he remembered it vividly. She ran after him and astonished him with a goodbye kiss as he walked away.[12] What could she have been thinking?

With Walter gone, Elisabeth prepared her evening. Perhaps Walter's departure prompted her to write a note for Kurt Muschan explaining that she expected two visitors, so he would need to go elsewhere for a while.[13] Later, between 6:00 and 6:30 p.m., she borrowed wine glasses from Frau Stö. to reinforce this lie. Elisabeth was not thinking straight or at least made yet another error. When Kusian returned them, the glasses were still dusty. Curious, the landlady thought, nobody drank.[14] But that was later; for now, all of her tasks done, Elisabeth could sit by her window to wait for Doris Merten and Kurt Muschan.[15]

As expected, Muschan arrived first. At about 8:15 p.m., he alighted from the #75 streetcar and saw Elisabeth's profile in the window. She was a vision. He flew up the stairs even as she hurried down. She apologized but insisted that he could not come in yet. Unfortunately, two old friends were visiting; she had to entertain them, no? Handing him the note she had written earlier, Elisabeth suggested he either see a film or go to the nearby Berliner Kindl for a bite to eat and a drink.[16] Having no interest in a movie, Muschan went to the pub, drank schnapps for about three hours, growing ever more annoyed and impatient. Two waiters shared responsibility for his table. Both tried his nerves. His detective instincts kicked in as he noticed that one of them had a red face and a drinker's nose. Is that why the two argued? One finally yelled at the other, "Go home. Why are you still here?"[17] Ever angrier, Kurt Muschan must have thought that this would not be a night to remember.

At about 11:00 p.m., Kurt Muschan dropped 80 Pfennigs on the table for his drink. Time to leave![18] Then, like a miracle, Elisabeth waltzed in. Muschan responded with a grumble. He wished he had stayed home with his family.[19] Thinking about how to calm him and make the rest of her night as pleasant as possible, Elisabeth wove him a tale of two visitors, Musch and Ulla. Musch had fallen ill after having had a drink. Of course, the women had to telephone Musch's son Horst to collect and take them home.[20] The women were real. They never, though, visited. Elisabeth Kusian's evening had proceeded quite differently.

Two hours before, at about 9:00 p.m., while Muschan was still at the Berliner Kindl, Doris Merten stepped onto the bus bound for Elisabeth's building. With luck, she could exchange the silverware for the required down payment and leave quickly. This second trip to Kantstraße was an annoyance that Frau Merten could do without.[21] After a thirty to forty-five minute ride, she let herself in unannounced and unnoticed. Though she expected their business to take no more than a few minutes, Doris Merten politely hung her coat, hat, and umbrella on the door hooks and made herself comfortable on the sofa, even smoking a cigarette, while Elisabeth stood by the oven, chatting as the radio played in the background. Merten then shifted to the business at hand. Here was the silverware and a receipt for the agreed-upon cash. Indeed, Elisabeth handed her two 20 DM bills and a 10 DM one. Then came the equivalent of 50 Pfennigs in East German change, the fee for setting up the instalment plan.

Her task finished, Doris Merten rose but then changed her mind, staying long enough to smoke one more cigarette. Maybe this extra moment allowed Elisabeth to make a final, fatal decision. She stepped to her table, opened the drawer, and removed a length of pre-cut clothesline.[22] Elisabeth insisted that Merten quickly lost consciousness after a brief struggle. Might this belief ease her conscience? Forensic evidence showed that Merten struggled.[23] Though Kusian initially claimed she then dragged Merten's body into the room of another of the building's subletters who happened to be out of town for the weekend, she later admitted to stowing the corpse under the bed. There was no time to do anything else beyond opening the windows before going to Berliner Kindl to fetch the disgruntled Kurt Muschan.[24]

Would Kurt notice anything amiss, perhaps suspect something odd? Elisabeth asked him to wait outside the door for just a moment, explaining that she wanted to begin their night together with lit Christmas tree candles. Their glow would emphasize the season's warmth and beauty; they might even dispel the horrors of her earlier actions.[25] Festive lights in the tree and a still-cooling corpse under the bed produced an irony beyond Elisabeth's grasp. As the candles blazed, the still annoyed Muschan stomped around Kusian's room, noticing things that seemed out of place. Rather than remarking on the tree or the candles, as he hung up his jacket he asked about the coat and hat hanging on her door. He had never seen them before. Her quick, illogical response was that her visitor left them behind to be taken to a shop for alterations.[26] When Muschan commented on the umbrella and unused wine glasses, she claimed that the umbrella was hers, just back from being repaired. Were her lies too blatant even for Muschan? Elisabeth Kusian sensed that he did not believe her: "He was a little weird with me and peevish all evening."[27]

To shift her lover's attention from the dry wine glasses, Kusian insisted on inviting Frau Stö. and her mother over for a quick visit. Elisabeth popped into the shared kitchen to brew coffee, then knocked on the landlady's door.

Was it real "bean" coffee or Muckefuck? This second, derogatory, term meant both weak coffee and a hot drink made with some mixture of coffee, chicory, rye, or barley. In 1949, West Germans drank, on average, 164.8 litres of Muckefuck versus only 57.8 litres of real coffee. Real coffee stood for prosperity; Ersatz for a continuation of the hunger years. Only two years earlier, a kilo of real coffee had cost 1,100 Reichsmarks on Berlin's black market, almost twice its 600 Reichsmark price in Stuttgart in the West. Elisabeth certainly would have wanted to serve the former, if only to reinforce the image of bourgeois prosperity and "culture" that she was trying to conjure. Given her willingness to pay absurd prices to create the illusion of a good life, she likely did so.[28]

Apologizing for any tension between her and her "fiancé," Kusian invited the two women over for a brief, friendly visit to clear the air. Mother and daughter were happy to accept, and the foursome chatted politely. How was Herr Muschan's trip to Frankfurt am Main? Kusian had told the woman that Muschan had been travelling for business, a lie that should explain his odd absence over Christmas. "No," Muschan corrected her. He had been in Frankfurt an der Oder, not Frankfurt am Main. This new detail both covered and expanded Kusian's tale.[29]

The atmosphere lightened after the women left, and Elisabeth decided the time had arrived for her to give Muschan his typewriter. He was "amazed and astonished" but not particularly thrilled. Muschan had to leave the typewriter behind. The still grumpy detective knew that he could not invent a plausible explanation for his wife about how he had gotten it. Had Elisabeth's horrors been for nothing? Maybe the silverware for his wife would improve things. Muschan began to wonder about this generosity. Elisabeth could only lie about a fictional rich uncle in Gera who gave her 4,500 DM East.[30] To end their night, Kusian and Muschan spoke for a long while, then slumbered above Doris Merten's stiffening corpse.[31]

The next morning, 27 December, the couple awoke sometime between 9:00 and 9:30 a.m. As Elisabeth arose to wash, she had Muschan promise to stay where he was.[32] What could be worse than his looking under the bed? They then spent a nerve-wracking morning together before she sent him home to his family, not to see each other before New Year's Eve.[33] When Muschan arrived home to hand the silverware to his wife, he brazenly told her that he had purchased it. Regardless of its appearance, he insisted, it was cheap. Frau Muschan did not believe him and feared its real back story might be problematic enough to cost him his job. Her unhappiness convinced the detective to remove the cutlery without explanation. He would never mention it again.[34]

That evening the twenty-six-year-old nursing student Hertha S. visited Elisabeth to enjoy a coffee and chat. With Kurt Muschan long gone, this student would provide a pleasant diversion or perhaps a profit. Hertha S. arrived at about 6:30 p.m. and stayed until 10:00 p.m. As the two chatted, Elisabeth poured Hertha a cup of coffee after which she felt oddly tired, so tired that Elisabeth had her lie down to rest. At about 8:00 p.m., as Hertha relaxed, Elisabeth's "brother-in-law," Walter Kusian, knocked at the door to fetch two rucksacks. They were still at the hospital, Elisabeth apologized, and needed a thorough cleaning before they could be returned. Walter then asked for the return of the 20 DM he had loaned her.

Hertha S. saw how unhappy Walter's arrival made Elisabeth, as if his arrival had spoilt her evening. What could this mean? Elisabeth sized up the situation, then decided that Walter was interested in Hertha. Her mood lightened, perhaps his roving eye could be turned to advantage.

Elisabeth Kusian brewed a second pot of coffee for everybody, a pot which Hertha thought tasted very different from the first, brewed just for her.[35] She wondered about it at the time. Perhaps, she thought while drinking another cup, the previous night's shift left her exhausted. Later, though, upon reflection, she decided that she had been drugged. At about 9:30 p.m., Walter accompanied her to Zoo Station to catch the streetcar for her night shift. His arrival might have saved her life. In the coming weeks and months, she came to believe so.[36]

Elisabeth Kusian had time to think about lost opportunities. After her two visitors left, she turned yet again to the dismembering and disposing of a corpse. Perhaps after turning on the radio (Had she done that? She could not remember.), Elisabeth injected herself with morphine, waited for the drug to calm her, and pulled Doris Merten's remains out from under the bed.[37] How might she proceed? First came Merten's wedding ring, then another ring, and finally Merten's clothes. All these tasks were complicated by rigor mortis.[38] Elisabeth stepped into the shared kitchen for Frau Stö.'s knife. Her experience with Hermann Seidelmann's body had taught her to prepare a rag, bucket, and newspapers for the night ahead. Elisabeth removed Frau Merten's arms, cut her legs off at the knees to simplify transport, and then wrapped the limbs in newspaper to prevent too much blood from escaping. Finally came decapitation and covering the torso with the same blanket that had covered Hermann Seidelmann. Then it was time to pack the body into rucksacks she would cover with dirty hospital scrubs.[39]

After tossing Doris Merten's clothes into a suitcase, Elisabeth began to clean her room, washing the floor as best she could, then pouring the bloody water down the toilet. She would, however, keep the decomposing corpse in her room for several more days.

Although she had not used the heat for a while, the room was beginning to smell. She opened her window to let in as much fresh air as was possible. Like so many of her actions, this was only partially successful. Christa S. (who rented the room next to Kusian's) wondered about the odd, sweet smell coming from the room. Kurt Muschan, who would return on New Year's Eve to spend a couple of hours with Kusian, found her open window odd for this time of year, especially as she had run out of coal and could not heat her place.[40] Nevertheless, it did not occur to the detective to follow up on this hunch.

After dissipating the smell as best she could, Elisabeth's priority was to inventory Doris Merten's resources. The wallet held 82 DM East and 5 DM in cash, an identity card, and an interzonal pass.[41] Elisabeth took the money, burned the cards in her oven, and turned to the remaining tasks. The strangest of these was typing a series of letters putatively from her mother that spun tales of life in Thuringia and her family's desire for Elisabeth to make a good marriage and rise in the world. These notes all dated from the first half of 1949 and reflected both the world that Elisabeth Kusian wished for and the one from which she imagined she escaped. They all discuss an imaginary clinic belonging to a non-existent uncle. They also discuss "Wolfgang," a fictional physician who wanted to marry her. Finally, they ask about her medical studies, a source of concern to Elisabeth's imaginary mother. Elisabeth, it seems, was giving her invented mother headaches.

Sprinkled in with these stories were real concerns, concerns about which Elisabeth must have thought. The context in which the mother in the letters tried to convince Elisabeth to come home had verisimilitude. She worried about her grandchildren, whom she felt Elisabeth ignored. Just as importantly, she sent Elisabeth warnings about Kurt Muschan. Why, she asked, did Elisabeth defend him so much, this man who seemed to want nothing more than to avoid all problems? Indeed, in a pointed question to herself, Elisabeth's "mother" asked her where her womanly pride was.[42] These letters must have represented a way for Elisabeth to analyse the relationship that, in her mind, allowed her to move from relatively minor crimes to murder. The only certainty is that she wrote them, tore them up, and tossed them into the wastebasket. Here police would later find them and painstakingly tape them back together.[43] When, several weeks later, Kriminalkommissar Menzel, her chief police interrogator, pressed about them, she refused to make any comment. She would not even admit that she wrote them.[44]

Wednesday, 28 December 1949

Maybe the confusion and unhappiness that prompted her to write these letters inspired Elisabeth Kusian's 28 December attempt to withdraw her letter of resignation from the hospital where she worked. As we learned in chapter 1, when she first applied for a job at the hospital, Kusian had provided the usual short autobiography, a verifiable record of her training, and previous places of employment. In her statement, Elisabeth named her three children. She then added that, as a girl, she had attended a Lyzeum in Altenburg, Thuringia. Furthermore, she claimed she had heard no news of her husband since 1943. The Lyzeum lie was a con. It polished a fake middle- or upper-class status and set of educational accomplishments. Mothers with missing husbands received 60 DM per month Kindergeld payments on top of their salaries. Had Elisabeth Kusian kept her job, she would have received an automatic pay raise of 7 DM in May 1950. However, this amount would not have come close to replacing the fraudulent state payment due to the widowed mother of three children.

It was too late when Elisabeth Kusian changed her mind on 28 December and tried to retract the resignation. With the matron's agreement, the hospital's works council (Betriebsrat) refused to continue her employment. The personnel department had nagging doubts regarding the story about her missing husband and wanted an affidavit. Without such an affidavit, which she of course could not provide, they would stop payment of Kindergeld. In addition, Kusian was not especially popular with her colleagues. She had alienated herself from them by borrowing money without repaying it.[45]

On the same day that Elisabeth Kusian attempted to continue with her current life as much as possible, Doris Merten's family began to worry about her whereabouts. Merten's two teenage nieces and a Glaubitz boy dropped by Charlotte Strach's home to pick up their Christmas gifts. As they chatted, Strach asked them where their Aunt Doris was. They were caught short by this question. They thought she was with Strach. They then told her the story of their aunt's quick visit to their house with a nurse's house key and a net bag of silver cutlery given her as surety. Because Strach was ill, she sent them to the Beigang shop to look for Doris, then thought no more about it.[46] The next day, 29 December, Frau Glaubitz called Frau Strach to tell her that the children found the shop locked with no sign of Doris Merten. Strach, still with no particular fear, thought that her sister must have visited her husband, still living in Cuxhaven. If she was not with him, she was probably with some other family in the "Zone," a name some used to disparage the German Democratic Republic.[47]

Herr Glaubitz though was alarmed. That same day he went to the criminal police at the local station, Spandau's Precinct #114, to file a missing person's report.[48] Although the police took his statement, the West Berlin murder squad still saw no reason to combine the case with Hermann Seidelmann's. As mentioned in chapter 2, West Berlin police issued a warrant for Gertraud A., a divorcee who had known Seidelmann for a long time. They thought it was her brown hat that they found among his things at Seidelmann's brother's place. She was, they had heard, known to owe him money. Although her apartment offered no clues, local gossip connected her to many men. Her floor sported fresh paint that detectives viewed with suspicion. This was yet another dead end. At around 9:00 or 9:30 p.m., Gertraud A. was set free. Police pinned notices around the city offering a reward of 500 DM for information about Seidelmann's murderer.[49]

At the same time as the notices were appearing, Kusian put Doris Merten's limbs into a rucksack, strapped it onto her back, and walked to Zoo Station. She caught the tram to Alexanderplatz near the ruin at the corner of Memhardtstraße and Prenzlauerstraße, her chosen disposal site. She would return to this same site

Figure 3.2. The ruins in which Doris Merten's dismembered corpse was found.

two nights later to finish her task. Before she could do that, though, she had to return home to transfer Merten's torso into the now-empty rucksack.[50]

New Year's Eve came and went without much seeming to change. Volkspolizei detectives finished going through the train tickets from Berlin to the Flöhe region, yet another dead end.[51] Although Herr Glaubitz's anxiety about Doris Merten grew, nobody else in the family was especially concerned. When Frau Strach visited them that day, she was surprised to learn about the missing person's report he had filed. Still, Glaubitz could not shake the idea that the silverware might have made Merten a target for thieves.[52]

New Year's Eve was also to be consequential for the Kusian couple. That afternoon, Walter Kusian had met his landlord's daughter in the kitchen to exchange a few pleasantries. He planned to telephone Elisabeth later that day.[53] As the two spoke, Elisabeth left the hospital with Kurt Muschan, who had dropped by her floor to walk her home. As they strolled along Fasanenstraße, still about 100 metres from her place, near the former location of the destroyed synagogue, she asked him to slip into a shop to buy a coffee cake while she went home to straighten up.

Muschan made the purchase, and when he arrived, he looked up, noticing that her right window was wide open, and wondered about it. Although not especially cold, he thought that the temperature was low enough that Elisabeth would want to shut the windows.[54] She, however, was doing her best to dispel any smells that might alert Muschan to the corpse that still lay rotting under her bed.

Probably after Muschan left, Walter Kusian finally reached his ex-wife on the telephone. Would she like to come by that evening? No, Elisabeth lied, she would be on the floor until 11:00 p.m. Her shift, however, ended at 7:00 p.m.[55] For her final night at the hospital, Elisabeth arrived on time with alcohol, or something else. Did she want to be friendly or cause a last bit of trouble? Once situated, she made a pot of spiked coffee, then poured some for a nursing student who became so ill she could neither give a shift report nor hand over her patients to her replacement.[56] Walter dropped by at 7:00 p.m., thinking he had plenty of time to catch her. Had Elisabeth left when she had hoped, they would have missed each other.[57] Unfortunately for her, though, they ran into each other, and he escorted her home. Her words describe that night:

> My husband accompanied me to the front door. He wanted me to take him upstairs or come back down [presumably after she had changed] and go with him to his apartment. This, however, I refused to do, and after we had talked for about fifteen minutes outside the door, I went into the house, locked up behind me, and went upstairs. Once upstairs, I looked out the open window and noticed my husband standing on the street below. He remained standing for quite some time. It may have been about 12:30 a.m. when I turned out the light and sat down in the corner by the stove. Before I turned off the light, I first injected morphine; how many cc I don't remember. I fell asleep and then woke up again shortly before 4:00 a.m. I had already thought the night before that I absolutely had to get rid of the body parts, and for this reason, I had not lain down.[58]

Walter's neighbour heard him arrive home by midnight, leaving Elisabeth to her night, a night in which she hoped to finish disposing of the evidence of her second murder.[59] She made two more trips to the ruin she had visited earlier in the week. On the first, she laid out Merten's remaining limbs. On the second, she brought Merten's torso.[60] Kriminal-Anwart Reichmuth from the West Berlin squad timed the trip from Kusian's room to the discovery scene and back. He calculated a time of about 4½ hours, which would have brought her home at 8:30 a.m. on New Year's Day.[61]

By coincidence, Walter Kusian arose on New Year's Day morning at about 8:30 a.m., quickly went into the apartment's shared kitchen to make coffee, exchanged New Year's greetings with his landlady and her daughter, then headed to Elisabeth's place. About 10:00 a.m., he met Frau Stö. at the front door, then climbed the stairs to his former wife's room.[62] As they chatted, Elisabeth complained about losing her job, then shifted the conversation to the new orphanage where she had placed the children. Nothing strange about this conversation, thought Walter, but the atmosphere was odd and out of place. Freshly washed stockings and underwear hung drying by the stove. Why were his two rucksacks, rucksacks she had told him were at the hospital, lying on the floor? Elisabeth recovered quickly, if oddly. One was soaked with rabbit gore. She would have to wash it. He could take the other. Walter, probably still wondering about this, moved towards the door when Elisabeth stopped him. She had done something horrible, "but she could only confess it on her deathbed." He had heard such dramatics before. This was yet another of her "fantastic tales."[63] He took his leave.

Now that Walter was gone, Elisabeth Kusian could brood, think, and plan. She had disposed of Doris Merten's body, but so much was still undone. The hanging underwear and bloody rucksack reminded her of the clothing yet to sell or give away.[64] She had already started this task, though, which provided some relief. For days, she dragged her clothes-stuffed suitcase around the city. Walter had wondered about this suitcase when she opened it at his place.[65] Whether it showed arrogance, carelessness, or guilt is impossible to say. In the end, after Walter's visit, she took the bag to the Moabit Hospital, again opened it, and tried to sell a pair of suede shoes.[66] Her next stop was Anni Glißmann's.

Once there, she concocted a story about the contents belonging to a colleague who owed her money and wanted to sell the articles, presumably to clear the debt. This kind of delivery was nothing new. Soon after Elisabeth Kusian carried Doris Merten's body to the ruin, she had given Anni a brown-red hat and red shawl to sell.[67] Glißmann took this new batch of clothing and was on her way. She sold Doris Merten's shoes at a bakery. She negotiated a deal to sell Doris Merten's coat and sundry for a combined 40 DM to a used clothing store in the old industrial district of Alt Moabit, but when she contacted Kusian about the price, Elisabeth balked, and Anni returned the clothes to Elisabeth, who then gifted Merten's coat to Glißmann as a thank you. Glißmann quickly returned to the shop with this windfall and sold it for 12 DM. She held onto the receipt from the transaction, later handing it to West Berlin detectives. This selling and giving away, though, only scratched the surface of what needed to be disposed. So much remained to be sold, gifted, or tossed before Elisabeth Kusian could once again feel relatively safe.

Elisabeth Kusian was desperate for cash, with debts both significant and growing. At 11:00 a.m. on 3 January, she brought yet more clothing to a laundromat to wash and prepare for sale. About an hour later, Anni appeared at the same place to peddle shoes. Even if the women had succeeded in turning these clothes into money, they would not have earned enough to cover Elisabeth Kusian's needs. That same morning, Hedwig Schrö. appeared at Kusian's room to demand the rest of the money still owed for the furniture "sale."[68] If only she could dispose of the evidence, she knew that she could pay her debts and move forward. Yet nothing in her behaviour showed any intention of stopping her killing and crazed spending. She must have thought that she could continue to evade the police. This time she was wrong.

Only one hour after Kusian tried to prepare the last of Doris Merten's clothing for sale and move on, her worst nightmare happened. Children playing in the cellar of a house ruin on the corner of East Berlin's Prenzlauerstraße and Memhardtstraße ran into the street in horror, then caught VP Wachtmeister Walter Baudasch to tell him that they had found a corpse. The discovery began a three-day combination of hard work and luck that took investigators from complete mystification to solving two murders.[69] When VP Kommissar Beutter of the Mitte District's criminal police got the call, he joined Baudasch at the scene. The pair then descended into the basement to find a dismembered body they believed had belonged to a woman between thirty and forty years old. Although all of its parts were in one spot, somebody had detached the arms, legs, and head from the torso. Also peculiar was that the torso still wore underwear and pyjamas. Certain that it was a homicide, they telephoned the murder squad at about 12:35 p.m., only half an hour after the children made their first report.[70] Ten minutes later, VP Kommandeur Rockstroh and the rest of his team arrived to survey the ruin, an empty iron monger's shop across the street from a bombed-out Hertie Department Store on Alexanderplatz.

This ruin marked yet another of the cruel historical echoes that plagued this case. Both the Hertie building that overlooked the site where Doris Merten's remains lay and the business that it had once housed had already witnessed German horror. Hertie, founded by Oscar Tietz in 1882 as one of the first prominent Jewish-owned department store firms in Germany, had once been known as the Hermann Tietz Department Store.[71] This particular branch opened in 1905 on one of the most significant city squares in Germany, if not in Europe. The firm flourished for decades; it even supplied goods to the German military in the First World War. Like so many of its contemporaries, it had suffered significant losses during the Depression.[72] By 1933, it was in deep financial trouble, 85,000,000 Reichsmarks in debt, and Adolf Hitler would have been happy to see it fold. Only when Minister of Economic Affairs Kurt Schmitt convinced him of the firm's value to the German economy did Hitler relent and allow a credit line of 11,000,000 Reichsmarks. The price of that loan was Aryanization and renaming. The company passed into the hands of Georg Karg as Hertie. The larger population soon forgot its Jewish heritage.[73]

The building, too, reflected both a more majestic past and a broken present. Had pedestrians walked by the store in 1936, they could have gazed upon the monumental, indeed proud, architecture, topped by a globe perched on a clock, itself on the building's roof. If the same pedestrians walked by in January 1950, they would see the building as one more sign of the broken present. The right side of the building's façade was gone, leaving only a yawning, gaping hole. The globe that once stood proudly on the clock now sagged to the right. It looked almost as if it wanted to leap off and fly away. The clock was gone. Theirs was a time out of joint. Detectives, though, lacked the luxury to think about this earlier crime. Their attention turned to the ruin across the street.

Debris piled up, stacked so high in places that navigating a path to the corpse was almost impossible for adults. The strewn remains of iron goods lay rusting among the stones that had broken from the former walls. As the squad moved further into the site, they found the pile of rubble behind which lay a female torso encircled by a knotted tricot undershirt and bloody pyjamas. Behind this horror lay a woman's head on a pile of bricks positioned in a corridor about 7 metres deep by 1.5 metres wide. Her hair was brownish-red. Her mouth was open, missing several teeth and sporting a single gold crown. Nearby was the rest of the body, close to but not touching a rose-coloured blouse. Detectives quickly determined that the victim did not die in this rubble cave. However, the scene provided no further clues for their eyes or the summoned police dog's nose.[74]

When the detectives finished, they sent the corpse to the morgue for an autopsy that they hoped would provide some clues to the cause of death.[75] The few describable features of the corpse's head were the only immediate clues to the deceased's identity. Investigators included their descriptions (hair, teeth, crown) in a teletype sent later that day to Volkspolizei stations.[76] On 5 January, short notices published in the East German press detailed many of the same points.

Elisabeth Kusian passed her time before the notices appeared in relative peace; among her activities was writing a note full of lies to her children. In it, she explained why she had not spent Christmas with them. She had, she claimed, visited their ill grandmother. If that were not enough, she wrote that she was in the hospital suffering from an old leg wound that had reopened and needed another operation. She assured them, though, that she would be discharged on 6 January.[77] Kusian was not in bed. Instead, she was delivering the typewriter to Kurt Muschan at the police station where he worked, a task that probably gave her both pride and pleasure.[78]

This delivery might have been Kusian's last congenial task. West Berlin's Kriminal-Sekretär Blüme wanted to speak with her. While tracking Doris Merten's movements before her disappearance, Blüme contacted the Moabit Hospital to get details on Nurse Kusian, whose name Paul Glaubitz had provided as Doris Merten's last-known contact. Hospital officials informed him that she no longer worked there as of New Year's Eve. They could, though, provide him with her address. Thus armed, Blüme arranged for her to come to Precinct #131 at 9:00 a.m. on 6 January to give detectives any information she might have.[79] She would have found the summons annoying but not alarming. Elisabeth Kusian knew that it was not a murder investigation. She did not realize that Merten's corpse had been found and had no reason to think that she would not be able to con her way out of any complications. Blüme was simply following standard police procedure to determine Merten's movements. Neither he nor his colleagues saw any connection between Doris Merten's disappearance and the second corpse that the Volkspolizei had found.

Thursday, 5 January 1950

Elisabeth Kusian and Kurt Muschan started 5 January with a stroll to the laundromat, a small romantic treat after Muschan's night duty ended. Meanwhile, Berlin's two police departments began another day of still-separate inquiries.[80] The separation was about to end. By afternoon, teletypes and newspaper articles made the squads aware of each other's activities. Once Kriminal-Sekretär

Blüme saw the Volkspolizei circular and noted it in his files, he began to consider whether the murder and missing person's cases might be one. The Volkspolizei's description of the body they had found differed slightly from the description family members had given him of Doris Merten. It was, however, close enough to prompt him to contact Paul Glaubitz and Charlotte Strach.[81] Blüme also made several unsuccessful attempts to reach Merten's employer, Herr Beigang, whom he surmised was on vacation.[82]

Helene V. provided the final key to the investigations' next stage. Herr Beigang had asked Frau V., his shop's regular custodian, to clean on 2 January. Cleaning should have been easy for the business was closed. The always reliable Doris Merten was supposed to unlock the shop for her. Frau V. found her absence to be exceedingly odd. She returned again and again for several days to no avail.[83]

The *Telegraf* article, "Body Found in a House Ruin," struck her when she realized that the description sounded much like Doris Merten. Frau V. alerted the West Berlin police, who redoubled their efforts to contact Beigang, still without success.[84] That morning, detectives in charge of the Merten disappearance decided they had waited long enough for Friedrich Beigang's return. They brought a locksmith to let them into the shop. By sheer coincidence, even as the smith was opening the door, Beigang showed up. He had just returned from his ski trip, went to check on his shop, and was understandably surprised to see them. Kriminal-Sekretär Wetzel understood his shock and showed him the *Telegraf* notice. He then explained Frau V.'s anxiety. Wetzel assured him, though, that the police were simply working to eliminate possible explanations. One of these was that Frau Merten was inside the shop, perhaps the victim of an unfortunate accident. A quick search of the premises determined that she had not been there for days. With few options left, the West Berlin detectives telephoned their Eastern counterparts. Beigang was on his way. He might be able to make an identification.[85]

Friedrich Beigang drove across the border, arriving a little after noon to meet with Hauptwachtmeister Schiller of the Volkspolizei's murder squad and look at the body they had found.[86] He and Merten, Beigang explained, had known one another for twenty-four years; she was an old hand in the typewriter industry and had worked for him since the previous September. There was no question but that he would entrust the shop to her while he was gone. Beigang told Schiller how surprising it was to find West Berlin police at his shop. Schiller responded with details that the West Berlin police seemed not to know. For example, Merten's sister, Charlotte Strach, had asked Frau V. if she knew anything about the missing woman's whereabouts. Strach's uncertainty only increased Frau V.'s anxiety. After they spoke, VP Hauptwachtmeister Schiller showed Beigang a photograph of the recovered corpse. Beigang immediately and without a doubt identified it as Merten and told them what he knew about her activities before her disappearance. Most important among these details was Doris Merten's appointment to deliver a small typewriter to, and collect payment from, a nurse named Elisabeth Kusian. He did not know whether Merten had made the delivery or received the scheduled payment.[87]

While awaiting Beigang's return from East Berlin, West Berlin Kriminal-Sekretär Wetzel and his squad proceeded with their investigation. Among their first steps was to call Charlotte Strach. When they could not reach her at home, they left instructions with her landlord for her to telephone upon her return, then followed up that request with a note to the same effect.[88] Charlotte Strach was unavailable that 5 January because she was working with the Volkspolizei.[89] She had had a horrendous day. First, Frau V. told her that police had found her sister. Once Friedrich Beigang viewed the corpse, Frau Strach's local police station telephoned to inform her that a police unit was on its way to transport her to the morgue to make her own identification. She left the morgue to speak with VP Polizeirat Pohl at Volkspolizei headquarters.

In her statement, Frau Strach explained that her sister Dorothea (her real name) had only returned to Berlin the previous August. Doris Merten had lived in the city until the end of the war. Then, between the end of 1945 and August 1949, she had been in Altenbruch, a district of the port city of Cuxhaven in Lower Saxony, where she found herself stranded after Germany's collapse. It took her four years to get official permission to return. Her legal residence in Berlin was a Laubenkolonie.

The Laubenkolonie, or garden colony, is still a Europe-wide phenomenon of garden allotments that allowed urban dwellers access to the soil and the ability to grow their food. In most places, these allotments were quite basic. As Mark Hobbs reminds us, they were often much more substantial in Germany. Such an allotment could represent "adapting the functional tool shed standing at the centre of the allotment into a more substantial structure: a summerhouse."[90] Aerial bombardment had destroyed much of Berlin's housing stock in the Second World War. West Berlin's official statistical record for 1950 estimates that, of the city's 1,061,846 inhabitable units in 1946, 42,084 were in such Laubenkolonien. Thus it is not surprising that Doris Merten lived in such a unit.[91]

For the previous month, though, her residence was a legal fiction. The two sisters had been living together in Charlotte Strach's Weissensee apartment; Laubenkolonie shacks would be too cold for the winters. Frau Strach told police about how, on Christmas Eve, Doris Merten returned home with a portable typewriter that she would have to deliver to a nurse named Kusian the day after Christmas. At least, Doris told her, she was looking forward to the lunch Kusian had promised in exchange for the favour.[92] Frau Strach then related the by-now-familiar details of the nurse, the typewriter, the missing person's report, the visit of the Glaubitz girls, and her assumption that Doris had been out visiting family. Even as she told the story, she continued to chastise herself before VP Polizeirat Pohl. "Why," she wondered aloud, could she not see what should have been so obvious? How was it possible that Herr Glaubitz was alert enough to contact the West Berlin authorities even though he believed everything was probably fine, but a sister did nothing?[93] After her heartbreaking soul searching, Strach confirmed Merten's identity. She ticked off details such as the red-blond hair dye Doris used to cover up her premature grey, grey like Strach's own. Strach then pointed to Merten's torn underwear, hand-repaired with a strip of blue-green cloth that almost matched. When the police showed Frau Strach the corpse's dental prosthesis, she confirmed that it had belonged to Doris, eliminating any lingering doubts the detectives might have had.[94]

Because neither the police nor her family knew why anybody would murder Doris Merten, Charlotte Strach provided an addendum to her initial statement and identification. It detailed her sister's life and personality. She hoped that such details would help identify the murderer. Strach told of the sisters' many conversations in the weeks when they lived together. These conversations led Strach to tell Pohl that, as she understood it, Merten was libidinous, yet had not slept with her husband for four years. Because she needed sex in her life, she frequently went out in the evening, always with a male companion. Herr Steg. was among the names that often came up in their evening conversations. According to Strach, Merten told her that, when Herr Beigang left Berlin for vacation on Christmas Eve, he left very little cash in the shop that she could use to buy or sell. Disappointing as that might be, it was not a problem for her plan to earn some money on the side. With a wave of her hand, she had told her sister that she could always do some business with Herr Steg. Although she knew very little about him, comments like this led Strach to assume that he was also a businessman. Frau Strach also believed that Doris Merten met him through her job and that he might be Merten's lover.[95] Lastly, and almost in passing, Strach told VP Polizeirat Pohl about her sister's impression of Elisabeth Kusian. "From the conversation, I could tell that she didn't think much of the nurse either. I said to her, when she mentioned the nurse's name, that it was a strange name. She replied, 'Yes, she is also a strange woman.'"[96] Clearly, Elisabeth Kusian barely figured in Charlotte Strach's thoughts.

Charlotte Strach closed her exhausting day by providing yet another police officer with a detailed description of the clothing worn by Merten when they last saw each other. She described Merten's brown mole coat with its small collar. She then listed the following:

round brown fur muff with a zipper (pocket muff) that didn't match the coat
red scarf

pink petticoat
rust-brown, patterned, unbelted dress
brown silk stockings
size 39, black suede pumps
gold wedding band
large smoky topaz (yellowish, transparent) ring
big brown patent handbag with a broken clasp
pair of worn brown leather gloves.[97]

That same day, VP Hauptwachtmeister Böhlandorf brought Charlotte Strach and Paul Glaubitz to Doris Merten's Laubenkolonie cottage in Spandau. The police kept hoping for further clues. Anna D., Merten's neighbour, used the key Merten had given her to let them into the cottage. As expected, everything was in its place and dusty. Nobody else had come by to search or disturb anything. Merten's notebooks recorded her attendance at Nazi meetings. Her photos were from the Weimar Republic. These worlds were gone – and not germane to the present.[98] Once Böhlandorf and Strach returned to the police station, Strach confirmed that the clothing police had found next to the corpse belonged to her sister.[99]

The Volkspolizei then returned to Friedrich Beigang. What was his opinion of Dorothea Merten? Did he have any thoughts about her personal life or her dealings with Elisabeth Kusian? Beigang insisted that Merten's contact with Herr Steg. was purely professional, never romantic. Herr Steg. was a self-employed typewriter representative. He met Doris Merten when they both worked at the Mercedes typewriter factory's branch office on Xantener Straße in Berlin's Wilmersdorf district. His thoughts on Kusian were far vaguer. He had only met her once. Yes, she had come by the shop more than a few times but had always worked with Frau Merten. His most significant memory of her was when Merten asked his opinion of Kusian's trustworthiness.[100]

That same day, other Volkspolizei asked Paul Glaubitz to come by to help them map out Merten's activities on the day of her disappearance. Having spoken again of Merten's visit, silverware, and her final walk to the bus stop, Glaubitz then mused about Merten, the person. She was a quiet but worldly woman who knew how to take care of herself but would never have any improper relationship with men. She was not such a woman! Besides, he added, she had not been in Berlin long enough to strike up any romantic relationships.[101]

The difference of opinion between Herr Beigang and Herr Glaubitz on the one hand and Charlotte Strach on the other regarding Doris Merten's sexuality had to strike the Volkspolizei as curious and worthy of further investigation. Perhaps Beigang and Glaubitz were simply trying to preserve Merten's conventionally moral reputation. Strach may have assumed that her sister's life and sexuality, at least as she understood them, might have led to her murder. A possible connection between the elusive Herr Steg. and the horror visited on Merten made perfect sense. Gender norms and masculinity were topsy turvy in occupied Berlin.

In 1949, Dorothea Groener-Geyer noted that "after Stalingrad, there is no aspect of life in which the actions of German men have protected German women from want, misery, and poverty."[102] The new "gender imbalance" at the war's end seemed to ensure either a surplus of women or a shortage of men, depending on how one chose to view the numbers. In 1950, "there were 1,400 women for every 1,000 men in the age group twenty-five to thirty-nine."[103] Such numbers must have destabilized Beigang's and Glaubitz's sense of masculinity. It also might have reinforced their desire to believe that Merten lived according to a predetermined, conventional set of marital norms that would reassert men's traditional, dominant roles as the heads of households. As Elizabeth Heineman reminds us, "the family's 'imaginary' nature contributed to its appeal. In the midst of hardship, it was easy to idealize an imaginary family life."[104] The same destabilization might have led Strach to see Merten's desires as perfectly fine in these new, unstable times. Frau Strach could both hold this world view and worry about what men were capable of in a new post-war world defined, in many ways, by confusion, want, and rubble.[105]

At 4:00 p.m. that day, West Berlin's Kriminal-Sekretär Wetzel seemed to have given up waiting for Beigang to return and called the Volkspolizei, who informed him that Beigang had provided an identification. Parallel cases merged as the police departments began to concentrate on Elisabeth Kusian. Not surprisingly, she knew nothing of this intensified interest. Her mind was elsewhere. Could she dig out of this hole or at least postpone the inevitable? That afternoon, the last they heard from her, Kusian called the Schrö. family. She would pay the rest of the money owed for the furniture.[106] She then paid a birthday visit to Anni Glißmann. Instead of a gift, Kusian brought a brown briefcase inside of which lay a bloody rucksack. Glißmann didn't give this a second thought; Elisabeth and her "brother-in-law" often went about with bags of slaughtered rabbits.[107] Certainly it was illegal, but British occupiers had instructed police not to enforce the Reich game law that allowed the prosecution of "any person who snares or catches wild rabbits in the British sector of Berlin on land occupied by him or with the consent of the occupier of the land." Rabbits destroyed food crops. Unstated but likely just as important was that the rabbits would themselves be a valuable source of protein.[108]

The next day, 6 January, a troubled Elisabeth arrived at Walter's workplace in Hallesches Tor with a mid-sized, brown suitcase and a notice that looked as if it had been ripped from a notebook. What could this mean? Was it serious? The ominous note required her to provide a statement to aid Friesenstraße Station detectives investigating a missing person's case. Did Walter know about this? When he told her that he knew nothing, she asked him to watch her suitcase while she was with the police. He declined. His job – he operated a steam dredger – made that impossible. When he asked why she had the bag, Elisabeth answered that she needed it for her visit to the laundry to retrieve her nursing uniform and then deliver it to the hospital. Did she hope to plant the incriminating evidence on Walter? Regardless, he never again saw his ex-wife as a free woman.[109]

Having spoken with Walter, Elisabeth Kusian began the day's rounds of interviews with West Berlin's Kriminal-Sekretär Blüme, who hoped that she could help with what his department was officially treating as a missing person's case. She provided details about the typewriter's purchase and delivery, and her use of silverware as a surety. This tallied with what Blüme thought he knew. When she finished by describing how the women walked together to the Zoo Station, Kusian added fabricated details for authenticity's sake. Doris Merten was concerned about making her train connection at Alexanderplatz. Then, almost in passing as she was about to leave the police station, Kusian "remembered" that Merten had forgotten her umbrella. All of Elisabeth's attempts to return it, spread over several days, had failed.[110] After Elisabeth breezed out of the station, Blüme decided that the investigation would have to pick up Merten's movements after leaving Elisabeth's room. Kusian, on the other hand, must have thought she had conned her way out of another serious situation. If her troubles were not entirely behind her, they would be once she had crossed the city border and spoken with East Berlin authorities.

Elisabeth Kusian was wrong. At this seeming moment of relief, the two investigations fused into one. While she was crossing the city's invisible border, the odd team of West Berlin Kriminalkommissar Schulz and VP Hauptwachtmeister Schiller visited the Moabit Hospital to learn about Nurse Kusian. The more they uncovered, the more suspicious she began to appear. Kusian's former supervisor expanded on her unprofessional, dishonest conduct. She (the supervisor) had to spend too much time dealing with complaints about this "notorious liar." This unexpected turn raised the detectives' interest; what, if anything, might it mean?[111]

Later that day, having been informed about this turn of events, Elisabeth Kusian's landlady let VP Polizeirat Pohl into Elisabeth Kusian's room to summon her to East Berlin police headquarters for a discussion about Doris Merten. Pohl, a keen observer, quickly took in the details of the empty one-room flat. He noted a displayed photograph of West Berlin police detective Kurt Muschan, something his West Berlin colleagues missed.[112] The picture convinced Pohl and VP Kommandeur Rockstroh to approach Muschan, which they probably did at the same time as their colleagues VP Hauptwachtmeister Wriedt and VP Hauptwachtmeister Schiller sat with Kusian. Muschan's name was of great interest and might represent a propaganda coup of the highest order. Could Muschan be involved in a crime? Assuming that he was not involved in the murder, what would he, a fellow detective, be able to tell them that would help them with their case?[113] Before they could look into it, though, other East Berlin detectives spoke with Elisabeth Kusian.

Sometime during that mid-afternoon, Elisabeth Kusian appeared at Volkspolizei headquarters to make her statement "on her own account."[114] In what would become a pattern for her, the document wove a web of truths and lies. The lies were not merely about her involvement in the crime, which would be completely understandable, even expected. They touched on all aspects of her life. For example, after providing her birthdate, address, salary, marital status, and the number of her children, she made a brief autobiographical statement. Among her lies, she spoke of having attended a Lyzeum for a year and a half, an accomplishment that would imply at least a middle-class background. She never mentioned the menial jobs she held as a girl. She insisted that she left the Moabit Hospital because of personal differences with her supervisor.[115] Police could check all of these statements. All were lies.

After this quick recapitulation, Kusian turned to the matter at hand. As she told her well-rehearsed story, the Volkspolizei detectives asked her about Kurt Muschan, a topic she could not possibly have prepared. She explained her acquaintance with him by remarking that his precinct was close to the Moabit Hospital. She must have been thinking frantically about why and how they thought to ask about him. How might she bring him into her story? What did the police know and want to know? Perhaps to cover a momentary flustering, Elisabeth Kusian told the detectives that this was her second interview that day. She had spent the morning at West Berlin's Friesenstraße Station speaking about what she thought was a missing person's case. Kusian soon saw how different this discussion would be.

Turning to the topic of her lover, she spoke of how useful a typewriter would be for his job, but she lacked the cash to buy such a gift outright. She had lit upon the idea of finding a shop that took instalment payments. At the Beigang shop, she met Frau Merten and offered up her plan. In her telling, when Merten explained that she had no authority to make such a deal, Kusian turned to Beigang, who approved the scheme and explained how the purchase would work. Kusian pondered the commitment, deciding to go forward with the purchase on 22 December. The parties agreed that she would provide a down payment of DM 50 on Christmas Eve, pick up the machine, and take it home.[116]

Elisabeth told the officers that her hospital work shifts ruined the original plans to pick up the machine, forcing her to telephone Beigang sometime between noon and 1:00 p.m. on Christmas Eve to make alternate arrangements. Unfortunately, the store would close at 2:00 p.m. Could, she inquired, the typewriter be left somewhere for her to pick up? That way, she would still be able to present it on Boxing Day. She claimed that Beigang responded with a generous offer: Frau Merten could deliver it. Although this was convenient, Kusian claimed to hesitate. Was there no way that she could pick it up somewhere? Recasting the offer to bring the typewriter by her apartment was a clumsy attempt to divert suspicion. She must have thought that, if the delivery idea had been Beigang's, detectives would not suspect her of planning murder. Kusian presented herself as a caring nurse who thought about others' inconvenience rather than about what would benefit her.

The "caring nurse" continued. Dorothea Merten brought the typewriter on schedule and stayed for about forty-five minutes, drinking coffee as the two women chatted about the machine. Elisabeth continued that she had to give Frau Merten some unfortunate news. She was 10 DM short of the 50 DM owed to the Beigang firm. Could Merten wait a bit? Kusian was happy to leave and exchange enough DM East to finish the deal. Merten declined the offer, explaining that she was already late for her visit to the Glaubitz family in Spandau. Perhaps Frau Merten could leave the typewriter? She had made it clear that she had no desire to haul it to Spandau. Again "No." Herr Beigang deserved some guarantee for letting Kusian have the machine. Finally, Elisabeth claimed, she lit upon the idea of giving Frau Merten some valuable silverware, which she told the detectives that she had owned for a long time. Elisabeth also loaned her the house key so that Frau Merten could easily let herself back in. Assured that Kusian had every intention of paying for the machine, Frau Merten left the apartment at about 1:00 p.m. for the #75 streetcar.

In her telling, the rest of Elisabeth's day was busy but uneventful. She visited Zoo Station to trade 230 DM East for about 39 DM, more than enough money to pay her bill. Next came the post office, then a phone call to a fellow nurse with whom she had planned to spend Christmas. After hanging up, she went straight home, prepared a snack for Kurt Muschan's expected visit, and stayed put for the rest of the afternoon and evening. Sometime between 9:15 and 9:45 p.m., Frau Merten returned, letting herself in with Kusian's key, exchanged the still-wrapped silver for two twenties and a ten, and was off. Adding more detail to enhance plausibility, Elisabeth added Merten's complaint that Kusian still owed a 1.50 DM transaction fee. Kusian paid with 9 DM East. Their business concluded when Elisabeth Kusian signed the receipt for the typewriter.[117]

Elisabeth then landed on another embellishment. She noticed that Frau Merten had a bag of sorts on her return that she did not have earlier. Perhaps this detail might lead detectives to conclude that thieves had murdered Merten. Then, as if struck by memory, she paused to say that she had forgotten another detail. Returning to the subject of Kurt Muschan, Elisabeth thought that her interviewers would want to know that he showed up at her apartment around 9:45 p.m. She sent him to the Berliner Kindl restaurant near the Zoo Station and promised to collect him later. Elisabeth Kusian confided to her interviewers that Muschan was not supposed to see that she was buying on the instalment plan. Such a transaction, Kusian claimed, would have bothered her lover.

She then returned to the story of Merten's visit, backtracking to add even more minor details. Merten, she claimed, only stayed for about fifteen minutes, just enough time to smoke a cigarette. Then the two women walked to the Zoo Station. Frau Merten explained that she was in a hurry to get to her sister's place and hoping for a quick connection at Alexanderplatz Station. They parted at about 10:35 p.m.; Kusian went to Berliner Kindl, picked up Muschan, and brought him home. Back at Kantstraße, they ran into her landladies, whom Kusian said wanted to see the couple. After a coffee and a half-hour chat, the two women left. Elisabeth gave Muschan the typewriter, and he spent the night, leaving the following afternoon.

Seemingly done, Elisabeth again claimed to remember several forgotten points. The nurse with whom she was supposed to spend the days after Christmas was Nurse Hertha. The typewriter remained in her possession until 5 January, when she took it to Muschan at his station in the Derfflingerstraße. Seemingly unable to help herself, Elisabeth then added yet more details. Merten had forgotten her umbrella, but, try as she might, Kusian could not contact Merten to return it. With a concluding flourish, Elisabeth discussed the day of the month on which she was to pay the remaining instalments for the typewriter, finishing with an invitation from Doris Merten to meet up after the holidays.

Her tale told, Elisabeth Kusian shared "a confidence" with the Volkspolizei. She had said nothing about Muschan while at West Berlin's Friesenstraße Station, hoping to spare him any possible embarrassment. That may have been her reasoning. It is equally plausible that she thought that police would trap her, and Muschan might provide some kind of protection. Redirecting police attention from one type of potential legal issue to another might distract them, even recast their investigation. Rather than looking at a murder, there might be more advantages to looking into a West Berlin police scandal. Maybe Kusian saw how the investigation was proceeding and hoped that she could take Muschan down with her. Regardless of her motives, the detectives remained unmoved.

Turning to her own life, Elisabeth Kusian told the Volkspolizei that she received her last salary payment of 275 DM on 19 December. She added that her monthly rent, including utilities, was 50 DM. Beyond everyday expenses, she paid 75 DM East per child to the Mutterhouse Teltow. She would soon pay off a two-year-old debt of 30 DM that she owed to a former colleague. Such details emphasized how tiny her debts were.[118] Minor money problems were never so severe as to drive her to murder. Indeed, she claimed she never borrowed money from patients and quit her job because of personal differences with her supervisor. Having signed her statement, Elisabeth expected to go home. She was, however, kept longer.[119]

As VP Hauptwachtmeister Wriedt and VP Hauptwachtmeister Schiller interviewed Elisabeth Kusian, VP Kommandeur Rockstroh and VP Polizeirat Pohl took Kurt Muschan's statement about the night. Muschan repeated his memories of the evening.[120] Nothing that Muschan had to say indicated that he might be involved in the crime. He appeared of his own free will on that 6 January to clarify his relationship with Elisabeth Kusian and recount events of the night of 26 December.[121] Why, the detectives wondered, did Muschan never think twice about the envelope that Elisabeth had so obviously prepared in advance? They said nothing, though, as he told of the couple's hosting the two older women for a coffee and short chat before they retreated to their rooms.[122] Far more important for them was that he noticed the new-to-him woman's hat and coat hanging on Kusian's door.[123] This observation gave the Volkspolizei something concrete upon which to act.

As the conversations with the nurse and her lover continued, VP Kommandeur Rockstroh detailed VP Hauptwachtmeister Schiller and another officer to contact Kriminal-Sekretär Meiser and Kriminal-Sekretär Repenning of Charlottenburg's crime squad to conduct a joint search of Kusian's room. Although this first search did not turn up any concrete proof of Kusian's guilt, it certainly raised even more suspicion. As expected, they found the items described by Muschan, a woman's watch, and a man's striped tie. All of these items seemed to be out of place.[124] This preliminary visit set up a much more thorough forensic visit the next day.

To make matters worse for Elisabeth, Muschan told Wriedt and Schiller about the dry glasses in Kusian's room. When they later asked Kusian about them, she answered that she laid out the glasses for her, Muschan, and Merten to use. Indeed, the more she spoke, the more awkward became her story.[125] It is, of course, possible that Kusian did not intend to murder Doris Merten or that the murder at least hung in the balance. Perhaps both last-minute desperation and a premonition that things were spinning out of control pushed Kusian to think murder would solve her problems. Murder would allow her to keep both the money and still give the typewriter to Muschan. None of this, though, would matter.

Elisabeth Kusian's tangled stories of 6 January ended any chance she would be allowed to return to her life. After Kurt Muschan finished his statement and the search of her room ended, Wriedt and Schiller returned to Kusian to ask follow-up questions about the coat, the hat, and the wine glasses. Up to this point, the Volkspolizei likely had told her that Muschan was curious about the clothing's provenance and nothing else. Her answer otherwise makes no sense. There is little to no chance that the detectives told her they saw Merten's clothes hanging from her door.

Nevertheless, she seemed to grasp the significance of this line of questioning. Wriedt and Schiller questioned her for hours; she responded with stubborn silence. At first, she would only say that she did not want to involve anybody else in the issues that would ensue from such buying and selling. Finally, she explained that she had bought the clothing near the Zoo Train Station for about 230 DM East, then resold it on 2 January in much the same manner.[126] This clue broke open the investigation as it was the first concrete, irrefutable evidence of Kusian's lying.

With that, the detectives invited Kurt Muschan into the room where Kusian sat. He joined the other three in their conversation. Elisabeth seems to have been confused. She must have understood she had trapped herself. She turned to Muschan and said, "That is the terrible part of it. I want to add … I also want to help you, but I just can't. What more can I say? I can't think anymore. I can't tell the truth because I lied to you. Because my testimony would be so improbable, I'd rather say nothing at all."[127] She then reiterated her now-tattered claims that she had left Merten at the Zoo Train Station at about 10:30 p.m.[128]

Elisabeth Kusian finished all of her conversations at about 12:30 a.m. on 7 January. She chose this moment to request permission to visit the morgue. It is hard to imagine the impression she must have made when she said, "I would like to see Frau Merten again." Once she confronted Merten's remains, she added, "It is terrible. One can hardly believe it. I would not recognize her by her face."

The police were not about to let her go; she was under provisional arrest. As officers led her from the morgue to the women's prison on Barnimstraße, she neither showed emotion nor commented further.[129] The next day police from both departments began their forensic examinations of Elisabeth Kusian's room. The murder cases were seemingly solved, but more remained confused and confusing than was clear. As both the West Berlin and East Berlin forces worked to prove the case against Elisabeth Kusian, their understanding of her would only grow murkier.

chapter four

Building the Case: Berlin's Police Departments Investigate Elisabeth Kusian

Saturday, 7 January 1950–Monday, 9 January 1950

Would they transfer her to West Berlin custody? The world was changing so quickly. What might come of her case? Which half of the city would be a better, safer place for her? So many concerns swirled around Elisabeth Kusian's case as she sat on this cold, drizzly day in East Berlin custody.[1] Without access to what the police departments knew or shared, it was impossible to develop a plan in which she could have much confidence.

The two investigations proceeded apace, parallel but separate. Elisabeth's almost accidental capture allowed police from both sectors to begin the painstaking task of interviewing and then re-interviewing witnesses to construct a narrative that would make sense to them, the prosecutors, and ultimately to a tribunal that Elisabeth Kusian was guilty of murder. Detectives would stumble over each other, creating confusion and misunderstanding. In early January, Walter Kusian found himself caught in this mess. On the morning of 7 January, he visited Elisabeth's room to give her a rucksack of coal to heat her apartment. As Frau Stö. and her mother let Walter in, he expressed surprise at Elisabeth's absence. This surprise turned into shock when they told him that she was under arrest for murder.[2] Speechless, he walked to the local police station. The station's officers directed him to Friesenstraße. Here, he could ascertain what was happening.[3]

Figure 4.1. Elisabeth Kusian's mugshots.

As Walter made his way to the station, the departments continued their painstaking work. VP Kommandeur Rockstroh began the paperwork necessary to arrest Elisabeth Kusian, though she had not confessed.[4] Guards paraded Elisabeth Kusian before a panel of judges. She stoically stood by her original declaration of innocence, even as she prepared for another round of questioning (a round that would not occur for a few days).[5]

Kriminalkommissar Menzel's 7 January afternoon took a surprising turn when he picked up the telephone and heard a voice from Charlottenburg's Precinct #131 on the other end of the line. VP Kommissar Steffen had visited the West Berlin police precinct responsible for Elisabeth's district to inform his opposite numbers of his intention to conduct a forensic examination of Kusian's room. What a curious turn of events, one pregnant with possibilities. Kriminalkommissar Menzel alerted Kriminalkommissar Griebsch, and the two immediately drove to the precinct to meet the East Berliners. Menzel met Steffen at the precinct, alerted the Friesenstraße homicide squad's chemical investigation team, and discussed the facts of the case. The mixed unit then proceeded together to Kusian's room.

Kriminalkommissar Griebsch quickly took charge of the forensic investigation, directing chemists and other investigators who spent three hours in the room. Detectives seized several articles of men's clothing (including underwear, a shirt, and a pair of socks) as evidence and questioned Frau Stö. They then began their search for traces of blood.[6] Menzel noted that, during the investigation, he "cut the floorboard cracks to the right of a couch with a pocket knife. The material – putty and small wood chips – were given to Kriminal-Sekretär Oehmke of the Friesenstraße laboratory for immediate examination utilizing benzidine. The benzidine reaction was positive, that is, the required blue coloration occurred immediately to a strong extent, from which it could be concluded that it must undoubtedly be blood." The East Berlin forensics experts who were present agreed.[7] West Berlin forensic technicians removed additional materials from the apartment, including a rubber glove, for further laboratory testing. Unfortunately, they failed to find a knife that Elisabeth Kusian might have used for Dorothea Merten's and Hermann Seidelmann's dismemberment.[8]

Then, in an unexpected arrival, Kriminalkommissar Schulz from the Tiergarten Precinct appeared on the scene with Kurt Muschan in tow.

The Tiergarten district and its police precinct took their name from Berlin's Tiergarten (Animal Park), an urban park that originated as a royal garden. The Prussian Elector Joachim I purchased the land in 1530 to use as a game preserve. By the end of the nineteenth century, Tierpark was a 600-acre green space – Berlin's largest urban park. In the wake of the Second World War, the park was almost deforested. Bombing and the need for firewood wreaked havoc on the area, but the British occupation forces (the district lay in the British Occupation Zone) gave permission to plant new trees. The district lies close to the city centre and the museums, making it a relatively peaceful hub, indeed a prosperous bourgeois living quarter in the otherwise bustling city and a centre in its own right.[9]

Muschan told the gathered detectives that he had already spoken with the Volkspolizei criminal division. The chagrined detective then repeated how he removed his coat and hat and then saw a woman's coat and hat hanging on a hook inside the door.[10] None of this surprised the West Berliners. Muschan's following line, though, did. He told his fellow detectives that officers from the Volkspolizei had visited Kusian's room the night before and confiscated a woman's umbrella and watch.

While Muschan spoke, the assembled detectives were increasingly delighted with what they had been able to accomplish together. They wanted the two departments to cooperate as the multiple cases collapsed into one. When VP Kommissar Steffen suggested that detectives re-examine Frau Stö., the West Berlin squad not only assented, but its members also agreed to forward its report to the Volkspolizei.[11] Yet Muschan's revelation deepened tension between the two departments. The irony is that the West Berlin department's ineptitude, not politics, heightened interdepartmental tension. While telling his story, Kurt Muschan explained how precinct detectives permitted Volkspolizei detectives to visit Elisabeth Kusian's room just the previous night. Detectives from the two departments went together but failed to inform the western murder squad of the outing. In short, the first serious friction between the western and eastern investigations resulted from bureaucratic problems within the West Berlin police rather than any Cold War chicanery.

As their somewhat problematic meeting broke up, the Volkspolizei returned to their headquarters for another discussion with Elisabeth and to tie up other threads. Unsurprisingly, Kusian began with yet another claim of innocence. "That's impossible. I don't believe you that there is blood in my room." When they showed her the forensic report, she responded coolly, "I don't know where the blood could have come from. Frau Merten did not bleed. I have eczema on my knee, which I often scratch, and then it bleeds. It can't be Merten's blood. She did not bleed. She was not sitting on the couch. She didn't get sick, either. The blood on the comforter is from my knee."[12] With this absurd statement, Volkspolizei halted their work for the rest of the weekend.

Showing his displeasure with the turn of events, West Berlin Kriminalkommissar Menzel asked Kurt Muschan to accompany him back to West Berlin headquarters to provide an official statement. Menzel also wanted to follow up on another of the room's odd clues. As detectives tossed Elisabeth Kusian's trash can, they found the torn remnants of an official registration form belonging to Alfred Brandt. This name was new to all concerned. Menzel mused about the investigation's next stage. He would have to follow up on the Brandt question. Perhaps this new Herr Brandt was yet another victim of Elisabeth Kusian.[13] Menzel assigned Kriminal-Assistant Sonntag the task of identifying and finding Alfred Brandt. The torn form listed all cogent information. Brandt's birthday was 26 June 1922. He came from Graudenz – a Prussian town before the First World War; Germans were expelled in the wake of the Second World War. Brandt worked as a bricklayer. In 1949, he was single and living in Berlin's Charlottenburg district, about 3.6 kilometres from Kantstraße 154.

Neither the city registration office nor the local police precinct had a record of a Brandt at the address Kriminal-Assistant Zimmermann, who was working with Sonntag, showed them. Although Sonntag found two men named Alfred Brandt, neither shared a birth date, address, or profession with Kusian's Brandt.[14] He was yet another figment of Elisabeth Kusian's fertile imagination, another dead end.

After this not-unexpected disappointment, Kriminal-Assistant Sonntag and Kriminal-Assistant Zimmermann turned their attention to some concrete evidence that would link Kusian to her victims. They began by visiting a cigarette shop that ran a side business blocking and reconditioning hats. They retrieved the hat left by a nurse and took it to Hermann Seidelmann's sister, who identified it. They then visited the laundromat that Kusian used. Frau Ka., the owner, showed them a list of laundry items that Elisabeth had dropped off in early January, then spoke of a young woman who had stopped by to try to sell a pair of women's shoes. This woman reappeared on 6 January with a young girl in tow to try to sell a brown dress. Although Frau Ka. had no interest in the items, she remembered the mysterious young woman who told Frau Ka. that Elisabeth Kusian would come by later for her laundry. Unfortunately for the detectives, Frau Ka. could not identify her any further.

It seemed to be time to work directly on building a three-dimensional portrait of Elisabeth Kusian. Sonntag and Zimmerman moved from apartment to apartment, speaking to landladies and former fellow tenants. Marja Sobe. told the officers that, although Kusian had rented from her, she expelled her from the apartment for noise. Frau Sobe. sent the detectives to another apartment. After knocking for what seemed to them a long time, a young child came to the door. Mommy, he said, was out shopping. Grandmother was sick in bed. They waited 2½ hours until "Mommy," thirty-five-year-old Anni Glißmann, returned. When they saw Glißmann, they knew she was the woman described at the laundromat and had a story to tell. Anni Glißmann had almost made a career selling and pawning clothes for Elisabeth Kusian. Dropping into shops and finding random buyers in train stations allowed Glißmann to conduct a series of quick, black-market-like transactions. Here – a lightning-fast exchange of a coat for a fistful of cash.[15] There – worn but clean clothes exchanged for cash and pawn tickets. The detectives needed no encouragement to bring Glißmann to the station for Kriminalkommissar Menzel's consideration.

This Berlin native intrigued Kriminalkommissar Menzel. She stood at the centre of Kusian's dealings.[16] The two women met when Elisabeth Kusian lived in the same building as Glißmann. She sublet a room from a Frau Nee. until Pentecost (early June) 1949. Kusian's fondness for children cemented her friendship with Glißmann. Just as important, though, were Elisabeth's stories; they were titillating and vaguely scandalous. Among these was the tale she told Glißmann about a box stolen from Frau Nee. Although Nee. suspected her of the theft, Kusian remained in the apartment for a while. Nee. never pressed charges. For the longest time, Kusian's luck held out. She avoided punishment even when others noticed and suffered from her deeds and misdeeds.

When Frau Nee. could no longer bear having Elisabeth in her home, Anni Glißmann helped her move to a new room on Birkenstraße, where she sublet a room from Frau Sobe. Glißmann recalled that, while still living with Frau Nee., Kusian took a lover. He was a physician or a medical student – she either couldn't remember or never knew – who wanted to open a practice. His name? It was unfamiliar, difficult to remember, but it sounded Polish. The couple was always together during Kusian's free time. The building's cleaning woman, Frau Plagw., once told Anni Glißmann about Frau Nee.'s stolen jewel box, gossiping about how police arrested the unknown Kusian's doctor friend for the crime. Glißmann, of course, asked Elisabeth Kusian about this arrest. A disappointed Kusian rued that she paid his legal fees; he repaid her by escaping from prison, leaving her holding the bag for his legal debt.

As the evening wore on, Anni Glißmann balanced her shrinking patience with police questions against her joy at being the centre of attention and the opportunity to speak about this romantic friend. She remembered the physician's name. It sounded like "Borislawski." Thinking further, she remembered Kusian telling her that he lived in the "Zone." One day, Elisabeth Kusian involved Glißmann in her affair with this man. Would Glißmann meet Boguslawski's sister to ask for a table, bicycle, and chair? Of course Anni would.

This romance, love, sex, criminality, scandal, and mystery had to appeal to the young Berlin mother. In the end, though, Frau Sobe. evicted Elisabeth Kusian from her apartment because she was too loud. Unsurprisingly, when Kusian left, she still owed 40 DM rent. When Elisabeth Kusian moved, the women lost touch for a while. They reconnected when Glißmann dropped by the hospital where Kusian worked to collect a 5 DM debt. Elisabeth Kusian's colleagues informed Glißmann that Kusian was now renting in the Kantstraße. At some point in November 1949, Glißmann visited Kantstraße to collect. Kusian was not home to receive the visit but returned the compliment the following Sunday and invited Glißmann for tea. Glißmann accepted the invitation and waited four hours; Kusian never showed. However, when Glißmann returned to her home, Kusian left an envelope that bore the words, "Wait, I am coming." From this point forward, Kusian visited three to four times per week, often bringing her son and leaving him for the day. This pattern of visits lasted about two weeks, to the point that Kusian trusted Glißmann enough to leave her son overnight.

Glißmann lingered on Kusian's dramatic biography as she knew it: the physician husband who died in Paris during the war, her father-in-law's clinic in Thuringia. Then, though, she returned to what were for her mundane details of sold coats, shoes, and more.

Kusian could be a stern taskmaster. She was frequently unhappy with the amounts that Glißmann received. Still, Glißmann must have thought that this passing disapproval was a small price to pay for the excitement. Tales of clothes led to a story of silverware. Kusian, she noted, was disappointed at the failed pawning. The failure led to Glißmann's borrowing money from Frau Stö. Even this silly transaction had elements of melodrama. As Glißmann passed the borrowed cash to Kusian, the nurse began to weep as she explained that Muschan was married and had children. Kusian would have to spend Christmas Eve alone. Glißmann invited her to the Glißmann house. Kusian accepted, adding that she could not come until 9:00 p.m. The two separated, Glißmann watching as Kusian drifted towards Zoo Station. Kusian never showed up for Christmas Eve. The friends would not see each other until after Christmas when Elisabeth Kusian brought a suitcase, complete with a broken lock, to Anni Glißmann's building. In it was Doris Merten's clothing, ready to sell.

Glißmann offered to give everything she still had to the police. Could Kriminalkommissar Menzel trust her honesty? No, he could not. He admonished, perhaps threatened, her to tell the truth in all its details. Immediately, she remembered a new, potentially significant point. The suitcase was bloody.

Anni Glißmann had far less to say about Kurt Muschan. She claimed she had only seen him come and go a few times when Kusian still lived in Frau Nee.'s apartment. Perhaps Frau Nee. could speak in more detail about him. She did not even know what Muschan did for a living. Some neighbours, though, claimed that he worked for the police. She finished her statement at about 10:30 p.m., leaving Kriminalkommissar Menzel even more confident that Kusian killed Hermann Seidelmann and Dorothea Merten. Had she, though, acted alone? Was she involved in even more crimes? At 10:45 p.m., he took Glißmann to her apartment to collect some goods and dropped by the neighbour's for the blood-stained suitcase. Glißmann left him with lingering suspicions of her. Might she warn some of her contacts about police interest in their activities? Menzel ordered her into police custody.[17] Glißmann had to be earning money from her transactions.[18] That alone justified keeping her.

As the day drew to a close, the Berlin press had not yet fully processed the story but understood how it might unfold. One headline screamed, "Nurse Arrested as Double Murderer." Another informed potential readers that the "Victim Was Strangled with a Clothesline." She used the proceeds from selling her victims' clothing and valuables on herself. But nurses were angels of mercy. What could this mean? The case's drama and horror would soon unfold in the public eye.[19]

8 January 1950

Kriminalkommissar Menzel started his cool, damp Sunday, 8 January[20] by thinking about Glißmann from the previous night. She had been very cooperative. She handed over all of the suitcases and the blood-flaked blanket that once had wrapped coal. Nevertheless, her motivation for helping Elisabeth Kusian still puzzled him. What could account for all the aid she gave to the murderer? Did she profit from all the trading she did on Kusian's behalf? With no obvious answer, he decided to keep her in custody.[21]

Pushing this puzzle aside, the Kriminalkommissar turned his attention to the man whom Glißmann believed was Elisabeth Kusian's brother and whom she thought lived on Wollankstraße. Menzel contacted the nearest precinct station, which directed him to Walter Kusian, a forty-nine-year-old waiter residing in the Sternstraße area. Menzel's first surprise was that Kusian was Elisabeth's ex-husband. He recovered and asked the precinct to dispatch two officers to detain and drive Kusian to an interview with the murder squad, then search his room. At 1:15 p.m., even as the precinct contacted Menzel with the disappointing news that they were unsuccessful in their search for Kusian, Walter walked into Menzel's office. A shaken Kusian explained that Frau Stö. had informed him of Elisabeth's arrest, and he wanted to make an official statement. As a former Nazi, he understood that he could not create problems for Berlin's new authorities. Indeed, Menzel noted the "relatively reasonable impression."[22]

Walter Kusian's 4½ page, typed, sworn statement provided investigators with some intriguing first glimpses into the personality and background of his ex-wife.[23] He spoke of their meeting, marriage, and move to Berlin, as well as his job with a Nazi bureaucracy to which his long-term membership in the Nazi Party entitled him.

After the outbreak of the war, Walter Kusian joined an army medical unit. According to him, Elisabeth began to drift from the kind of life he had imagined into something wilder and altogether more problematic. On one visit home, Kusian found a piano in the 3½ room apartment. Elisabeth told him that she had rescued it from a bombed-out dwelling. He discovered later that she was renting it by the month. On another, she asked him to take two rings to a jeweller to engrave. After this, it dawned on Walter Kusian that Elisabeth was having extramarital affairs. Kusian told Menzel about her suicide attempts (he was unsure whether she tried to overdose on sleeping pills or hang herself) and her stay in the Heilanstalt Wittenau.

Heilanstalt Wittenau was founded in the Weimar Republic as a treatment facility for children with intellectual disabilities. By 1941, it was part of the Nazi T4 Program, which mandated that these children should be medically murdered because of their lack of value for the Reich. It is impossible to know if Elisabeth was aware of Wittenau's role in the Holocaust, but if she was, this knowledge surely contributed to her instrumentalization of, and lack of interest in the dignity of, human life.[24]

Walter claimed that, after returning to Berlin from captivity in an American POW camp, he tried to restart his marriage while employed as a construction worker during Elisabeth's stints at the Rudolf Virchow and Moabit Hospitals. They divorced by mutual agreement in 1947 or 1948 (he could not remember which) and then did not see each other for about 1½ years. Kusian now worked at construction for about 50 DM per week, from which he paid about 60 DM per month to the Catholic Children's Home in Pankow-Niederschönhausen, where their three children stayed until August 1949. He thought Elisabeth Kusian earned 260 DM per month. He knew of Elisabeth's illegitimate Kindergeld payments. Perhaps, he pondered, such cheating led to her dismissal at Moabit Hospital.

Turning to thoughts of his children, he explained that, after they left the Catholic orphanage, he spent more time with the whole family. Walter knew of the long-term affair with Kurt Muschan but seemed to think little of it. The preliminaries completed, Walter reflected on the rucksacks filled with coal he often brought to Elisabeth's room. Menzel perked up as Kusian explained the details. Elisabeth had borrowed two from him (at this point, Menzel showed him one such rucksack, which Kusian identified as his), which he had tried to get back after Christmas; Elisabeth claimed to have left them at the hospital. When he was surprised to see them in her room on New Year's Day, she said that she had not been able to return one of them as she loaned it to somebody to transport rabbit pelts. It reeked, so Elisabeth wanted the borrower to clean it properly before she returned it to Kusian. Walter showed Menzel the clean rucksack, adding that he had taken it when he left the bloody one behind.

Walter's thoughts turned from rucksacks to clothing that Elisabeth wanted him to sell for her. These articles, she claimed, belonged to a friend of one of her colleagues, Erna. Walter was led to believe that this woman had escaped from the Soviet Zone and needed cash. Then began a web of details about rucksacks, Christmas, Elisabeth's appearing in a nursing uniform at her door, and gifts he wanted to send to their children. What might her forlorn goodbye kiss, which she gave him as he took his leave of her, have meant? Probably the knowledge that she would soon kill Doris Merten. Walter Kusian did not wrap himself in glory. He neither knew where his children lived nor pressed the issue with their mother. He was more concerned about detailing the money he gave Elisabeth and thinking about her lying ways. Money issues, he claimed, underlay their divorce. Ultimately, Walter thought about her last words to him when she came by to visit. "About eight days ago, but it could also be longer, she told me during a visit to my apartment that she had done something terrible but could only confess it on her deathbed. Since she often tends to fantasies, I gave these, her words, no particular value."[25]

As Kusian mused, the West Berlin team fanned out to conduct yet more interviews. Charlotte Glaubitz discussed her twenty-year-plus friendship with Dorothea Merten and details about her living arrangements. She could not stop thinking about how she had hated Doris Merten's accepting silverware as surety for a typewriter. It was odd and boded ill.[26] Anni Glißmann added a few details to her previous statement, the most notable of which was that she had noticed Elisabeth Kusian's bloody left knuckles, acquired, Kusian claimed, in a fight with her brother-in-law. Long in the habit of giving her money, this man declared she belonged to him. When Elisabeth Kusian told Anni Glißmann this story of blows and choking, she cried. The best thing, she said, was for her to commit suicide.[27]

Not knowing that Walter Kusian had gone to headquarters, and with Anni Glißmann's words still ringing in his ears, Kriminal-Assistant Sonntag and a colleague visited shops to collect evidence, before trying to find Walter Kusian, the "brother-in-law."[28] When they showed up at his Sternstraße 11 address, Kusian's landlord set them straight about the Kusians' relationship and described Walter as a reticent, orderly man who never caused any problems.[29] The other detective on the street, Kriminal-Assistant Weisheit, had an equally frustrating Sunday. He used it to visit the hospital floor on which Elisabeth Kusian worked, look into the Kusian children's living arrangements, and visit a pawnshop in Wilmersdorf. Dr. Kühn, the physician in charge of Elisabeth Kusian's ward, was no help. Kühn simply referred Weisheit to his supervisor, Dr. Hintze, who grudgingly admitted that, although theft was possible because of the hospital's size and complexity, such tools were also easily purchased from medical supply companies. A floor nurse who claimed to be a friend of Elisabeth Kusian's explained that she knew nothing about Kusian's personal life, then referred Weisheit to the floor's charge nurse, who happened to have the day off. Weisheit never found an administrator to tell him Kusian's salary, why she left, or, indeed, anything. He ended his fruitless trip with an admonishment ringing in his ears. Dr. Hintze took the detective aside to warn him not to mention the hospital's name in any press reports. It would be awful if the public thought that the murders took place there.[30]

Kriminal-Assistant Weisheit's next, equally frustrating visit took him to the "Maria-Frieden" Home to examine the children's living situation. Here, he learned that the orphanage only allowed girls. None of the home's officials with whom he spoke knew where Elisabeth Kusian had placed her son. Although he did learn that she paid 2.30 DM per day for each child's upkeep and that she had removed the children, nobody knew where they went.[31]

A small, hard-won success may have redeemed Weisheit's day. Joined by Kriminal-Anwart Reichmuth, he visited the pawnshop on Wilmersdorf's Badenerstraße 48.

> Wilmersdorf was, and in many ways still is, a district that recalls much of the twentieth-century history of the city. Before Berlin's post-unification political reshuffling of districts, which created Charlottenburg-Wilmersdorf, Wilmersdorf was the home of sites that, in different ways, exemplify the troubled and troubling past. Here was the home of the Olympic Stadium, built to house the 1936 Olympic Games in which Jesse Owens shone. It is also the site of the so-called Teufelsberg, the second-highest spot in the city, reaching 120.1 metres above sea level.[32] The Trummerfrauen (Women of the Rubble) built Teufelsberg from the rubble, transported from every corner of the city, of about 16,000 buildings that were destroyed during the bombing of Berlin.[33]

In this pawnshop, they hoped to find Hermann Seidelmann's watch. The employee at the shop sent them to the director's home, but Herr Kr. was away. When they finally contacted him about the pawn ticket for the watch, he told them that he did not have the key to the shop's safe and referred them to the appraiser, Herr Br., whom they visited at home. In what might have been the only satisfying moment of the day, Herr Br. accompanied them back to the shop to hand over the timepiece.[34] The crowning frustration of Kriminalkommissar Griebsch's day was his failed attempt to telephone East Berlin detectives to discuss the case. Nobody was at headquarters to take his call.[35]

9 January 1950

Snow and rain mixed on a cold, grey 9 January as West and East Berlin detectives returned to the case.[36] As Kriminalkommissar Menzel oversaw a second forensic investigation of Elisabeth Kusian's room, some West Berlin homicide detectives interviewed yet more witnesses. Others continued tracking and retrieving the clothing she stole from her victims. All the while, detectives from the two squads spent a great deal of time on the telephone trying to coordinate investigations and prevent miscommunications.

Menzel and his team met Frau Stö. at Kantstraße 154a, where she let them in and acted as a witness. They hoped to find the murder weapon and perhaps even more blood stains and other physical evidence. Although the search did not locate a probable weapon, it yielded valuable and puzzling details. When they opened up an umbrella hanging on Kusian's door, the team found a ring with a stone that Charlotte Strach later identified as belonging to Doris Merten, two syringes, an ampule of chloroethyl, and a waste basket containing the torn letters seemingly sent by Kusian's mother.[37]

The squad experimented to understand why nobody had heard either of the victims struggle or scream. Menzel and his colleagues went into Frau Stö.'s room. After they were gone, Kriminal-Assistant Sonntag cried, "Help," first softly, then ever more loudly from inside Kusian's room while they listened from the adjacent rooms. Only when Sonntag yelled loudly was he at all audible. With Kusian's radio turned on, nobody heard him.[38]

The search and experiment were interrupted by a married couple, Paul and Hedwig Le., who appeared at the door, hoping to find Elisabeth Kusian. It seems that Kusian borrowed 500 DM, a not inconsiderable sum, from Le., a seventy-year-old haulage contractor, who had been her patient at the hospital. Kusian had told the couple that she needed the cash to send her children away and that her father-in-law was good for the debt. In what might have revealed the real reason for the loan, Le. told the investigators that, although he knew that Kusian was active in the hospital's admissions department, he denied any possibility that she did anything to help him get sick leave. After the couple left and the detectives finished searching and collecting, they resealed the room and departed.[39]

At about 10:00 a.m. that morning, Kriminalkommissar Griebsch returned a telephone call from VP Kommandeur Rockstroh to have yet another discussion about clothing. Kriminalkommissar Menzel had already shown some of it to Seidelmann's widow, who confirmed it as his.[40] Were there any doubts in West Berlin about Elisabeth Kusian's guilt, they were long gone.[41] Menzel thought about what he and his detectives had learned from their work and conversations with Eastern counterparts, then wrote to the Generalstaatsanwalt to request that West Berlin seek Kusian's transfer to Western custody without delay.[42]

As West Berlin authorities attempted to move Elizabeth Kusian across city lines, East Berlin detectives crossed the invisible border to interview her Western colleagues and customers. VP Kommissar Steffen appeared at the Tiergarten Station with three requests. He wanted permission to compare investigation notes. He also asked to speak with Kusian's "Oberin" (matron/head nurse) at Moabit Hospital. Steffen hoped to visit several shops where the Volkspolizei believed Kusian and others had taken some of the clothing. Although Kriminalkommissar Schulz, the precinct's chief of detectives, was open to the idea, protocol required him to telephone the murder squad's Kriminal-Assistant Weisheit for permission. Weisheit informed him that the murder squad had the evidence. Frustratingly, it was too late to prevent an unnecessary couple of stops that VP Kommissar Steffen and VP Kriminalpolizeirat Schwarz (who accompanied him) would make as they had already left.[43]

After VP Kommissar Steffen made his pointless trips with his West Berlin companion to several shops only to find the evidence already in the hands of the West Berlin authorities, his superiors issued him an uncomfortable order.[44] An unhappy Steffen informed his opposite numbers that he was sorry but soon he would no longer be able to work with them. West Berlin files noted his regret. Not surprisingly, this regret did not appear in Steffen's report.[45]

It is possible, but unlikely, that the miscommunication was a deliberate slight of East Berlin authorities. The murder squad's records show bureaucratic infighting in the West Berlin department was more important than were Cold War issues. VP Kriminalpolizeirat Schwarz made no effort to hide his frustration. Despite Schwarz's urgent request, Menzel hid details about his squad's collected objects. He only disclosed that "Friesenstraße had identified a woman who had pawned Seidelmann's wristwatch at a pawnshop on behalf of the arrested Kusian. The disclosure of the name and address of this woman was also refused."[46] Menzel viewed the departments' cooperation issues very differently. When VP Hauptwachtmeister K. Schiller appeared at the Tiergarten Station with two of Doris Merten's sisters, Menzel insisted that Schiller hold his discussion at the murder squad headquarters. Ostensibly, this was to allow the sisters to see the clothing West Berlin police had gathered. Just as significantly, using his offices would help Menzel centralize control of the investigation.[47]

Meanwhile, Kriminal-Assistant Zimmermann interviewed some of Elisabeth Kusian's former neighbours from around Berlin. Twenty-six-year-old Marja Sobe., an unemployed stenotypist, had sublet a room in her Birkenstraße 13a apartment to Kusian. Berlin's Housing Authority assigned her the apartment in 1946 when her husband returned to Berlin from a POW camp. Their income, however, made it impossible for them to pay the rent without help. Marja Sobe., Elisabeth Kusian's former landlady, had nothing good to say about her tenant. She certainly still remembered Kusian's misuse of and theft from Sobe's mother as well as the 32 DM that Kusian still owed her for rent and utilities.

After Sobe.'s tale of the theft and unpaid rent, detailed in chapter 1, and perhaps to get a fuller picture of the suspect, the Kriminal-Assistant shifted the conversation to Elisabeth Kusian's visitors. A still annoyed Frau Sobe. responded that Muschan dropped by two to three times per week. More interesting was that another small and stocky man, probably between forty-five and fifty years old, came by almost daily to help Kusian's children with their homework. They called him "Uncle." His identity was a mystery to the former landlady. After Elisabeth Kusian moved out, the man returned carrying a full rucksack, looking for Elisabeth, but not knowing where to find her.

At this point, Frau Sobe. added personal details about Kusian to her statement that confirmed Elisabeth Kusian's desire to construct a middle-class, educated identity. Elisabeth Kusian would tell stories of her father-in-law's private clinic in Thuringia, her husband who had died in a Soviet concentration camp, and the comfortable Gesundbrunnen apartment the Allies had confiscated.[48]

Gesundbrunnen was an apt district around which to weave a tale. Its name came from a spring (Brunnen), first found in the eighteenth century. As the story goes, the spring's healing properties were discovered by King Frederick I in 1701. In 1750, the chemist Andreas Siegmund Markgraf studied the water, "as the mob has long been shouting for a healthy spring." The hoped-for majestic public bath was not built, though. Rather something much simpler opened in 1760 with the name "Friedrichs-Gesundbrunnen" (Frederick's Fountain of Health). The baths soon closed, were reopened, and closed again. During the Weimar Republic, Bauhaus-style apartment blocks were constructed there. During the Third Reich, the area was reconceived yet again. This time, it was to be the site of a "garden city for soldiers." Much of the area was eventually levelled by bombers. Each of these stages in the area's development fits well with Elisabeth Kusian's image of herself and her life – from unfulfilled dreams to destruction.[49]

Frau Sobe. was still not done. In an appendix added in response to further questions from Zimmermann, she added details about Herr "Borislawski," whom Kusian had once mentioned. Kusian wove a story for her landlady in which the mysterious Boruslawski and Detective Muschan were the only men she had ever loved. Her love for the mysterious man led her frequently to hide him in her previous apartment because of his black-market activity. When questioned, Frau Sobe. said she had seen a photograph of this foreign-looking man with a pencil moustache wrapped inside a bundle of papers that Kusian had given her to burn.[50]

Kriminal-Assistant Zimmermann later returned to Kusian's room to speak further with Marie Schön., Frau Stö.'s eighty-six-year-old mother, who told the story of Anni Glißmann's trip to collect some cash. Frau Schön. added the unsurprising detail that Kusian made no move to repay the loan until Schön. forced the issue with a written reminder.[51]

Others had even more prosaic jobs. Kriminal-Assistant Sonntag tried to locate Hermann Seidelmann's coat and shoes.[52] Another pounded the streets to confirm details with witnesses and secure more evidence. Perhaps more interesting, but certainly more fraught, some had to liaise with their East Berlin counterparts to sort out some confusion and maintain lines of communication. At about noon, VP Kommissar Steffen arrived at the Tiergarten Precinct to compare investigation notes, speak with West Berlin witnesses, and collect evidence. The precinct's Kriminalkommissar Schulz assigned Kriminal-Sekretär Schwarz, who shared a common German surname with the Volkspolizei detective, to accompany Steffen in his investigations. Unfortunately for the pair, Schulz did not yet know that the murder squad had already collected the evidence.[53] This oversight, annoying but seemingly meaningless, would have consequences later.

The mixed pair of detectives began with a visit to Moabit Hospital to round out their sense of Elisabeth Kusian's work life. The hospital administrator with whom they spoke discussed problems that both she and a certain Dr. Freyaldenhoven, a then thirty-five-year-old physician, created for the hospital in 1948 and 1949, when they came under suspicion of having performed abortions. To make matters worse, administrators suspected Freyaldenhoven of morphine addiction. The hospital fired him in April 1949 while he was in the midst of preparing his paperwork for denazification proceedings. His then current problems played no role in his denazification process, and his Nazi Party membership raised no eyebrows at the hospital, making Elisabeth's concerns about her ex-husband's membership seem to be at least a little overblown.[54] Might Elisabeth Kusian and this mysterious new name have had an even more problematic connection? Each interview raised as many questions as it closed. The detectives left the hospital to continue their rounds of the Moabit district. First came a fruitless trip to an umbrella shop.[55] In response to what looked like a West Berlin run-around, VP Kommissar Steffen spoke with the murder squad's Kriminal-Assistant Weisheit to tell him about his regrets that he would soon have to stop working on the case unless he had special permission from his superiors.[56] VP Kommissar Steffen's assessment was cagier. Noting that he had observed all formalities before beginning his work in the West, he wrote nothing about any regrets about further cooperation with his Western colleagues.[57] Reports back to Volkspolizei headquarters emphasized missteps rather than cooperation.

Later that day, more Volkspolizei detectives contacted the Tiergarten Precinct at about 3:45 p.m. Kriminalkommissar Schulz reached Kriminalkommissar Menzel to inform him of VP Hauptwachtmeister Schiller's interest in Doris Merten's sisters. Menzel readily agreed to arrange an interview with them at the murder squad's building. There was sense to this decision. Police stored Merten's clothing in squad headquarters as evidence.[58] Indeed, Doris Merten's family spent much of the day identifying clothing.[59] Once Charlotte Strach finished with Merten's clothes, police inventoried them. Then, it was Frau Seidelmann's turn to view some wardrobe. She recognized the hat, shoes, clothing, watch, and more as "without a doubt" belonging to her late husband, Hermann. She added that, before the murder, she had never heard Elisabeth Kusian's name.[60]

At about 10:00 a.m. that morning, Kriminalkommissar Griebsch of the West Berlin squad had spoken with VP Kommandeur Rockstroh. Rockstroh told Griebsch that Elisabeth Kusian had still not confessed to the murders. Griebsch responded with details about the evidence in Western hands. He acknowledged Western authorities' conviction that Kusian was guilty of murder. In what seems to have been a pretty straightforward set of bureaucratic manoeuvrings, Kriminalkommissar Menzel requested that West Berlin's Generalstaatsanwalt (district attorney) work to accomplish the transfer without delay.[61] Although the bureaucracy was seemingly perfunctory, the transfer took longer than the West Berlin authorities wished. The East Berlin detectives had an independent agenda for the case that would last a few days. At 1:00 p.m., three hours after Kriminalkommissar Griebsch and VP Kommandeur Rockstroh spoke, VP Hauptwachtmeister Wriedt, VP Polizeirat Pohl, and VP Kriminalpolizeirat Schwarz had Kusian led out of her cell in the Barnimstraße Women's Prison for a conversation that would proceed her official statement.

Interdepartmental cooperation allowed the three detectives to inform Elisabeth Kusian that Western authorities had possession of Dorothea Merten's and Hermann Seidelmann's stolen clothes. Even more to the point, they had proof that these items had been in her possession. In her rambling response, she bridled against the accusations of murder. How could she even be capable of such gruesome deeds? Playing the victim as well as her circumstances allowed, Elisabeth Kusian displayed so much emotion about the accusation that she would not even speak about the murder that day. She demanded that the detectives take her back to her cell. Would this give her time to develop a new plan that might still get her off the hook? After all, she had managed to slither out of her previous problems.

The detectives were unmoved. They calmed Elisabeth Kusian enough to allow her to speak further. She did not, though, say much of value to the case. Kusian rattled off a series of peculiar statements and claims, some of which had to strike her listeners as absurd beyond belief. Over the next few hours, her story would swerve into ever-widening gyres, spinning out of control. She claimed Dorothea Merten gave her a fur coat she no longer needed. Interviewers asked about the coat found in her room. Kusian simply refused to answer. Of course, she said, her guests had a few drinks. The alcohol was for them, not for Kurt Muschan. She also explained that Doris Merten was not her only visitor on the day after Christmas. When detectives pressed for more details, Elisabeth Kusian blurted, "I can't believe it myself. This person has three children of his own. I can't blame him. I don't know if he did it."[62] Would this scatter-shot series of statements be at all helpful to her? Could this vague accusation, probably aimed at Kurt Muschan, help? Might the police start to see her as a wronged woman? It certainly could not hurt to try this approach. After all, she was already in jail. She then told the Volkspolizei interrogators that West Berlin police would probably not have arrested her. They would have been happy to stop by to provide daily updates.

Elisabeth Kusian again tried to control her narrative. She asked the detectives if the public knew of her arrest. In response, they showed her a headline from the 9 January edition of *Der Abend* that screamed, "Nurse Arrested for Double Murders!" Now, she had to understand both the seriousness of her case and her horrifying reputation.

The detectives then pressed her. They insisted that she did the deed alone. She possessed the professional skills necessary for such a dismemberment. She replied in what must have been a sarcastic tone, "I did the deed alone; the newspaper writes that I am the murderer, and you told me I'm capable of it. I put ten Phanodorm tablets in a cup of coffee and gave it to Merten to drink. Then, when she fell asleep, I cut her up and then put her where you found her."[63]

The detectives believed they had reached some resolution. When they pressed for more details, Elisabeth Kusian fell into her familiar dodge, "Tell me, how was she killed?" Feigning annoyance, they accused her of trying to protect Muschan. He was, after all, the only person she was ever close to in her life. What would be the best response to such an implied threat? Kusian shot back, "Leave Herr Muschan out of this. He had nothing to do with it. I'll tell you the truth." This sterile back-and-forth went on for hours. Once it became clear that nothing would come of this seemingly unofficial chat, VP Hauptwachtmeister Schiller and the others shepherded Elisabeth Kusian to VP Kommandeur Rockstroh, who conducted a ninety-minute official interrogation.[64]

Elisabeth Kusian's monologue, a tissue of facts and lies, lasted from 10:30 p.m. until 2:30 a.m. the following day, when she was too tired to continue.[65] She rehearsed the details of her life, both factual and fabricated, to enhance her class status for these detectives from a newly Communist German state. Again came the tale of her father, the career military officer, padded with details about her brothers who fell in the Second World War, a sister who was really a cousin, her mother's pension, her attendance at a Lyzeum, and more. Next, she wove a tale of being a nurse before the war, her marriage to an "Unterarzt" (a rank given to a qualified physician), who was a long-time Nazi Party member.

She then spun what would become a familiar tale of the war that discussed her husband's POW status, her heroic work in the streets of Berlin, her post-war divorce, her children, her career as an artist and nurse in this new Berlin, and her father-in-law, the physician. She finished her "autobiography" by telling of personal enmity with her superior at the Moabit Hospital and her disinterest in politics.

Having finished one set of lies mixed with truth, Elisabeth Kusian began a second set, chatting into the night about the murders for which she stood accused. She started her story with a chance encounter with Hans Boguslawski on 31 January 1948. In her telling, Boguslawski claimed to be an engineer. She met him, she said, at a business party hosted by Siemens on Gotzkowskystraße. They hit it off so well that Boguslawski often visited her for evening tea and chats at the hospital where she worked and lodged. Later, when she sublet a room in an apartment, Boguslawski would visit, often arriving early in the morning, soaked with sweat. When Kusian asked about this, he claimed that he worked nights. In her telling, Boguslawski would spend time in her room as she worked but claimed to have a flat on Schillerstraße and sometimes lived with his sister on Mindener Straße. Hans Boguslawski brought radios and large sums of cash that he said belonged to his employer. Elisabeth Kusian's attempted cunning self-portrait imagined a naive young woman sadly besotted with the wrong man. To round out this image, she explained that her hospital colleagues told her he was bad news. She ignored them. Throughout their acquaintanceship, Boguslawski introduced her to several men. One purported to be a certain Dr. Hiller, like her, a medical professional. Another time, he introduced her to a photographer whom he told her lived on Nollendorfplatz. She constructed a group portrait of a criminal gang, possibly with her lover as its mastermind.

In a melodramatic plot twist, three months after they met, on 25 April 1948, Boguslawski spent the night. The following day, two members of the criminal police showed up, arrested him, and interrogated Kusian about the radios and a phonograph stashed at her place. At first, she claimed that these belonged to her. Elisabeth Kusian later recanted, claiming they were Boguslawski's.

Elisabeth Kusian told her interrogators that she first believed Boguslawski was not a criminal and paid a defence attorney, Dr. Warnow, 300 DM to defend him. Once Kusian discovered that he was twenty-six, not thirty-six, she decided he probably lied about the rest. Nevertheless, she insisted that she had forgotten to tell Dr. Warnow about her disillusionment. He sent her a bill for legal services over Christmas, which she had still not paid. Adding to the tale of financial woes that she wove for her interrogators, she claimed that Boguslawski once bought her a 3,000 DM fur coat. Imagine her shock when, even as he served an eighteen-month prison sentence, she received a bill for the present that landed her even deeper into debt. Her created Boguslawski was much like her. He was, she explained, a thief, a liar, and a con artist. Elisabeth Kusian would, she told detectives, have nothing more to do with him.

At this point, Elisabeth's story takes on even darker, more ludicrous tones. Fate would not allow her to lead an uncomplicated life. Although she managed to get rid of Boguslawski, her woes only increased. The photographer she had mentioned earlier turned out to be Boguslawski's accomplice. One day, his wife showed up at Kusian's door demanding that Kusian turn over some of the things the pair had stolen or hand over some money. How could Elisabeth Kusian, faced with such extraordinary debts, comply with such a demand? She refused. In yet another absurd claim, Elisabeth Kusian told her interrogators that the photographer's wife threatened to tell Kusian's supervisor that Boguslawski had falsified his employment book in a way that would allow him to purchase more than the amount to which he was entitled. This threat forced Kusian to give her a further 300 DM, deepening her financial woes. She never explained why such a move would have any effect on her supervisor at the hospital.

At this dark moment in her story, when all seemed to be beyond salvation, Elisabeth Kusian's white knight appeared. Kurt

Muschan, one of the detectives investigating Boguslawski, and she met while he was gathering evidence. At last, here was the man with whom she could start a new life. Yet even his appearance could not rescue Elisabeth Kusian from her myriad woes. The mastermind Boguslawski returned to her life after Christmas 1948 to demand that she return all of his goods. Although she could produce some of it, circumstances forced her to sell the rest to pay her mounting debt, for which Boguslawski was morally responsible. He then threatened her over her relationship with Muschan. Elisabeth Kusian feared the worst. Her breathless story proceeded like a runaway train, unimpeded by facts or even an attempt to appear truthful.

In yet another gyre, one day during Christmas week 1948, when Kusian expected a visit from Kurt Muschan, Hans Boguslawski arrived at the door. Perhaps flustered, she let him in by mistake. During this invented visit, Boguslawski took the opportunity to sneak into the room of her landlady, Frau Nee., and, she claimed, steal her jewellery. Once again, Elisabeth Kusian could weave fiction into fact and shift responsibility for her crimes onto another. Might the detectives believe this tale? It ceased to matter. Elisabeth Kusian told the interrogators that she understood her moral obligation to repay the debt and did so at the rate of 40 DM per month, which she could maintain until November 1949. Although Boguslawski never returned to her apartment, she claimed he would accost her on the street, both demanding money and that she end her relationship with Muschan. He threatened that he and Dr. Hiller would take revenge on her children and Muschan using a gun that the two of them had (which Kusian claimed to have seen).

Elisabeth Kusian's story of Boguslawski and Hiller spun ever more out of control. Wolfgang Hiller, a thirty-two-year-old figment of her imagination, often visited Elisabeth in her sublet room. Hiller lived with a woman named Emmi Seifert, had two children and a brother who owned a small, sometimes black-market, food shop near the Börse S-Bahn Station (later Marx Engels Platz, now Hackescher Markt).

Might there have been an anti-Semitic aspect involved in choosing this locale? The entire area was once part of the old Jewish Quarter. There is something audacious in choosing it as the locale in which to place fictitious swindlers. Hackescher Markt had its own sad history. It was one of the first developments beyond Berlin's city walls. Before the Industrial Revolution, it was a barn district (Scheunenviertel), as Berliners were not allowed to keep animals within city walls. By the turn of the twentieth century, the term "Scheunenviertel" was synonymous with poor, Eastern European Jews, while the nearby Hackescher Quarter became an upscale area, attracting many of Berlin's wealthier citizens. In the Third Reich, the local synagogue would function as a deportation centre to death camps.[66]

Detail piled upon detail to give credence to the tale. Much of it seemed designed to address the forensic evidence she must have suspected was in the hands of the West Berlin police. Wolfgang Hiller visited her at the hospital and even invited her to accompany him to one of his favourite hangouts, the "Alten Ballhaus." She probably meant the Ballhaus on Chausseestraße, situated in what was a business and entertainment district before the Third Reich.

The Ballhaus was a legendary nightclub in Berlin, even appearing in the television series *Babylon Berlin*. The building's front was bombed to rubble during the war, but it reopened in 1949.[67] Recalling evenings there from a later moment, Regine Sylvester dreamed of luxury from another era, a luxury that would fit into Elisabeth Kusian's fantasies.

As Sylvester remembered it, "the Ballhaus Berlin, with table telephones, that was something! We danced, we flirted, we had a good time. It was something special, something grown-up to be there. Sometimes there was a ladies' choice. You'd take heart and approach someone, but nothing ever came of it."[68]

In yet another attempt to lay down a smokescreen and squirm out of her trap, Elisabeth Kusian told Kriminalkommissar Menzel that, in late November or early December 1949, Hiller visited her in her room in Kantstraße to secure a suitcase because he wanted to go away. Probably because she suspected that the police had already approached Anni Glißmann, Kusian discussed how the pair borrowed a suitcase from Glißmann's neighbour. The following day, at about 9:00 a.m., Hiller purportedly showed up and took the suitcase. She of course didn't want to give it to him, but he told her he would need it to disappear from Berlin. His coming disappearance, Kusian claimed, gave her some peace, so she let him have it. So now a man who never existed had a suitcase. He returned it the next day, filled with a bloody shirt and more. Hiller also gave her a separate package with even more clothing. Again riffing on her activities, Elisabeth Kusian gave Hiller's purported explanation. He and Hans Boguslawski had been transporting rabbits and slaughtered black-market birds to sell in Berlin. The detail about the birds expanded her original story. Hiller demanded that she sell these items quickly as he and his brother needed cash. He then handed her a watch to hold onto for the time being.

Could she come up with a different, more likely story than the one she had used for Anni Glißmann? It seems not. Try as she might, Elisabeth Kusian could add nothing new or convincing. The rest of her story overlapped with Anni Glißmann's, including furtive sales at train stations. It only added the detail of mysterious black-market traders.

The goods, she claimed, did not sell for as much cash as Dr. Hiller had wanted, so he forced her to add 5 DM of her own money to the money she and Glißmann had received for their various sales. She said that she had taken the rest of the clothing to the laundry. It was now in her room.

Perhaps because the detectives believed there was nothing more to gain from this line of inquiry, they drew a line under it and moved the conversation to the typewriter that Kusian had purchased. Hiller was too vivid a character to abandon. Soon he intruded into this aspect of Elisabeth Kusian's story in ways that made even less sense than the rest of the tale. After Elisabeth Kusian detailed her "perfect" job of arranging the machine's purchase on Christmas Eve, she segued to an encounter with Dr. Hiller on the street. In this tale, she told him about the typewriter. Hiller countered by immediately inviting himself to her house and then again for Christmas. The mysterious, non-existent Hiller visited her on her hospital floor on Christmas Day to say he would be at her apartment the next day for the typewriter transaction. His presence infused every detail of the story. Hiller showed up on Boxing Day morning, took her desk key, and ordered her to give some kind of surety to Frau Merten when she arrived. Hiller informed Kusian that he would be present for the afternoon transaction.

Merten arrived after the fictional Dr. Hiller. Elisabeth Kusian explained that she had no cash. Within the story's logic, Hiller's locking of the desk drawer kept it away from her. He was behind her use of the silverware as a guarantee of payment and joined her for a 4½-hour wait until Dorothea Merten arrived. In addition, he posed as Kurt Muschan and drank wine and schnaps with Frau Merten. All the while, Elisabeth Kusian paid for the typewriter. At about 10:15 p.m., this Hiller drove away with Doris Merten but returned nearly half an hour later with her hat and fur coat. She would, he told Kusian, return later to pick them up. Now, though, the couple was going out to celebrate.

Had her imagination run into a dead end? Elisabeth Kusian broke off her statement and told the detectives she could not continue; she did not want to make any mistakes. VP Hauptwachtmeister Wriedt, who served as the stenographer, noted the following at the bottom of the statement: "Closed with the note that the interrogation was terminated at 2:20 a.m. due to total fatigue of the defendant."[69] That much is undoubtedly true. The task she gave herself must have been exhausting.

If Elisabeth Kusian's day was an exhausting series of discussions, challenging questions, and failed lies, Walter Kusian's ended on an entirely different note. As he returned to his apartment building, he encountered his landlord reading the newspaper about his former wife's arrest for murder. Coelestin He. looked at Kusian, showed him the story, and only said, "Herr K. Hold your head high." This advice would become ever more challenging to take as Elisabeth's story progressed.[70]

chapter five

Finalizing the Case: Berlin's Police Departments Finish with Elisabeth Kusian

Tuesday, 10 January 1950–Monday, 13 February 1950

10 January 1950

As they adjusted their coats to deal with yet another day of wintry mix and temperatures ranging from sub-freezing to barely 6 degrees Celsius, Volkspolizei detectives prepared for another day of tracking down evidence.[1] VP Hauptwachtmeister Rudat had Hermann Seidelmann's widow identify some of her late husband's clothing, which must have compounded the suffering she had gone through the day before when she did much the same in the West. VP Kriminalpolizeirat Schwarz spent his day looking for Wolfgang Hiller and Emmi Seifert, whom Elisabeth Kusian tried to paint as the true culprits. Later, he joined VP Polizeirat Pohl and VP Kommissar Steffen in another discussion with Kusian. Meanwhile, VP Kommandeur Rockstroh began the mind-numbing paperwork that the East Berlin authorities assumed would wrap up their involvement in the case and hand over Kusian to the West.[2]

VP Kriminalpolizeirat Schwarz's assignment was undoubtedly the most interesting. Even before Elisabeth Kusian finished her statement of the night before, the Volkspolizei began to look into Hiller and Seifert. Frustratingly, the vaunted German bureaucracy seemed to let him down; neither name was listed with the Einwohnermeldeamt (Residents' Registration Office). A telephone call, however, soon established that a Helmut Hiller operated a fruit and vegetable shop at Dircksenstraße 16, located very close to Alexanderplatz.[3] Looking into his story, though, would wait. First came the attempt to find the Hiller whom Kusian had fingered. After he finished her interrogation, Schwarz drove Kusian along Dircksenstraße. She could not identify any of the buildings. Could this story of Hiller have been made up out of whole cloth? Perhaps to keep the tale at least partly alive, Kusian said that she had never been to the shop where Hans Boguslawski and Hiller allegedly met. Schwarz continued to drive her around the area, but she also failed to locate the house where she claimed Hiller and Seifert lived. Again, her tale seemed to lay in tatters. Perhaps "her" Hiller lived elsewhere. To test this possibility, Schwarz asked six precincts to comb their records for Hiller and Seifert without success.[4]

The Volkspolizei eventually turned their attention to the Hiller they could find, Helmut, a thirty-eight-year-old greengrocer.[5] Helmut told VP Polizeirat Schwarz about his twenty-eight-year-old brother and their stepsister, with whom he lost touch in 1932. This Hiller trained as a young man to be a fruit and vegetable merchant and worked in this field until 1939, when the army drafted him. In an irony that may have saved his life, the army expelled him in 1940 when records emerged that showed he had a Jewish mother. Hiller spent the war working in the produce business. Legally forbidden by the Nazi regime to marry earlier, he wed after the war and was, by 1949, the head of a household. He avoided politics but knew his rights in the post-war world as a victim of the Nuremberg Laws. In a small victory, he could help his mother regain possession of the apartment that the Third Reich had requisitioned. Mostly, though, he seemed to live a quiet greengrocer's life, first co-owning a shop with his brother. Later, when they lost their lease, they went their separate ways.

When VP Kriminalpolizeirat Schwarz turned the conversation to the matter at hand, Helmut Hiller immediately shed light on Kusian's accusations. His brother Rolf once had a relationship with Elisabeth Kusian. Helmut never met her, but Rolf told stories of a morphine-using nurse named Elisabeth at the Moabit Hospital. She wanted to be a physician and was given to spinning yarns about running a clinic in Thuringia. The name Boguslawski meant nothing, and neither he nor his brother owned a car. Helmut did not think that his brother Rolf possessed a gun.

Later, VP Polizeirat Schwarz invited Rolf to the police station where he told much the same story as his brother, albeit with some variation and more specifics.[6] Rolf, the younger and seemingly wilder of the siblings, met Elisabeth at the Alten Ballhaus. This beautiful woman claimed to be a medical student whose uncle owned a clinic, but Rolf Hiller did not believe these "fairy tales." Something about her charms attracted men; Rolf was no different – they were together for about three months. In the end, though, she was too "motherly." The last straw was that she dropped into his shop and his mother's house with a cake for him. Even after he married another woman, Kusian telephoned him, angering Hiller's wife. Rolf did not know any Boguslawski, told Schwarz that he had been with his wife over the Christmas holidays, and finished his statement by saying that he had not seen Elisabeth Kusian in 1949.

When Rolf finished his statement, officers led Elisabeth Kusian into the interview room. What was he doing there? What had he told the police? How could she deal with this unexpected turn of events? Elisabeth Kusian looked at him and blurted out, "Where is Wolfgang? Finally, tell me. I'm done with this. You've already done enough to me."[7] When Hiller reproached her for her "nonsense," VP Kriminalpolizeirat Schwarz asked whether she wanted to implicate Hiller. In what must have been a muted tone, Elisabeth Kusian responded that she wanted peace. "Peace" was the only reason Kusian dredged up his name. Indeed, as officers pressed her about Rolf Hiller's possible involvement in Dorothea Merten's murder, she said he had none.[8] The Hiller story evaporated as quickly as it had emerged.

A now exhausted Kusian, seeking some kind of quiet, finally confessed that she alone murdered Hermann Seidelmann and Dorothea Merten.[9] She dismembered them. She invented the Dr. Hiller who hunted and haunted her. She invented him and the rest of the tales in the interview room where she now sat. The horrifying details spilled out when Elisabeth Kusian decided to tell something more like the truth.[10]

She spoke of meeting a currency trader in the Zoo Train Station and inviting him back to her room for a second exchange, of coffee and garrotting with a clothesline, of dismemberment and wringing out gory rags in a toilet, of a suitcase and rucksacks full of body parts, of multiple trips over several nights to locations in both East and West Berlin, of burning documents in her room's oven. Selling used clothes should have solved her financial problems, but it did not. Her story then turned to the murder that tripped her up. She rehearsed the now well-known details of the typewriter she wanted to buy on the instalment plan, the silverware that would bring too little money from a pawn shop, and a second murder. She wailed in a moment of self-pity, "I have to say that, now that I have already done something so serious – I cannot go on. I do not understand myself anymore. Why I have done all this?"[11] Why did she implicate innocent people and fictional characters? She bristled at the thought that she was protecting an accomplice. In her mind, the murders just happened. They were necessary for her to live her life as she wanted.[12]

Between 20 November 1945 and 1 October 1946, the International Military Tribunal (IMT) – convened by the victorious Allies – tried, and convicted, high-ranking Germans of "subjugation, exploitation, and extermination of subject populations."[13] As Katharina von Kellenbach reminds us, it was commonplace in the war's aftermath for churches to ascribe such horrors of the Nazi regime to an aberration, a fall from God, a fall that Christianity could both cure and prevent.[14] Kusian's statement is a variant of this trope. She had lost her moral compass. The lack of something had made her actions possible. She was, like so many of her contemporaries, grasping for an answer that both explained her crimes while trying to exculpate herself. The crimes of which she stood accused were post-war. Her relationship to and explanation of them were rooted in the previous historical moment.

Indeed, 13 million Germans filled out forms in the American sector alone in the hopes that they could distance themselves from their past. Of these, 3.5 million required further investigation. The historian Lutz

Niethammer has shown that, in the American Zone, there were more former Nazis in the civil service than there had been during the Third Reich. What might all of this mean? Historians like Alf Lüdtke and Wolfgang Benz discuss the decade after the war as a time of forgetting – a kind of cultural amnesia. Robert Moeller, on the other hand, sees it as a time of memory, but memory of German suffering rather than Germans causing the suffering of others. Both interpretations are of value in understanding the attitudes towards Elisabeth Kusian. The horror at her actions speak to a public that was ready to cast itself in the role of victim of some kind of seemingly innocent, disguised horror, while at the same time trying to forget that her motivations and social contract (violence in the service of self-aggrandizement and self-promotion) were the guiding logic of the period that had just ended.[15]

When Elisabeth finished her statement, VP Kommandeur Rockstroh and his colleagues took her to the ruins on Memhardtstraße, Borsigstraße, and Chausseestraße to identify the disposal sites, which she did with relative ease.[16] They then went to the East Berlin morgue to present her with Merten's corpse. An angry VP Kommandeur Rockstroh accused her of this "gruesome deed" and mutilations. Kusian replied cooly, "I did the deed and dissected the body, but I did not make the cuts (at this, she pointed to the many dissection cuts on the body parts)."[17]

Although the Volkspolizei case was concluded, the situation's politics still needed to be massaged. How could Rockstroh laud his squad, properly regard the help they received from the local West Berlin authorities, and yet still condemn the West? After some reflection, he wrote:

> Thanks to the excellent support of the Charlottenburg and Tiergarten criminal investigation departments, the Volkspolizei were able to obtain further evidence to convict the perpetrator. When the investigation reached this stage, the Friesenstraße homicide squad became aware of the situation and immediately intervened in the further investigation. It refused to hand over the evidence secured by the Volkspolizei

and did not even provide information about the objects seized by the Friesenstraße Homicide Unit on the initiative of the Volkspolizei.[18]

West Berlin murder squad members had no time for such reflections. They were still trying to understand Elisabeth Kusian as a nurse and a parent. Multiple frustrating trips to Moabit Hospital reinforced what they knew. Elisabeth Kusian was a liar, a cheat, and a thief. Her nursing colleagues did not trust her. Physicians were somewhat kinder but quick to say they did not know her well. There were rumours, but the doctors seemed to imply that they were above such gossip.[19] The floor's chief medical officer (Oberarzt), Wolfgang Hintze, expressed his amazement and dismay at the deeds of which Kusian stood accused, then quickly emphasized that he was a married man and did not know her well. The detectives told him that his name appeared in a letter in Kusian's wallet, supposedly from an uncle who owned a clinic, saying she would inherit the clinic if she married Hintze. The physician was shocked. How could their names be linked? He had never been to Gera or heard the stories of Kusian's uncle or his clinic in Thuringia. He concluded by saying that hospital rumours abounded of Kusian stealing with an accomplice, probably her police detective boyfriend.[20]

Nurses painted a rather rounder and nastier portrait than did the physicians. Supervisors set the tone. One volunteered that Elisabeth was courteous, polite, and respectful and that the patients liked her. Indeed, the patients were horrified to hear about her deeds. She very easily could, though, have stolen equipment from the floor.[21] A second added that she was scatterbrained and self-absorbed, but the patients liked her.[22] Floor nurses were not much more charitable. One didn't like Kusian because she was always exceedingly friendly – such people usually have something to hide.[23] Others remembered the bags of clothing she constantly seemed to be bringing. A pair of young nurses were confident that Kusian had drugged their coffee, but her newly earned notoriety might have accounted for their unsurprising suspicion. One student nurse spoke at length about Elisabeth's suspicious brother-in-law (really her ex-husband). She discussed the jewellery stolen from Frau Nee. Kusian had told this gullible young woman that Nee. believed the student nurse had stolen it on a visit and that she would have to reimburse Nee. or face charges. The student nurse also told the detectives about a wool cloak she lent to Kusian, a cloak for which Kusian promised to pay. The student never saw the cloak or the money.[24]

Two interruptions made the day of interviews even longer. First, reporters descended on the hospital to speak with the detectives and staff. After the detectives sent the journalists on their way, they faced a much more formidable presence. The hospital's medical director, Professor Erwin Gohrbandt, buttonholed them to register his annoyance that the Moabit Hospital had appeared in news reports about the Kusian case.[25] Dr. Gohrbandt modelled democratic, bourgeois propriety in his chiding of the detectives. After he left them, the detectives finished the interviews knowing more details but with their portrait of Elisabeth Kusian intact.

Kriminalkommissar Menzel had about as much luck as did his men. Having filed a report about the previous day's repeat search of Elisabeth Kusian's room, he turned to Olga Maus, who, claiming to be a close friend of Dorothea Merten, came to the station to report on a mysterious, suspicious man named Walter.[26] After listening to her prattle, he turned his attention to the much more promising Kurt Muschan, who arrived at Friesenstraße headquarters with the silverware and typewriter given to him by Elisabeth Kusian.[27] Kriminalkommissar Menzel added these effects to the ring found inside the umbrella hanging on Kusian's door and the clothing that officers had gathered.[28] It had to be embarrassing to explain to Kriminalkommissar Menzel that, until recently, he was still telling his wife that he was involved in a murder case.[29] Still, it was time to come clean and add more details to his statement of 7 December. Muschan's first interaction with Kusian had been little more than a clumsy flirtation.[30] Kurt Muschan again related his story of Christmas Eve and silverware. This story illustrated Elisabeth Kusian's desperation to have him in her life and the extent to which she would go to keep him around.

As Kriminalkommissar Menzel spoke with the chagrined Muschan, Kriminal-Assistant Sonntag crossed the city to the

Kinderheim "Morgensonne" at Lichterfelder Straße 45 to talk with the Kusian children, who ranged in age from ten to thirteen. They told of their lives, spent in and out of religious orphanages and with their mother in Frau Nee.'s apartment on Turmstraße.

How odd it must have been for the Kusians to be among children who had once had name tags around their necks, or who had names sewn into their clothing so that their parents could find them, or worse, those – the majority – who were unidentifiable. That they were in an orphanage, among other children who had been abandoned, made them doubly unusual. Often other children could not reunite with their parents because their father was a POW or their mother was held in the east as a forced labourer.[31] The Kusian children had simply been dropped off.

Many of their peers must have been like those described by Morris Troper in a letter to Eleanor Roosevelt, "tired, wan, broken little old men and women. One of the most pathetic sights I have ever seen was that of these children, freed of restraints, trying to learn to play again."[32] Indeed, about 13,000,000 European children lost one or both parents in the war.[33] As they came to know of their mother's actions, though, perhaps they found themselves in agreement with Günther Grass when he wrote, "To have been born … on an unknown day, to Mother Unknown, begotten by Father Nowheretobefound, was far preferable to being the child of German parents after the war."[34]

Elisabeth's children claimed that their mother's romantic life was a closed book until Dieter remembered going to the zoo with "Uncle Kurt," presumably Kurt Muschan. This memory refreshed the girls' memories. They chimed in about going to the zoo with him as well. Although they knew he was a police officer, they never saw him in uniform. Still, they liked him and were happy in his company.

On the other hand, they told Sonntag that they had no particular interest in their father who was a mystery. The last they had heard from him was a letter in which he said he would soon be leaving the POW camp. Was he still alive? They did not know.

Whom they thought Walter Kusian was remains a mystery. In their telling, their mother took wonderful care of them. She protected them from strange adults, warned them away from a janitor at the Moabit Hospital whom they liked, and did not want them to spend time with the Stö.s. They loved their mother and their visits to her at Kantstraße. When could they see her? When would they get the Christmas presents that she had promised them? They had no idea of Elisabeth's newfound infamy or circumstances.[35]

By day's end, police had collected all the evidence and seemed to conclude their interviews. In short, the second stage of the Kusian Affair began to wind down. As if to signal the case's conclusion, Berlin reporters descended on Elisabeth Kusian's neighbours in their investigations that appealed to the public's love of the lurid. Did anybody hear screams in the night? Reporters wanted these details and more.[36] Other Berliners had their own personal or business interests in the case. The owner of the shop that had sold Kusian the radio she used to mask any sounds was thrilled to hear from the police. He wanted to know when he could retrieve it. In what had become a familiar refrain, he told the officer who called him that Elisabeth Kusian had once invited him to her room to collect the money he was due. He assumed that she was planning on killing rather than paying him.[37]

Wednesday, 11 January–Friday, 13 January 1950

Like so many cases, Elisabeth Kusian's settled into a routine, becoming a matter of filing reports for the officers involved and lurid reporting for the public. People gossiped about the city's newly uncovered murderous nurse. When Kurt Muschan's wife visited some friends, the subject of killer nurses dominated the conversation. Her friends were shocked that a trained caregiver could act so coldly. As Frau Muschan heard at least once in such discussions, "But nurses really have to be good people."[38]

Police lost all interest in Hans Boguslawski, whose incarceration provided the best possible alibi. They dropped him from the case.[39] Hedwig U., who sold Elisabeth Kusian the silverware, showed up at Friesenstraße to get it back. She left disappointed; it was material evidence and would not be going anywhere.[40] In short, at least from the police perspective, the morning of 11 January began with the firm knowledge that there was nothing new to discover, only reports to write. The confidence changed at 11:00 a.m. when the prison in which Elisabeth Kusian sat telephoned Volkspolizei headquarters. In the wake of her lost dreams, capture, and humiliation, Elisabeth Kusian slit her wrists in her cell. Officials transferred her to the prison hospital.[41]

The case's drama ticked up again on 12 January. Volkspolizei detectives descended on Elisabeth Kusian's hospital bed to learn as much as possible about her motivation, suicide attempt, and activities. Perhaps there was yet more that had to be investigated, unearthed. In retrospect, it should have come as no surprise that Elisabeth Kusian had wanted to kill herself from the day of her arrest. She seized her chance when one of the prison attendants brought her a knife to use when cutting her rolls. The blade comforted her; it meant her ordeal would soon end. She again implicated innocent people, hoping to finish the endless interviews as quickly as possible and kill herself.[42] The press had a field day with this news.[43] The Volkspolizei were more interested in untangling the attempted suicide and learning who, if anybody, helped her.

Elisabeth's suicide attempt turned suspicion back onto her ex-husband. The Volkspolizei began searching for Walter Kusian, only to be surprised by the news that the West Berlin police had already arrested him on suspicion of murder.[44] Nevertheless, officers went to his residence, only to learn that he was a quiet man who kept to himself. His employers could add nothing to that comically stereotypical assessment. Frustrated, the East Berliners quickly turned to the police authorities in Wedding (the French-controlled district where Walter lived) for permission to continue their investigation.[45] Precinct-level police further ratcheted tension between the departments when they told the chagrined Volkspolizei that Friesenstraße forbade them from speaking with Kusian. The West Berlin murder squad alone would interact with him.[46] From the squad's technical point of view, it made perfect sense. They did not want to share access to a suspect.

One of Elisabeth Kusian's neighbours raised their suspicion when she told them that she had seen the Kusians together, carrying rucksacks, at 7:00 or 7:15 a.m. on 1 January on the commuter train from Alexanderplatz to Friedrichstraße. Perhaps, West Berlin detectives reasoned, the pair spent the night together, then jointly carried Merten's corpse to Alexanderplatz. For the murder squad, this tidbit was a "smoking gun." Western detectives also accepted the Volkspolizei argument that the peculiar dumping ground for Merten's dismembered corpse meant that two people could have disposed of her in one trip.[47]

If Walter Kusian's arrest simplified matters for the police, the arrival at Kantstraße 154a of reporters from *Der Tag* complicated them. Residents flocked to tell their stories. Frau Marie Sch. claimed she had heard a scream from the front of the building. She also claimed to have seen Kusian and a man carrying rucksacks around 11:00 p.m. one day at the end of December. Frau Sch., a woman with "a very nervous, sickly appearance," lived so far back in the building's courtyard that police did not believe she could offer any helpful information. What little confidence they might have had diminished even further when they learned that this "witness" had suffered a skull injury in a 1935 auto accident and that her pride lay in being an inveterate reader.[48] As one officer said to her, "Frau Sch., we won't be angry with you if you tell us the truth now, that is, if you have told the reporters about the man and the backpack to get rid of them." She countered, "I didn't make it up; it's actually true. I have certificates in my hands, from which it is clear that I have always been honest and reliable."[49] Detectives escorted her to a lineup that included Walter Kusian and Kurt Muschan; she could not make an identification.[50] Journalists were less troubled by her problems as a witness. She made for a good story.

Such "witnesses," though, were a nuisance, a sideshow. The main concern for the Volkspolizei was to keep Elisabeth Kusian alive. They assigned her a minder who would hand her a comb, brush, toothbrush, bar of soap, and so on while she used the toilet, then collect these items again when she had finished with them. The Volkspolizei would not give the West Berlin police the satisfaction of losing the case's chief suspect.

Meanwhile, West Berlin authorities continued to work on the angle that Walter Kusian might be involved in at least one of the murders. They searched his room and found sheets taken from the Moabit Hospital, a rucksack, syringes, and a few letters. They yanked him out of his cell and made him observe the search. Might this humiliating exercise make him confess? When they finished, they simply returned him to his cell. They had a far less significant discussion with Friedrich Beigang, who appeared at murder squad headquarters that day to retrieve his typewriter for possible sale to another customer. Deciding on Beigang's request was easy. Herr Beigang would have to wait.[51]

West Berlin police activity slowed again the next day, 17 January. Detectives returned to the Moabit Hospital to hand over receipts from the bedclothes they confiscated from Walter Kusian's room and to ask about the uses for some medical devices they seized from Elisabeth Kusian's room. The hospital's chief of medicine explained that the equipment, including dilators, catheter tubes, 5-gauge hypodermic syringes, and a dissecting knife, was commonly used for abortions (a crime at the time). The found drugs, though, were not. They included yet more narcotics – probably for Elisabeth Kusian's use – and an ointment to treat the common cold.[52] All of this was useful in building a rounder picture of Kusian's activities and aiding prosecutors in deciding what charges they might bring against her.

VP Kommandeur Rockstroh and some colleagues did the day's most significant work when they conducted yet another long interview with Elisabeth Kusian. Her lies and truths ranged across the subject of her children, marriage, career, love affairs, drug use, and crimes. Why had Elisabeth Kusian never told Walter Kusian that she placed their children in Teltow because West Berlin options were too expensive? Although he was a violent father, Walter provided some child support. When they told her that the West Berlin police had arrested him, she insisted that neither he nor Kurt Muschan had anything to do with her crimes. Still, he was an embarrassment and a problem in this new world. His Nazi Party membership, she insisted, would make it difficult, if not impossible, for her to get a job. His sudden reappearance while she was still living at Birkenstraße was an embarrassment. But at least he paid 60 Reichsmarks per month in child support.[53] Notably, she did not tell the officers that she could collect Kindergeld from the hospital as a purported war widow by constructing this story about her husband. Inventing a husband's death to get a job seems designed to elicit sympathy that stealing from the hospital would not.

As to the murders and her attempt to hide them, Elisabeth explained how she hid the evidence of Doris Merten's body under the bed by leaving the window open to conceal the increasing smell of the rotting corpse. This story, in turn, led to a discussion of her drug addiction and its consequences, a conversation she started in response to a question about the length of rope she used to strangle Doris Merten. Kusian tried a blatant, clumsy bid to elicit sympathy. She admitted to lying in her statements but quickly added, "Now I don't want to lie any longer. I spent a lot of money on morphine and coffee. When I had the courage, when I had injected, I didn't know much anymore."[54] The detectives pushed her on her drug use. How long had she used morphine? Why? Where did she buy it? She answered in a way to reframe herself as the real victim. Shooting up gave her some psychological escape from Walter Kusian's beatings, beatings that began when they still lived on Sternstraße.

> You know, I would like to talk. I would like to vent. I want to tell you how everything was. I have lied to you very much! I'd like to be brought before the court soon. I want the death penalty, but not life imprisonment. Believe me, the children's father has nothing to do with it. Muschan also doesn't know that I injected.[55]

After quickly explaining where one could buy morphine, she returned to her narrative:

> The worries at home. The children have been beaten. They no longer dared to go home. I was always supposed to take them with me. Then I also lied to be [able to stay] at the hospital at all. The fear of discovery. My husband had lost his nerve. On the other hand, he had meant well again. Since that time, I've used morphine. I started with half a cc. Then 1

cc. Now I got up to 8 cc. For 1 cc, I paid 3 DM. Also, here in the East. You get it everywhere, even on Tauentzienstraße. I would shoot up at home.[56]

Colleagues warned Elisabeth Kusian that administrators suspected her of using drugs. At the very least, she feared that police would search her room. Still, she continued to shoot up over Christmas. She even shot up right before Doris Merten's arrival. When Merten asked if she was alright, Elisabeth Kusian knew she no longer understood how she appeared to others. In short, she explained she had no choice but to murder Doris Merten. Merten's money would buy more morphine.

Even with the money, Elisabeth would still have many concerns. Walter Kusian had threatened to report her drug use. She thought he was going to speak with the hospital authorities.[57] This comment marked a radical departure in their conversation. Elisabeth Kusian's interrogators did not know what to make of it. The nurse pressed on. Walter, she insisted, was morally responsible for her actions.

> I had the children with me. He had already threatened us then. He knew that I was taking morphine. He wanted to turn me in and also wanted to take away various things I still had from us. He had recently given me money. The money was not enough. I needed morphine. He then made demands with the money. I stalled him for as long as I could. If I had not known that the man had to take care of the children, I would have killed him. Maybe I am saying things here that I can't take responsibility for. For me, nothing can be made worse. But I can no longer think clearly, like a person who has never injected. I can't eat anymore; I can't think like this. I had a good talk with Merten even in the afternoon. But now I can't think anymore. I miss the morphine.[58]

When the detectives tried to turn the discussion to the silver she had bought, Elisabeth Kusian parried the question with a final story of her descent into hell. She might have believed it herself.

> That was such an idée fixe. With it, I wanted to cover up a debt again. A person who thinks normally wouldn't have done that, and I did it

> anyway. I went to our director and talked to him, asked him to take back the resignation. I knew I wouldn't be able to get another job. I had the kids and all the debt. I was desperate. The director refused. The horror, day in and day out. I could not talk to anyone. When he came (M. [undoubtedly Muschan]), it was only hours, then I always tried to inject myself. I wanted to give everything from the good side. I didn't want to get along with anyone else. I hated people so much because of my husband. I didn't want to hurt the man (M.). I didn't tell him anything, but he noticed something. I lied. I did not have the courage to tell the truth. I did not want to lose him. One thing led to another, and everything collapsed, that I made the man unhappy. He will curse the hours. For me, they were the most beautiful of my life. Perhaps everything would have been different if I had had the children with me. But they were torn down then, and I bought things without thinking. I started at the wrong end. I then borrowed. Everyone still had confidence in me. I hadn't incurred any debt before. Then they all came to me, "Sister Elisabeth, you must pay. Otherwise, we will go to the matron."[59]

At this point, VP Kommandeur Rockstroh ended the interview. He saw that Elisabeth Kusian either would or could not continue. In his final report on the case, Rockstroh noted that only with this interview did the Volkspolizei learn of her morphine addiction. Because she had already begun the withdrawal process, and after talking with a physician, they decided to continue her "cure."[60]

End of January–Beginning of February 1950

Like the Volkspolizei across the border, the West Berlin murder squad spent the rest of January tying up loose ends before Elisabeth Kusian's transfer into their custody. On 18 January, detectives spoke with Elise Nee. about her stolen jewellery. She did not recognize the recovered pieces. That could not have unduly surprised the detectives. Elisabeth Kusian's thefts were widespread and probably beyond their ability to sort out.[61] Moabit Hospital's

Dr. Hintze had no relatives in Thuringia and knew a nurse named Kusian but no medical student. He thought that the instruments found in Kusian's room might have been stolen, perhaps when she assisted in treating women who had suffered miscarriages. This cagey answer left no room for doubt; Elisabeth Kusian could easily have performed abortions.[62]

Three days later, on 21 January, the West Berlin district court issued an official arrest warrant for Kusian, beginning her transfer across city lines.[63] On 8 February, accompanied by VP Kommandeur Rockstroh and others, Elisabeth Kusian was driven to the Sandkrug Bridge, where she crossed sectors into Kriminalkommissar Menzel's custody.

When he arrived at the bridge, Kriminalkommissar Menzel duly signed the official forms that ended the Volkspolizei's official involvement in the case.[64] The following day, representatives of the metal goods company that sold the cutlery to Elisabeth Kusian officially requested that the goods be returned to them.[65]

Monday, 13 February 1950

Five days after her arrival in West Berlin, Elisabeth Kusian began her second round of confessions, now with Kriminalkommissar Menzel and his colleagues. This series of harsh interrogations put her on the spot. Menzel did not believe much of what she had told the Volkspolizei. He would hold her to a higher standard of truth. On 13 February, the first day of her interrogation, Elisabeth rehearsed her autobiography to Menzel, members of his squad, and Dr. Weimann. She started with her childhood. "Cruelty to animals was out of the question for me."[66] She was no sociopath. She then revealed her lies to the Volkspolizei, quickly bringing her story to Walter Kusian's return to Germany from the POW camp.[67] She lingered on her addictions. She would inject herself all over her body, sometimes intravenously, working up to a dose of 8 cc. Morphine helped her through the night. If she were too tired from the morphine to go to work, she would take Pervitin to survive her shift. Her affair with Boguslawski, her abortion, and abortions with which she might have helped brought her close to the present.

> As for the allegation that I performed abortions in the Robert Koch Hospital with Dr. Freyaldenhoven, I would like to note that I usually prepared the operating field and the instruments for this physician, who was on night duty with me in ward 11. The scraped-out fetuses went into a bucket in the usual way. Whether there were abortions among these cases, I cannot judge. I firmly reject the statement of the matron that I had participated in abortions in the Robert Koch Hospital.[68]

Here, Dr. Weimann left the room. On his return, she continued by telling of her relationship with Boguslawski and her theft from Frau Nee., which allowed the Western detectives to establish that Elisabeth Kusian was a long-time criminal. Police rejoined that her use and misuse of her acquaintances showed her to be a con artist. Kusian quickly blamed Boguslawski for her failings. Menzel and Weimann tried to build a story in which her murders were an almost inevitable conclusion to other crimes; Elisabeth Kusian refused even a hint of responsibility.[69] The interview ended in frustration, probably mutual frustration.

The next day, Elisabeth tried a different tack. When Kriminalkommissar Menzel wanted more info on her jewellery theft from Frau Nee., she refused to speak. Menzel snapped angrily, "Since you do not give any answer, I would like to ask you to break free and finally tell the truth. It is futile." Kusian responded, "Write what you want. The facts of this terrible matter are so terrible. It would be better if we dealt with that first. The other thing is so unimportant."[70] Menzel pushed, observing a gradual shift in Kusian's bearing. "Frau K. bows her head, looks in front of her, sits apathetically on the chair, and is silent. After minutes of silence, while Frau K. weakly wiggles her head back and forth, she says, 'I am so ashamed of myself for having done all this.' Frau K. bends her upper body forward, begins to cry, and rests her elbows on her thighs. She continues to cry." He gave her a moment to compose herself.[71]

She finally admitted guilt when Menzel would not let the subject go. Only then did their conversation turn to the murders. Menzel asked how and when she met Hermann Seidelmann. Kusian did not want to discuss the "small matters" before the murders. After a moment's pause, though, she responded, "I have already confessed in the case of Seidelmann and Merten. I don't want to touch on this point again."[72] Kriminalkommissar Menzel refused this dodge. Did she have any cash at home to exchange with Hermann Seidelmann? Kusian couldn't remember. Menzel retorted how unlikely that was. Kusian was known to walk home rather than take public transportation. He reminded her that 8 cc of morphine cost her 3 to 4 DM. Still, Elisabeth ducked the question, insisting that she was in a constant state of poverty. She further claimed that she "had received [her] salary, including child benefits, from the hospital on 19 November 1949." But she added, "At the end of November, I nevertheless borrowed 30 DM from my husband. He had no smaller bill and gave me a 50 DM bill. He later repeatedly demanded the remaining 20 DM, but I was unable to pay it back." Menzel pressed. How much did she hope to exchange with Hermann Seidelmann? Elisabeth had not been sure that he would come. If she had cash, why not take it to Zoo Station to exchange? Kusian replied tiredly, "You may be right."[73] Menzel was a bulldog. He believed she never meant to exchange money with Seidelmann. Murder was always her goal. Kusian stood firm. Until Seidelmann's arrival, she insisted that exchange was always the plan.[74]

Because the conversation went nowhere, Menzel changed tack. "For certain criminal, judicial, and forensic reasons," he told her, he wanted "to go into the course of events again because the information you gave to the CID in the eastern sector is obviously not entirely accurate." With this comment hanging, Menzel asked her to repeat her story yet again. Kusian refused, leading to a tense moment, when Dr. Weimann interrupted with his own question. "Frau Kusian, you knew that I had repeatedly given lectures at the Robert Koch Hospital. Did you attend these lectures?" Kusian answered with a surprising "Yes." Intrigued, Weimann probed even further. "Did you also hear the part and see the pictures I showed of violent asphyxiation, strangling, and so on?" This time, Kusian answered "No." She also claimed not to have heard him discuss how such a victim might lose consciousness. Weimann continued, "Your actions were otherwise tremendously dangerous for you, for you stated that you fell to the ground with the man." Kusian replied, "At the moment the sudden thought occurred to me, I did not know what was happening." Even this claim of impulse, though, seems very weak. The detective/pathologist team showcased her premeditation and acquired expertise.[75]

Menzel retook the lead. "Tell me, did you tie the cord right away?" Elisabeth Kusian stood up and walked excitedly around the room, refusing to answer while claiming she could not continue. Menzel and the others at least appeared to lose patience with her.

They understood. These were difficult questions to answer. Nevertheless, one interrogator volunteered, "You not only killed Seidelmann, but later, you also found the courage to kill Frau Merten. If you now want to act as if the killing of Seidelmann was so tremendously hard for your heart, then it was probably not necessary to kill Frau Merten later on. I, therefore, trust you to be able to describe the course of events concerning Seidelmann to us again during the interrogation. You are not a child or an inexperienced young girl." Impatient or frustrated, Elisabeth Kusian shot back, "I won't describe the Merten case to you any more than I will describe the Seidelmann case."[76]

Seeing no progress, Dr. Weimann again spoke to ask whether she could at least discuss the dismemberment. "I have already done that," she responded. Weimann countered, "I have dissected both corpses and was quite astonished." Menzel noted, "Kusian is silent, lowers her head, or wobbles her head back and forth." Weimann finally asked if she had injected a lot of morphine. "Yes," she had.[77]

In a handoff, Kriminalkommissar Menzel once again took over the questioning. "What did you do or talk about with S. in the two – two and a half hours? You are a woman. Seidelmann was probably a money changer, but it can be assumed that you had an effect on him as a woman. Did he try to approach you?" Elisabeth Kusian answered in one syllable: "No." Menzel responded that police knew from other testimony "that the man in question told you about his wife, that she was jealous and was searching his jacket for women's hair." Elisabeth Kusian responded with a kind of outrage. "Please do not relate this to S. I did not know that S. is married and has children. I was told these things by the lawyer Krautwald when he came to see me once in my apartment."[78] She would try anything to distance herself from incriminating knowledge of Seidelmann. Was he dead? She wouldn't even acknowledge that she knew that much.

Perhaps another of her interrogators tried to show that Elisabeth must have known Hermann Seidelmann. If, as she claimed, she had first spoken with him at 2:30 p.m. on 3 December 1949, why did she call Kurt Muschan at 1:30 p.m. that afternoon while he was at work? Why was it so important to cancel a meeting with him and tell him she had to meet a couple from Mahlow? Her confused answers led nowhere. "I just wanted to prevent him from coming that day because he always stayed for some time then. I didn't want to lie to him again. If he had come, he would have asked questions, and then I would have had to tell him to leave." When somebody in the room asked her why Muschan had to leave, she seemed to be at a loss for the best answer. "I've made my confession; you ask a question, and right after, you ask another. I don't want to say anything more."[79]

Her hesitation prompted interviewers to change direction to her children. Menzel told Elisabeth Kusian that the Western CID sent an officer, who pretended to be her friend, to her children's orphanage in Teltow, where her son and daughters talked about her Christmas letters to them. Why, Menzel asked, so many lies? "So my kids shouldn't wait for me at Christmas; I had no money to pay their upkeep." Menzel reminded her that she had written the letter after Christmas. Rapidly changing course, Elisabeth Kusian declared that she wanted to apologize for not seeing them on the holiday. Menzel would have none of it. What about the gifts Walter gave her to send to the children? Why did she not send them forward? "After I had committed the horrible act on S.," she replied, "it was impossible for me to face the children." A sceptical Kriminalkommissar Menzel challenged her. Somebody else could have made the delivery. Her final comment on the subject was, "For this way of acting of mine, I have no excuses."[80]

Still keeping her off balance, Menzel moved to the clothesline used in the murders, rigor mortis, the borrowed suitcase, and selling her victims' goods.[81] The Kriminalkommissar became ever more frustrated. "From her entire behaviour, it can be seen that she repeatedly tries to state untruths. In this context, it should be pointed out that Frau Kusian only admits what can be proven to her without a doubt. This makes her interrogation extremely difficult and therefore requires a great deal of time."[82] With this comment, he wrapped up the interview for the evening.

The next several days' interviews began with Kriminalkommissar Menzel chastising Kusian for not eating. That was a mistake, he scolded. He reminded her that the process would probably take several more days.[83] As their discussion proceeded, Kusian changed her story's details. She sat in a different chair when she spoke with Hermann Seidelmann. Her morphine addiction agitated her during the murders. She reminded Kriminalkommissar Menzel that it was an expensive addiction, though she lied to him when she claimed that the Volkspolizei knew nothing about it. Kusian clearly understood what a morphine addiction did to her body and health, and her ability to function as a witness to her activities. Perhaps she could make the addiction work in her favour. It was worth trying to see how the detectives might react to a frank discussion. "Since I started taking the M, I have often had menstrual irregularities. I also had a lot of difficulty with bowel movements in the beginning. I also have buzzes in my head from time to time when I am asked too much, and I would like to ask that I not be asked so much about things that have nothing to do with the facts."[84] Menzel would have none of it, asking her instead about the money she removed from Seidelmann. About her response, Menzel noted, "Frau K. was about to say something but began to cry, got up, and walked up and down the room. She returned to her seat after a few minutes."[85]

Nevertheless, Menzel believed that, for some reason, she decided to trust the West Berlin police who were interrogating her.[86] Perhaps it was because of her experience with the Volkspolizei. Sometimes, she complained the Volkspolizei would have sixteen people at her interrogations. Other times, the Volkspolizei would allow her to return to her cell and undress for bed. Then, as if to torment her, they would recall her for even more questioning. Perhaps most galling was when they paraded Kurt Muschan into her interrogation in shackles just to give the impression that he, too, had been arrested.[87]

Elisabeth Kusian continued refusing food through 16 January, despite Menzel's protests that she should eat. Kusian claimed that her confessions to him filled her. She was not hungry. When Menzel turned their conversation to Merten, Kusian made the shocking statement that she would tell the truth. This would be different from her discussion with the Volkspolizei. Whether she followed through is a different story. Menzel asked about Muschan's wish for a typewriter. "No!" Kusian insisted, "It is never true that Muschan expressed such a wish. If he has said so, he has lied. He probably once said that he needed a machine because he had to write everything by hand." She quickly added, "Yes, I bought the machine to give it to Muschan. But I had no money to pay for the machine and had to buy it in instalments. Leave Herr M. out of it; he has nothing to do with the fact that I did the business."[88]

She then told Menzel a detailed yet untrue story of moving Doris Merten's body across the hall into her neighbour's room to leave uncovered after the murder. Meanwhile, Kusian begged the detectives to quit asking questions. Only when Menzel and the others said that these questions would establish whether Muschan knew anything about the murders did she agree to answer.[89] The stories and lies must have exhausted her because she asked for and received a thirty-minute break before yet more questioning. Menzel's new interests seem to have shaken her. He told her that one of her colleagues, Hertha S., claimed she was to be Elisabeth Kusian's next victim. Kusian could only scoff at this. "I was with her all the time in the ward. People probably knew that she came to visit me, and even if she was wearing a fur coat or a valuable ring, the thought of killing her never occurred to me. If she wants to put it that way today, I can only imagine that she wants to make herself interesting or possibly wants to participate in the trial for sensational reasons."[90]

Yet, how different is this from the story of Doris Merten, whom many people knew planned to visit Kusian? Kusian had no answer. Furthermore, her linking Hertha S. to a fur coat and a ring only reminded her listeners of her strong desire for some kind of glamorous life. To keep her off balance, Menzel told her that she could not possibly have dragged and left Doris Merten's corpse across the hall. Her neighbour was teaching piano lessons when Kusian said she hid the corpse. That fact alone made the story patently ridiculous.[91] It was not her last lie; Kusian understood that the West Berlin detectives were unlikely to believe her stories, unlike the Volkspolizei. Nevertheless, lies were a constant part of Kusian's interviews. This one ended, perhaps, with Elisabeth Kusian considering what she could and could not do to foil Kriminalkommissar Menzel.

Menzel began the next afternoon's interrogation by pushing Kusian to admit she believed that Herr Beigang would deliver the typewriter rather than Frau Merten. She had hoped, Menzel argued, to murder Beigang. No – Kusian refused this interpretation categorically. Menzel responded that conversations with Walter Kusian led them to this conclusion. Elisabeth Kusian parried. She saw him as little as possible, generally when she needed money.[92] Seeing that this thread was a dead end, Menzel turned his attention to Kusian's possible participation in illegal abortions. She claimed never to have knowingly helped with abortions or euthanasia but had seen many deadly mistakes made by physicians. Indeed, the hospital had a lot of admissions for botched abortions. Menzel pushed; her supervisor's conviction that she helped with abortions had intrigued the Volkspolizei. Perhaps as a dodge, Kusian said that she knew of the rumours that Dr. Freyaldenhoven had served time for performing them, an accusation he rejected.[93]

While concentrating on other suspects and matters, West Berlin detectives left Kusian to cool her heels for three days. Menzel pondered the curious case of Walter Kusian, then had him arrested on 14 January for possible complicity in the murders. Walter Kusian had admitted to receiving and selling things for Elisabeth, yet claimed to know nothing of their provenance. He told police that she said to him that she had done a horrible thing, but she wouldn't elaborate. Witnesses saw a suspicious man near the ruin where Doris Merten's remains were displayed. None of this looked good for Walter, but there was not enough to hold him. West Berlin authorities released him on 20 January.[94] Even Elisabeth Kusian, who hated the man, stated that he had no role in the crimes. "Leave the man alone; he is still the only one who can care for the children." When further pushed, she added, "I have already told you what was, and I have added nothing to that. I have not told my husband anything; he has nothing to do with it. Other people have nothing to do with it either, and I have said nothing about it to others. Leave Muschan out of it, too, because you don't believe yourself that he has anything to do with it."[95]

Having settled the question of Walter Kusian's guilt, at least for the time being, the detectives turned their last interrogation, which was the next-to-last conversation with her, into an intensive discussion of her web of lies. She engaged on some points but refused on others. Menzel and a colleague pushed Kusian about all the lies she had told about her background. They hammered her on her spurious tales of her origins. They would not let go of her claims about the radio given to her by her fictional father-in-law. In response, she paused, silently bowed her head, and murmured, "I can't answer that; I lied about everything."[96] She claimed that she began this "web of lies," as the detectives called it, as soon as she left her mother's home but would not say why. She also refused to comment on her lies to Walter about her parents' background and to Frau Nee., whom she told that her mother was dead. They then showed her the printed notices she used to convince colleagues that she came from an upper-middle to upper-class background. Menzel said, "You listed yourself as a sufferer and called yourself stud. med. I submit this advertisement to you and ask for your opinion." In response, Kusian slammed the file with her right hand. "Thank you," she angrily retorted. She would not comment on the letters that she typed to herself. She would not even concede that she had written them.

One detective remarked, "You have, as far as we can prove here and from written documents, since at least 1948–49, moved on a level that has nothing to do with your circumstances, and these are manifestations that one usually finds with impostors. For example, you wrote letters from your mother to yourself as early as January 1949, and there is other correspondence that has nothing to do with your circumstances. There are letters from July 1948, for example, in which the place of dispatch is Gera. How did you come into possession of the letters presented to you here, or who wrote them?" She again refused to comment.[97] Her lies and the confidence tricks she had constructed over the years eroded in front of her.

Detectives pushed forward, if only to knit all the details together. They next turned to her financial and drug problems. Her monthly budget, including the illegitimate Kindergeld, brought her 275.10 DM. Out of this, she had to support her daughters in the GDR (for which they had no solid figure), Dieter (at 50 DM per month), and rent (just under 50 DM per month). They then asked her about the money she borrowed from patients. When she claimed to have always paid it back, the detectives reminded her about the money she "borrowed" to pay for upholstered furniture, asking why she did not bring the furniture when she moved. "Because I couldn't take it with me. I needed money." They again reminded her of how she had schemed to defraud the furniture company and her previous landlord. Elisabeth practically admitted her con job. "That's why I sold them, so that I could get some money back. I know that I have committed a crime."

Menzel and the rest did not pretend to empathize. They totalled her salary for June to December 1949, the money she had borrowed and effectively stolen, then reminded her that it was more than 2,000 DM. What, they asked, did she do with it? Kusian did not even pay her children's upkeep in the Teltow orphanage. After staring silently at the floor, Elisabeth Kusian claimed otherwise. "I paid back 290 DM to Leuschner and Wulf (*sic*), plus about 350 DM rent. I had to pay 700 DM East for the children's accommodations in Niederschönhausen. I had costumes made for 300 DM for the two girls. I bought two knitted vests for 80 DM. I bought shoes, underwear, and other clothing for the children. In addition, I lived somewhat carelessly when the children were with me at Birkenstraße 13a."

Did they believe any of this? Police interviewers never commented. They instead moved to her drug use. What did she do with the money stolen from Hermann Seidelmann and Doris Merten? It all went to morphine. What was the extent of her habit? "If I had a lot, I injected a lot. If I didn't have much, I could get by with 2 cc. If I had a lot of money, I spent a lot of money on morphine; if I didn't have any, I starved."[98]

She returned to her cell for another two days as detectives sorted out the mundane tasks associated with the investigation. They returned Hedwig U.'s silverware. They took Elisabeth Kusian's clothing from her room and sent it to her jail cell. Finally, they returned Frau Stö.'s room keys to her. Stö. wanted them for a new tenant. Frau Stö. would also, unsuccessfully, claim that Kusian's radio had become her property. The city courts rejected this claim.[99]

There was, ultimately, nothing left to do but have Elisabeth Kusian fingerprinted and photographed. Detectives avoided doing this earlier, assuming it would stop her from talking. While being processed, Kusian informed the technicians that she wanted to speak to the detectives again. Might this be valuable? The squad hurried to see her, curious what she might say. No new details, merely a question. She wanted to know whether Muschan "had known anything about the existence of her divorced husband before her arrest and also before that." The answer to this question mattered deeply to her. The detectives said that Muschan only knew that her husband had died in the war. This news, at least, was reassuring. Might she have anything else necessary to tell them? No, she had finished. When she wondered how they knew of morphine, Menzel referred to the Volkspolizei's case notes.[100]

Was it possible that the two competing departments shared case notes? What a shocking revelation in this Cold War moment, especially in such an iconically Cold War city. Any hopes she might have had about competing jurisdictions and playing one department off against the other vanished. This note of unexpected cooperation ended the murder squad's contact with Elisabeth Kusian. Detectives would have one more conversation with Kurt Muschan to clarify a few points. In what must have come as a shock, Volkspolizei detectives had informed him that not only was Elisabeth's husband alive, but he was a mason. Less importantly for himself, Muschan explained how Elisabeth prepared a lie for the landlady about his absence on Christmas. He seemed to miss the irony of being the victim of one lie and the co-perpetrator of another.[101]

The case was now in the hands of the Staatsanwalt, the public prosecutor's office, which needed to tie up some loose ends before a trial could take place. The prosecutor asked that the Institute for Forensic Medicine of the Free University of Berlin prepare an expert opinion on the accused's state of mind and criminal responsibility. In short, was she legally sane?[102] She was.

chapter six

The Trial of Elisabeth Kusian

On 11 January 1951, Berlin's newspapers began preparing readers for the circus that would be Elisabeth Kusian's trial, scheduled to start five days later. Western papers emphasized the scandalous. *Der Abend* rehearsed lurid details of cigarette smoke, bloody-water–filled bowls, a borrowed dismembering kitchen knife, bagged body parts, sex, and more to remind readers what they might have forgotten in the intervening months. The paper compared Kusian to two infamous murderesses: twenty-five-year-old Hermenegild Giesen, who robbed and strangled two elderly people, and thirty-five-year-old Johanna Behrendt, who pounced on and strangled her victim. As a nod to popular culture, *Der Abend* even compared Elisabeth Kusian to the murderer in the then-new Hans Albers film *Vom Teufel gejagt* (Chased by the Devil), the story of a physician who has lost control of his dark side.[1]

A piece in *Der Kurier* argued that Kusian's case illustrated Berlin's decadent political life by emphasizing the many people who wanted to buy tickets to the proceedings. It also reflected on Elisabeth's "double life" that hovered between "ruthless performance of duty and imposture." The purple prose left little to readers' imaginations:

> In this trial, we will see that a person may be the best mother, the most tender lover, the most self-sacrificing Samaritan, and yet be filled with an icy emotion that determines all her actions; that a person knows no measure in hospitality, in giving, in self-giving, and yet represents the

> embodiment of egoism. We will also be able to study, in this case, that strange degeneration of the "will to power" that can be traced in so many capital and violent criminals and which expresses itself in pathological craving for prestige, deceitfulness, "bragging," and the ability to create corpses. We will finally see in this trial how one can disregard all laws of morality and humanity to preserve the appearance of good bourgeois morality: and that this person can light the lights of the Christmas tree above the lovingly set up gift table, while next to it, under the couch, lies the corpse of the cruelly killed victim. It will turn out that devotion and egoism, sentimentality, and emotionalism are not contradictory.[2]

The Social Democratic *Telegraf*'s coverage was more restrained, emphasizing Kusian's social position while describing her as the child of an estate worker who developed a "strange love-hate relationship with these 'higher circles.'" Its rather conventional line compared her to her lover, "who had a wife and children to whom he was attached and for whom he had to provide. Elisabeth had nothing but debts." The same piece also emphasized the public's interest in Kusian's psychological state and the cooperation between Berlin's two police departments.[3]

Sunday, 14 January 1951

Sunday, 14 January 1951 saw the coming trial's first East Berlin coverage.[4] Perhaps because proceedings would not begin for a few days, *Neues Deutschland*, the official newspaper of the GDR's SED, focused its attention on stories seemingly worthier of note. The Kusian notice appeared on page 8, shoehorned between one story about children freezing to death in Berlin's western zone because the Western Allies were exporting coal from the city and a second that asked energy consumers to use less electricity during peak consumption hours.[5] *Neues Deutschland*'s readers would not have needed to dive this far into the paper to see the day's supposedly most critical issues. Page one informed them that the country's most productive chemical plant was to be renamed in honour of

SED General Secretary Walter Ulbricht, that the Chinese People's Army had surrounded American forces in Korea, and that West Berlin factory workers had staged a successful strike.[6] Readers who spotted the Kusian article would not be surprised by the paper's angle, which stressed the untiring work of the Volkspolizei, who had stood between this killer and the Berlin population. *Neues Deutschland* argued that the Volkspolizei did their job despite the city's division, cooperating with West Berlin authorities who tried to take credit while spending most of their energy troubling peace activists.[7] These details were but a preview of the coming coverage, which would begin two days later.

The trial's location was as telling as was its coverage. It would add a chapter to the history of the "New" Moabit Courthouse. The "Old" Courthouse, built in 1877, which had been adjacent to it, was destroyed during the Second World War.

The New Moabit Courthouse hosted much of Berlin's and Germany's modern criminal history. Its trials ranged from the ludicrous, almost comical, to the horrifying. Here is where Wilhelm Voigt, the notorious Captain of Cöpenick, stood trial for impersonating an army officer and robbing a municipal treasury.[8] By wearing the uniform of a Prussian army captain, Voigt projected enough authority to confiscate Cöpenick's treasury. Carl Zuckmayer immortalized the story with his comedic play about Germans' abject obedience to and respect for military uniforms.[9] In the Weimar Republic, notorious serial killer Karl Großmann, famed artist George Grosz, whose painting of a gas-mask–wearing Jesus on the cross prompted a charge of insulting God (Gottesbeleidigung), and three members of the Communist paramilitary Red Front Fighters' League accused of killing Horst Wessel – whom Joseph Goebbels would turn into a Nazi martyr – all stood trials within its walls.[10]

The neo-baroque building with its 77-centimetre–thick sandstone walls was – and is – as imposing as its history implies.[11] Approaching from the Turmstraße subway, a fifteen-minute walk away, one sees the 60-metre–tall towers immediately upon exiting the station. The building stretches 201.5 metres along Turmstraße. Its central, so-called

> Elephant Hall is 29 metres high and covers a 40 x 27 metre open area. The courthouse survived the war intact and was in use again as early as October 1945 for criminal proceedings; audiences sat wrapped in winter coats to witness trials held by candlelight in front of paper-covered broken windows.[12] Here, Elisabeth Kusian would have walked along the "Bridge of Sighs" (Seufzerbrücke), allowing her to move from her cell without wearing handcuffs or being bothered by onlookers.[13] As Benjamin Hett reminds us, Moabit stood for criminal law in the minds of Berliners, even producing a literary genre. "There were even Moabit folk songs and Moabit poems."[14]

In time, Elisabeth Kusian would become part of the court's lore.[15]

Monday, 15 January 1951

On a cool, drizzly 15 January morning, Elisabeth Kusian, pale with eyes showing large, looking at nobody, walked into the Moabit Criminal Court. The women's prison in which she was held and from which she would walk into court dated from the 1860s. To quote Benjamin Hett, "no one ever had a kind word for these buildings; they were stern houses serving a stern function. Little effort was made to make them comfortable."[16]

Popping flashbulbs, microphones thrust in her direction by reporters from across Germany and the world, and a courtroom packed with curious observers greeted Elisabeth Kusian.[17] The bulbs continued to flash even as she turned to speak with her attorneys, Doctors Weimann and Nicolai. Dr. Weimann was a peculiar choice to be the lead defence attorney. By an odd coincidence, he was the brother of Waldemar Weimann, the pathologist/psychiatrist who helped to find Elisabeth Kusian and then determined that she was legally sane. More importantly, Attorney Weimann was well-known in Berlin's criminal justice circles. In 1924, he became Berlin's youngest practising attorney at only twenty-four.

During the Third Reich, this Weimann practised as a defence attorney before the notorious "People's Court," known for trying, convicting, and often ordering the execution of the regime's enemies. Here he defended two members of the conspiracy to assassinate Adolf Hitler and end the Third Reich. The court sentenced both to death.[18] Weimann's reputation as an attorney was chameleon-like. As Stefan König argues about attorneys who appeared before the court, "hardly any among them would have dared to use harmless legal arguments to counter a death sentence for his client."[19] In König's estimation, of the attorneys defending those involved in the 20 July plot against Hitler, Weimann proved to be no exception.[20] Indeed, König noted that he was a "sure exponent of the Nazi Regime," that he attacked Carl Goerdeler rather than defended him, and that he was among those defence attorneys who believed that they had to be more prosecutorial than were the prosecutors themselves.[21]

At this moment in history, German criminal trials functioned very differently than did their Anglo-American equivalents. Rather than a jury determining guilt or innocence, then a judge deciding on an appropriate sentence, the German model had multiple professional judges, in this case, a chief and two associates serving alongside several lay judges. Trained judges adjudicated questions of procedure. Lay judges had no say in technical matters, but all the judges had equal votes in questions of guilt and innocence.[22]

Elisabeth Kusian's chief judge was Judge Korsch. One of his fellow jurists in the trial, Marion Gräfin Yorck zu Wartenburg, described him as a "good and somewhat impatient judge … and a level-headed and benevolent man."[23] Gerhard Schulz joined them. Certainly, Countess Yorck must have had thoughts about the trial's location. She had been imprisoned in Moabit in the late summer and early fall of 1944, only 6½ years earlier. The Gestapo had arrested her and her husband, Peter Graf Yorck zu Wartenberg, on suspicion (correct suspicion) of involvement in the Resistance's attempt to assassinate Adolf Hitler. She was eventually released. The same Nazi court in which Weimann practised had tried her husband, Peter, and then sentenced him to death.[24] At least some of those in the room knew her story. None could doubt her commitment to justice.

After officials ordered the photographers to leave so the judges could be seated, Judge Korsch began the proceedings by asking Elisabeth Kusian to tell her life story. All eyes were on her as, in her Thuringian accent, she started with fabricated tales of her sunny childhood in the vineyards of her mother, the Hungarian countess, and finished with detailed complaints and pleas for sympathy, sympathy due her for crushing debts and her addiction to morphine and Pervitin. In her words, it was "a dance from hell."[25] Kusian did not need to fear perjury charges with this tale spun out of whole cloth. In the German system, defendants technically do not testify and are never under oath.[26] She said nothing about the crimes of which she stood accused, stating that she had already confessed to the police and had no more to say. Her attorneys leapt in at this point, declaring that they would prove her innocence, claiming that her police statement was untrustworthy because "significant concerns have surfaced about the credibility of her confessions." Judge Korsch responded that he had no interest in getting involved with this issue. He then called for the day's witnesses.[27] The witnesses, members of Hermann Seidelmann's and Doris Merten's families, spoke of their loved ones' last days. Seidelmann had planned on returning home the day after his murder. Merten left a party to deliver a typewriter, then disappeared.[28] The first day was relatively drama free but hinted at what would characterize the days to come.

Tuesday, 16 January 1951

On the second day of the trial, witnesses provided the judges and onlookers – who may have paid up to 300 DM for tickets – a more well-rounded and confounding portrait of Elisabeth Kusian. Even before they could paint her character, Kusian also spoke, confusing onlookers with early and frequent outbursts, statements, and contradictions, bringing all activity to a standstill.[29] Her remarks touched on her morphine addiction, her husband's and her own Nazi pasts, and more.[30] At the end of her ramblings, she declared that all her previous statements to the police about her guilt were lies.[31]

Judge Korsch responded by trying to treat her in an "embarrassingly correct, even polite" manner, using the same kind of care one would use for "a raw egg."[32] Chief Prosecutor Kuntze, though, shot her a "hard, sharp, straight look," unsteadying her theatrical demeanour and causing her to babble in her Thuringian dialect as she asked the court for time to think and consider her further remarks.[33]

The day's testimony seemed to confirm her guilt. One former patient claimed that the two ran into each other on New Year's morning on the city train and that the awful-looking Kusian had a bag and rucksack with her.[34] Dr. Niedenthal, one of the physicians engaged to determine Kusian's legal sanity, testified that "neither physical ailments nor mental or nervous weaknesses are present in her. She was often unruly during the examinations and tried to play the two experts off against each other." In response, Kusian rose, shouting, "That's not true." Niedenthal continued, "All her life, she had tried to get into circles that were not open to her." He believed that she and Walter were a terrible match, so when the army drafted him, she could and did free herself from his restrictions. Dr. Niedenthal focused on her affairs and morphine use. "She became libidinous and unrestrained. And once entangled in impostor lies, she had to keep on lying. As to the deeds, it must be said that such a vivid description as she gave can only spring from her own observations." He concluded that, although she was peculiar, she was legally sane.[35]

The most momentous turn in the day's proceedings occurred when Elisabeth Kusian decided to blame Walter Kusian for the murders. The judges called Walter Kusian to the stand. His voice trembled as he detailed his marriage, which he claimed he had thought was and would remain happy. His tearful testimony soon moved to his discovery of Elisabeth's unfaithfulness and thievery.[36] He spoke through tears of a wife who was unfaithful and conniving. Among his tales of woe was the story of his return to the city on leave from the war, only to find Elisabeth celebrating her engagement to a butcher. Indeed, he claimed, she sent him to a goldsmith to pick up rings for her and her "groom." He also spoke of how she had an obituary of her still-living mother placed in the papers. Producing a wad of documents to show that he had paid far more child support than had been mandated by the court, Kusian turned to his role as a father, presumably after the couple's divorce. In short, he claimed that, although she was crazy, he had always acted honourably.[37]

When Judge Korsch asked about her drug use, Walter responded that Elisabeth often took sleeping tablets during their marriage. When pressed, he expanded, "She is a pitiful person. She has two souls. She was always attempting suicide, and I was always her nurse."[38] In short, he painted himself in the best light, especially given his Nazi past, which no longer shone brightly in this post-fascist Berlin.

Her former husband's testimony seems to have driven Elisabeth Kusian to the breaking point. After Walter's comments, the defence rose and announced that Elisabeth had a statement to make. "I want quiet. Now I will say what happened."[39] Rising "as if bitten by a tarantula," she hesitated, then approached the bench to declare, "Up to this point, I lied. I recant my confessions. My divorced husband carried out the two murders."[40] Elisabeth claimed her former marriage had been a martyrdom.[41]

The words spilled out of her. "I was held in detention for a year. I can't say what I went through. I want to make my divorced husband understand what I suffered," she said. "I came to know Seidelmann as a money changer from Zoo. He would greet me when we saw each other. One day he addressed me: 'Beautiful lady, why so sad?' He accompanied me on my way to the hospital, and I gave him my address while we chatted. He visited me on the evening of 3 December. While we were sitting together, chatting on the couch, suddenly my husband came unexpectedly."[42] Walter, she exclaimed, became insanely jealous. Then, she claimed, she left the room for a few minutes to defuse the situation. "When I returned, the room was dark, and Seidelmann was lying behind the desk, strangled."[43] "I was never a morphine addict," she added. "I use morphine now, though, because of this horrible deed."[44]

Figure 6.1. Elisabeth Kusian in court.

The judges wondered why she confessed. So that the children would have a father, she countered.[45] Judge Korsch urged Walter to respond.

WALTER KUSIAN: It's all lies from beginning to end. She's had a year in custody to think it all out. Why didn't she say this earlier?

JUDGE KORSCH: You heard. She says because of the children.

WALTER KUSIAN: I've never seen Seidelmann or Frau Merten.

JUDGE KORSCH: It's very strange, isn't it, that you continued to associate with your divorced wife?

WALTER KUSIAN: Why?

JUDGE KORSCH: So you still maintain that everything is untrue? Frau Kusian, you hear your husband says you lied again.

ELISABETH KUSIAN: Believe me, Mr. Chairman, I have lied many times, but I don't anymore.

ATTORNEY WEIMANN: I ask that the accused be given the opportunity to direct questions to the witnesses.

Elisabeth Kusian then walked forward to the barrier of the defendant's bench, leaned on it as if with the last of her strength, looked at Kusian with wide-open eyes, and began to speak monotonously and excitedly.

ELISABETH KUSIAN: I have done you much wrong, but please think of the children! I have suffered so much. Tell the truth now, tell it like it was.

The witness Kusian looked at her dumbfounded, shaking his head stunned.

JUDGE KORSCH: You are now hearing your wife's plea. You maintain that everything is untrue.

WALTER KUSIAN: Yes.[46]

Red-faced, Walter Kusian gesticulated so wildly that two court officials pulled him back in the witness chair. Elisabeth then claimed that Walter also strangled Doris Merten. One observer thought that her story barely held together.[47] Walter Kusian, wearing a melancholy smile, let himself be led away by guards to a jail cell where he would sit under suspicion.[48] After his removal from the courtroom but before being remanded to a holding cell, Kusian whined, "I can only imagine that my wife has gone mad … I am innocent. If I had committed a murder, I would not be so stupid as to keep the clothes of the murdered man in my room. I hope the trial is not postponed. I don't want to sit innocently in jail for weeks!"[49]

"Procontra," a pseudonymous columnist writing in *Der Kurier*, showed a grudging sympathy for Walter Kusian. The former Nazi was somewhat primitive, wooden, coarse, and ruthlessly industrious. Procontra thought that Kusian should be granted membership into a Protective Association for the Victims of Hysterical Women. Did Elisabeth's multiple suicide attempts represent a nervous breakdown, passing out, or simply comedy? The writer asked, then put aside, this question. Nobody, Procontra claimed, could understand why Walter would want to spend any time with Elisabeth, whose story that she falsely admitted guilt so that the children would have their murderous father "didn't sound like a novel. It's a story out of the insane asylum."[50]

After Walter Kusian's departure, the prosecutor's cautious approach demanded that Walter be remanded to jail. "On the one hand, the defendant admits that she lied a lot in her life. On the other hand, what the accused said could not be completely excluded from the truth. I, therefore, arranged for Kusian to be arrested so that he would not have the opportunity to obscure any possible traces."[51] He requested the press to help locate cab drivers who might have picked up a man with heavy baggage near Elisabeth Kusian's building on the night of 26 December 1949, adding his interest in anybody who might have seen a couple with heavy luggage at that location.[52]

When one judge commented that this development would amount to a request for a several-day adjournment, Attorney Weimann welcomed it. Perhaps he hoped the extra time might allow the defence team to develop a strategy based on this new turn. From this point on, Elisabeth Kusian's attorneys tried to prove that she was not guilty or, at worst, shared her guilt with others. After a consultation, they suggested that Elisabeth confessed to protect Kurt Muschan. The flaw in this argument was that the forensic scientist who searched Kusian's room explained that she had found Type B blood on Kusian's couch blanket and Type AB on her wool blanket and rucksack. Given this barrage of information and argument, the judges temporarily halted the proceedings, allowing officials to escort Elisabeth Kusian to the Robert Koch Hospital for blood typing. The lab at her former hospital determined that her blood type was A.[53] In conclusion, Judge Korsch chose this second day to ask reporters to disguise Kurt Muschan's name to protect his family from publicity (an East Berlin reporter believed it was to protect the West Berlin police department's reputation).[54]

After the day's events, some wondered whether Elisabeth Kusian's lawyers could convince the court to disregard her confession. Might the jury accept the possibility that she was trying to protect an accomplice? Berlin's general population thought that might be the case.[55] One anonymous observer writing for West Berlin's *Der Tagesspiegel* wondered if Kusian could differentiate truth from lies.

> During the hearing of evidence, she demonstrates a sure instinct for the trial's imponderables and reacts with a quickness and agility that always arouse astonishment. She is not a woman who fibs but an imaginative liar who backs up her statements so logically and so precisely that they initially seem like truths. In fact, it is a legitimate question as to whether Kusian even knows that she is lying, or whether she herself does not already perceive her lies as truths.[56]

This question of truth and lies had to have broader, if unintentionally ironic, resonance during a German moment when people recast themselves as victims rather than perpetrators or accomplices. What is guilt? What is responsibility? The observer never left Elisabeth Kusian's case to question post-war Germany. Interrogating broader questions of German truth and lies, self-deception and guilt, were never part of the Kusian episode.

As Robert Moeller reminds us, this was the moment when West Germans recast their collective memories of the previous years and their very identity around the stories of Communist brutality, expellees from the East, and German POWs still stuck in the Soviet Union.[57] Did Kusian know she was lying? Did her audience know that they were? For example, when expellees told their stories, they related "a history peopled with innocents in which a handful of zealous Nazis had deluded good Germans. Victims of Germans were not completely absent from these accounts, but when those who testified acknowledged the suffering of Jews at the hands of Germans, it was most frequently in order to establish a measure for the horror of their own experience."[58] How different was this from Elisabeth Kusian's tales that conflated perpetrator and victim, horror and pain?

Indeed, like so many of her contemporaries, ranging from the obscure to the famous, did Elisabeth Kusian not stress the apolitical and personal rather than look at the larger issues and horrors that helped influence and shape her decisions? Indeed, Kusian played the same role as many other celebrities who tried to recast their actions. Artists, in much the same way as Kusian, often claimed persecution or naiveté.[59]

As for observers in the courtroom, they could take comfort in the solidifying notion that promiscuous women were born of the occupation, not of the years that came earlier.[60] Most German observers could contemplate their own victimhood more easily than the specific suffering of others (Jews, "asocials," and Communists).[61] Perhaps the forgetting of the last group had something to do with the lack of interest in Herman Seidelmann's sufferings during the Third Reich and his survival, only to succumb to violence during the occupation.

One East Berlin newspaper, *Tägliche Rundschau,* used the proceedings to criticize West Berlin. It argued that the day's proceedings highlighted the exemplary work of the Volkspolizei and the failures of the West Berlin police. West Berlin authorities, it claimed, were notable in their attempt to provide cover for detective Kurt Muschan.[62] Rudolf Hirsch, its correspondent, added that the "Stumm Police" and the public prosecutor had wholly failed. Hirsch quoted Dr. Nicolai, who wondered about the judges' professionalism and complained to Judge Korsch, "Mr. District Court Director! In a trial like this one, it is unacceptable that none of the three professional judges of the jury court know the files."[63]

Even more acerbic and indeed overtly political was the East Berlin *Berliner Zeitung*'s "Cobra," who argued that spectators paying up to 80 DM to get one of the courtroom's seventy available seats were getting their money's worth. Others claimed that prices hit 100 DM. The trial, Cobra argued, satisfied both West Berliners' taste for American gangster-style gore and thrills, and was perfectly in keeping with the "American masters" desire to erase authentic culture. This film-like experience (Cobra imagined a movie with a title like "Sliced Up with the Bread Knife") would be perfectly in keeping with the Americans' desire to distract citizens from the real issues of the day – including Berlin's division, a possible West German remilitarization, and the looming threat of war. *Berliner Zeitung*'s take matched the rest of the East Berlin press, which added that the trial was designed to distract from American defeats in the Korean War, Western Allies' confiscation of Berlin apartments from their inhabitants, and the GDR President Otto Grotewohl's letter proposing a possible German reunification.[64]

By October 1950 at the latest, the SED leadership, including President Otto Grotewohl, had taken note of growing disenchantment among the West German public with some of the policies of West German Chancellor Konrad Adenauer. Certainly, this included mounting unhappiness due to the increase in West German defence spending. West Germans were also concerned about the war in Korea and what it might mean for Germany. One consequence was the growth of anti-militarism, specifically the "ohne mich" (count me out) movement. In response, the SED launched a campaign for a "national dialogue." To quote Dirk Spilker, "On 15 November 1950, in his official opening address to the newly elected People's Chamber, Grotewohl called for the creation of an all-German constituent assembly as the first step towards the establishment of a German central government and the signing of a peace treaty with Germany ... Two weeks later, on 1 December 1950, a formal letter signed by Grotewohl on behalf of the East German government was delivered to Adenauer. In it, Grotewohl repeated the proposals made in his speech of 15 November and called for immediate negotiations between the two German governments." The West German government summarily dismissed the proposal in January 1951, demanding free, Germany-wide elections as a precondition.[65] It is difficult to know if this move ever had any chance of success.[66]

One certainty is that Grotewohl's call for unification was nothing new. In October 1948, he gave a speech to the Deutsche Volksrat, entitled

"For an Undivided German Republik: Draft for a Constitution for the German Democratic Republic." This speech warned of the "wage slavery of foreign capitalist interests" and "dollar imperialism." Grotewohl reminded his audience that the language of the Allies during the war called for the destruction of the "Hitler War Machine, Nazi Party, and Hitler State," among other things. Reading into his argument that the West had abandoned these goals does not take much imagination. Grotewohl warned against the Western Allies' preference for a federal solution, which, he claimed, was the way to "annexation, colonization, and enslavement." Instead, he argued, Germany should embrace the Soviet ideas of demilitarization and denazification.[67]

The following month, Grotewohl gave another speech, this time blaming the West for the division of Berlin. Whether any of these had much social currency is debatable. There was hope that the fear of an inner German civil war, like the one in Korea, would push the Western public towards interest in unification on Eastern terms.[68]

Ultimately, all of these calls for a reorientation from the West to the East fell on deaf ears. The trial, and public interest in it, moved on.

Wednesday, 17 January 1951

Two competing narratives dominated the third day of Elisabeth Kusian's trial. As her attorneys argued that she could not possibly have done all of what she was suspected, prosecution witnesses incriminated her ever more deeply. West Berlin papers covered the events as if they were ripped from American noir. East Berlin writers focused on East-West tensions.

Defence attorneys brought Elisabeth Kusian's sleeping couch into the courtroom. Combining showmanship and poor planning, they thought the demonstration would prove she could not have hidden Doris Merten's corpse under it for days. To show the impossibility of her earlier confession, one of her attorneys, Dr. Nicolai, struggled but failed to fit underneath the couch, whose bottom stood 20 centimetres above the floor.[69] Nicolai, though, was a heavy man. One of the court's medical experts, Dr. Spengler, insisted a corpse could lie where a living person could not. Even this declaration, however, turned out to be unnecessary. A police officer and a court guard managed the feat with no difficulty.[70] *Tägliche Rundschau* scoffed that such a travesty might satisfy West Berliners' need for sensation while having no bearing on the truth.[71] The defence then filed a series of new motions to raise ever more questions. Who, they asked, owned the blue-striped sheets in which Doris Merten's corpse was wrapped? Did a taxi driver transport Walter Kusian to a destination near his apartment? Indeed, who was the woman whom Kusian's landlady claimed to have seen in Elisabeth's room on 26 December? Elisabeth herself undercut this move when she told the judge that this woman did not exist. "Why," Judge Korsch asked her, "did you tell your friend Kurt M. about her?" She responded laconically, "I told Kurt M a lot that wasn't true."[72]

In contrast to the defence, the prosecution brought a more sophisticated approach to the day's proceedings. Perhaps to match the defence's antics, the chief prosecutor again requested that the press and radio publicize the authorities' search for a mysterious taxi driver who might have picked up a couple in front of Elisabeth Kusian's building on 26 December between 10:00 p.m. and midnight, adding "if they do, in fact, exist." Walter Kusian sat and smiled, perhaps sardonically, at this request.[73] The morning's witnesses spoke of their interactions with Elisabeth Kusian. One former patient swore she saw "Sister Elisabeth alone on the tram on Alexanderplatz. I was riding home to see my husband. She had an empty rucksack under her arm. I greeted her, but got the feeling that she didn't want to chat because it would be unpleasant for her to be seen doing this on New Year's morning." Elisabeth retorted from her seat, "It wasn't a rucksack. It was a grey wool blanket that my husband had given to me."[74]

A former landlady spoke of Kusian's jewellery theft and Muschan's intervention:

WITNESS: Herr Muschan then promised me that he would deal with his girlfriend, and then Frau Kusian also made a written commitment to me to pay back 40 DM a month because the jewellery had already been sold.

Korsch then directed a question to Muschan:

JUDGE KORSCH: You always blindly believed the defendant, as you said, and now we hear that you considered her a thief?
KURT MUSCHAN: Frau Kusian was always known to me as an attractive, intelligent person. I knew that she was impulsive, but that she could commit theft was already unbelievable to me because of her good financial circumstances.[75]

Kusian's most recent landlady expanded the tale of Elisabeth's wealth with details of her fictional uncle's purported clinic.[76] Elisabeth listened "with downcast eyes," sometimes looking humble, other times insolent.[77] Her attitude continued when expert witnesses took the stand. After a chemist discussed the blood found in her rucksack, suitcase, and crevices between the floorboards, and on the kitchen knife, Korsch showed Elisabeth a rubber glove. She claimed to have used it for coarse work. She added that she had eczema; the discovered blood was hers.[78]

Psychiatric expert Dr. Niedenthal added that Elisabeth Kusian was a "hysterical psychopath," "intelligent, cold-blooded, and goal-oriented." Beginning with her childhood, he stressed what he characterized as her hereditary burden of an excitable father and unbalanced mother. He then skated over the tale of her desire to leave poverty behind, hopes – later dashed – about what marriage to Kusian might mean, her enjoyment of the war, lies about her background, and more. When pushed about her ability to commit the crimes of which she stood accused, Niedenthal discussed her attendance at lectures and exact knowledge of the cuts made to her victims. He was especially interested in what he characterized as her "lowered personality level." To his mind, this was especially evident in her wearing her uniform during the murders and her close observation of her victims' deaths. Nevertheless, Niedenthal concluded, "her aberrant dispositions remained within the bounds of what was still normal and, in his opinion, did not justify the application of paragraph 51 of the German Criminal Code."[79] If only to be dramatic, he added that "she doesn't have only two faces, as her former husband stated. She has more."[80]

Dr. Spengler established her ability to murder Hermann Seidelmann. "In such a case, the large carotid artery is cut off. The blood supply to the brain is immediately cut off. Although death isn't immediate, when a noose is thrown around a sitter's neck from behind, he can't respond immediately. Before he can rise and begin to struggle, he is already unconscious. People who are less powerful but skilled can kill people this way, no matter what their size or strength."[81] Spengler added that nurses knew how to move large, heavy bodies with relative ease.[82] To conclude the day's coverage, the *Berliner Zeitung* reminded readers that the "Stumm Police" had so muddled the investigation that Dr. Korsch needed to rely on the Volkspolizei's investigation.[83]

Friday, 19 January 1951

The trial resumed on Friday, 19 January with continuing fanfare. RIAS set up a microphone and giant loudspeaker in the courtroom's corner to make every word audible. Before its installation, many audience members could not hear Elisabeth Kusian's words.[84] Now, when she said, in her "melodic Thuringian tone, 'I want peace at last, I want to speak, I have lied and lied,'" it was clear to all present.[85] The prosecutor repeated his public request that "the cab driver who, according to the statements of the defendant Kusian, drove a man with a large tied duffel bag from the house at Kantstraße 154a to Sternstraße or its immediate vicinity in the north of Berlin on the night of 27 December 1949 is asked to come forward immediately."[86]

Newspaper readers heeded the prosecutor's call. Letters, many anonymous, poured into the court. "You're looking for a black woman?" read one. "I know a woman in Eberswalde who has … Maybe it could be her?" Another demanded the death penalty.

One wrote: "Regarding the K. case, I would like to draw attention to the fact that Frau X in Y Street had brought bloody things to the rag and bone dealer XY. Had brought. In the process, she said..."[87] Such cultural background noise did not stop the trial's third day.

The masses of forensic evidence made the work of Elisabeth Kusian's defence team even more difficult. The Volkspolizei presented a bundle of Doris Merten's bloody underwear to the court for examination. It was doused in the same blood type as that on Elisabeth Kusian's sofa.[88] Meanwhile, in the presentation of a discovery worthy of a detective novel, the court satisfied itself that Walter Kusian had nothing to do with the killings, a development duly reported by Procontra:

> A letter, torn to shreds, had been found in the murder room's wastebasket by the criminal police. They put the snippets together. What emerged is truly unique exonerating evidence for Walter Kusian. On the day he waited in vain for his wife, the showman Seidelmann was murdered. This evidence is finally sufficient for the court to release Walter Kusian from prison, after even in his apartment with the whole array of chemical aids, no traces of blood could be found that he could possibly cover up.[89]

The letter was full of Walter's longing for Elisabeth, whom he had not seen for a while. Its contents were enough to exonerate him.[90] The same observer quipped:

> Crime films prefer to end in a jury trial. Unforeseen events bite each other in the tail until, at the end, a grandiose proof of guilt or innocence, like a deus ex machina, like a thunderclap from the defence attorney's briefcase, clarifies the irredeemably confused scene to a happy ending. Reality, by contrast? In reality, the main hearing of a criminal case represents the public and oral recapitulation of the file's contents. This trial, though, is like in a crime movie. Here, thanks to the defendant's defence tactics, the court becomes the investigating authority: Let us hope for the grandiose clearing up of the jumbled scenery![91]

If Walter Kusian's release provided some drama, much of the rest of the day resembled nothing more than a black comedy. One friend of Doris Merten's claimed to remember a conversation the two had had while sitting under hair dryers in a beauty salon. Merten, she claimed, spoke of Walter Kusian, Kurt Muschan, and a typewriter sale. When pressed, the witness admitted that she had read about the murder in the newspaper and only then had the conversation in her memory.[92]

A woman who worked in Elisabeth Kusian's building declared:

> At noon on 26 December 1949, a gentleman was walking up the stairs. He was carrying a rucksack in which was a very long cardboard box. When I wanted to switch on the light in the evening, around 9:00 p.m., I heard slow steps on the stairs, as if someone was carrying a heavy load. It was Frau Kusian and the man I had already seen at noon. Again he was carrying the backpack with the long cardboard box, and he felt his way laboriously down the banister with the load. He caught my eye because of his Roman-Greek nose. He wore a brown leather jacket, grey-green mottled peaked cap, black pants, and new black leather shoes. The man was 5 centimetres taller than the woman.

When Judge Korsch asked if it had been bright enough for her to be sure, she responded, "There was a 15-watt lamp burning."[93]

Elisabeth Kusian quickly stood to say that her husband had no such clothes. Indeed, a year earlier, the woman had been unable to pick out Walter Kusian from a line-up of seven men. Also, the reporter noted that Elisabeth Kusian was taller than her husband.[94] Perhaps the most absurd episode involved "Rose," an astrologer. Like many others, she had written to the court about the case. Even members of the court smiled when she appeared. Judge Korsch asked, "Do you know Kusian?" She responded, "No. There you see again what you can think of astrology ... Go ahead and laugh. You'll see for yourself." Using a "scientifically" designed horoscope, she knew that Elisabeth Kusian was not guilty of the crimes for which she stood accused. A friend of hers was guilty. She finished by wagging her finger at the crowd and declared, "You are not permitted to laugh at me," then took a seat and handed out advertising material.[95]

The trial was scheduled to reconvene the following Tuesday, 23 January.

Procontra mused about and took stock of the case's significance. Quick to dismiss the East Berlin newspapers' criticisms of the trial and West Berlin justice, Procontra reminded readers of Hermann Joseph Flade's case. Flade, an East German teenager from the small town of Olbernhau, had been sentenced to death on 10 January, ostensibly for the attempted murder of a Volkspolizei officer but really for posting notices supporting a boycott of the first upcoming GDR parliamentary elections, held in October 1950.[96] Flade's crime, such as it was, was not codified until weeks after he mounted his protest. With this case in mind, Procontra asked whether Kusian's case deserved the ink spilled to bring it to the public's attention. Having posed the question, Procontra answered, "Is Frau Kusian worth so much fuss that she can justifiably dominate the headlines? The answer: She is not if the reporter limits himself merely to satisfying sensationalism by reproducing external details of the trial. She is certainly worth it if the reporting takes advantage of the general interest shown in this trial to dispel prejudices in the reader from the old *Gartenlaube* by exposing to view the dark dungeons of the subconscious, the soul, the motives."[97] The *Gartenlaube* was perhaps Germany's most popular nineteenth-century magazine, providing its readers with comforting notions of what a German was and what it meant to be German.[98] As the trial approached its second half, such comfortable certainties would continue to evaporate.

Tuesday, 23 January 1951

Camera operators from the *Neue Deutsche Wochenschau* brought their equipment to the day's session to film Waldemar Weimann's testimony and the reading of Elisabeth Kusian's confession to the police.[99] Weimann spoke of Kusian's charm – and guilt. A fellow inmate once told him of her indignity at the suspicion against this "innocent, this fabulous woman." Just days later, this same inmate told him, "I am downright idiotic! How could I believe this woman? She is the most horrible woman I know!"[100] The medical examiner's testimony revealed his professional expertise as a psychiatrist and pathologist, and his deep reservoirs of self-regard.

He emphasized his excellent rapport with Kusian during their interviews. He also spoke to police officials of her attendance at the lectures he gave, where he unwittingly taught her the theory of strangulation, theoretical knowledge she put into practice. Weimann seemed to be almost perversely proud of this indirect involvement.[101] He added that her descriptions of the deaths of the two victims were so precise that she must have witnessed them both.[102] The physician discussed her attempt to implicate her former husband, then added that she only changed her story when Muschan appeared in her jail cell during her confession.[103] Kriminalkommissar Menzel supported this conclusion by saying that no evidence of wrongdoing was found in Walter Kusian's room, even though officers had searched for two hours. He added that the police interviewed 206 people. He believed that all evidence pointed towards Elisabeth Kusian's guilt.[104]

Following the experts, Judge Korsch decided to have a several-hour reading of Elisabeth Kusian's confession to the Volkspolizei.[105] The reading allowed the listeners, cameras, and judges to hear Kusian's words as she told of how she killed her victims without help, her drug use, her love of Kurt Muschan, and her fear of life imprisonment.[106] Kusian had one exchange with the prosecutor in court that day, which only cemented her reputation as a very odd woman.

PROSECUTOR: Why did you write a card with "good wishes for the New Year" to Doris Merten, who had long since been murdered, on 4 January 1950, and ask her to visit you again soon?

ACCUSED: I wrote not just one but four cards. My husband told me to cover up the crime.

PROSECUTOR: You claimed you had enough money for the typewriter on 26 December 1949. But why did you try to pawn a box of silver?

ACCUSED: You ask questions, Mr. Prosecutor![107]

Kusian seemed to some to sit, head bowed, like a "sullen sphinx," aware of the corner into which such words had trapped her. "But while the inquisitive crowd gathered closer than ever by the entrance doors, and the press photographers' camera clicks could be heard ever more frequently, it was obvious that the tragedy had passed its dramatic climax and had now reached a sober, cathartic weighing, the purifying solution."[108]

Is life stranger than fiction? Jochen Harringa argued "that criminal cases, as every unmusical angle, each harsh juxtaposition of faith and nihilism, of love and crime, of delusions of prestige and poverty become visible," characterized modern life. As for Muschan, "he can never, of his own free will, break away from this capricious, dark-haired nurse with the singing Thuringian intonation. He does not know that wealth and the possibility of marriage are only lies, that her husband is alive, and that the magic of her strange buoyancy is only an effect of the morphine."[109]

The case's meaning was simple for East Berlin writers. The Volkspolizei cared about the city's safety; the "Stumm Police" did not.[110] Judge Korsch, seemingly fed up with the proceedings, declared, "We want to finally finish this," and no more evidence was taken.[111] The surprised prosecutor complained that he had not had enough time to prepare a final statement. Korsch relented, and the court adjourned until the following morning.[112]

Thursday, 25 January 1951

On the trial's final day, the prosecutor began with the following words: "It may be that the statement with which the defendant tried to incriminate her ex-husband on the second day of the hearing raised certain doubts about the charges against her. However, for those who know the accused, this explanation did not come as a great surprise. The defence has tried to prove that Elisabeth Kusian did not commit the crimes. I will now try to prove – on the basis of facts – that only the accused can be the murderess."[113] He spoke for more than two hours, proceeding in minute detail, discussing the dismemberment, the dual police departments' determination that the two murders were linked, Elisabeth Kusian's poor job of hiding the circumstances of Doris Merten's murder, the illogical attempts to implicate Walter Kusian, and more.[114] He then turned to arguments designed to sway the panel of judges. As to her drug use, Chief Prosecutor Kuntze argued, "Despite all the absurdity, she was not restricted for a moment in her free determination of the will." The motive, he argued, was simple greed. He concluded his statement by arguing:

> The accused committed the crimes in the way she first described them. Insidiously, and to cover up another crime, she murdered two people. In her catastrophic situation at the time, she had to get money at any price because she saw no way out of her sea of debt. She raised money – at the cost of two lives. The fact that she is a mother of three children cannot be counted towards her sentence as a mitigating factor. One must feel sorry for the children on whom she placed the burden of her fate but not for the mother of these children. One must have pity on the victims of this woman, not on the murderess![115]

After the prosecution rested, Attorney Weimann rose to speak. He counterattacked all who had condemned his defence strategy. "It is the defendants, not the defence attorneys, who determine the defence tactics, and no lawyer has the right to disavow his clients." Weimann acknowledged the general population's dislike of Elisabeth Kusian but then asked the panel not to be swayed by emotion. Her psychiatric evaluation, he argued, was weak. The state should have handled her like a schizophrenic. He claimed that the court must prove that she acted alone and was not merely an aide, a beneficiary, or a fence. Dr. Nicolai added to Weimann's comments, reminding listeners that Elisabeth Kusian may have lied to her attorneys as much as she had to the authorities. He then requested that the judges not base their judgment on her statements but only on the evidence. He reminded the panel of the building attendant's insistence that she had seen Elisabeth Kusian on the stairs with a man on 26 January, as well as other testimony that Doris Merten had mentioned Walter Kusian.[116]

The court only deliberated for forty-five minutes before pronouncing Elisabeth Kusian guilty and sentencing her to two life sentences and the loss of all civil rights, such as the right to vote and serve on a jury (bürgerlichen Ehrenrechte).[117] Judge Korsch's remarks showed no sympathy for Elisabeth Kusian:

> If this trial caused such a stir, it was because the defendant committed her misdeeds as a nurse. We judges can only condemn her crimes. But for what she did to her children and others, she will one day have to answer to her God.

As to Walter Kusian, Korsch added:

> With great conscientiousness, the detectives later pieced together stone after stone for their conviction. And if she accused herself of these acts almost to the end, it was certainly not because she wanted to spare the man she hated.[118]

Although stunned, Kusian accepted the verdict much more quietly than might have been expected.

> She swayed her head and upper body back and forth, but she continued to play the role of offended impenetrability with a dismissive face. Only when the chairman described how she was celebrating Christmas with her lover by burning candles in front of those she had murdered that she cried out shrilly: "My God, that's not true!" After the reasons for the verdict, she spoke briefly with her defence attorneys. Then she allowed herself to be carried away like a spoiled child who didn't get her way.[119]

Witnesses, officials, observers, and indeed the entire city were left to wonder what, if anything, the episode meant. Medical experts theorized that Kusian's early childhood experiences, relationship with her mother, and jealousy set her course of action.[120] Others felt that the case's only meaning lay in the pain that a new generation of children – the victim's, the perpetrator's, and the lover's – would suffer because of their connection to the events. This connection would follow them for the rest of their lives. Indeed, this argument went, Kusian's children lost both her and any faith they might have had in her.[121] Others mused that this case spoke to the necessity for, or horror of, the death penalty. One of the latter gratefully saw its recent abolition in the Federal Republic and West Berlin as a civilized distinction between them and the kind of state found in the GDR and the Soviet Union.[122] H. Schad mused that she could have been executed had West Berlin not abolished the death penalty three days before Kusian's sentencing.[123]

However, as soon as the trial ended, newspapers turned to stories of uprisings, renaming of squares, the construction of memorials, and more. Things moved on.

After

After Elisabeth Kusian's trial, East Berlin newspapers focused on other issues. Cobra wrote of how the trial coverage was the Western press's attempt to ignore West German Chancellor Adenauer's rejection of reunification with the East, West German militarization, West Berlin and West German strikes, and American preparations for war.[1] One anonymous commentator remarked that the trial had provided a diversion from West Berlin workers' demands and American militarization.[2] This comment would prove ironic. Only two years later, the East German state, with the help of its Soviet backers, would itself crush East Berlin workers who had taken to the streets to demand a better life.[3]

About a week after the proceedings ended, Friedrich Karl Fromm, writing for a West Berlin paper, attempted to take stock of both the trial and the cultural moment. The case's horror, Fromm mused, lay not only in Kusian's profession but in how it combined with her brutality and willingness to violate the unwritten code of how one ought to treat guests. For him, though, the true nightmare lay in the fact that women could now act as brutally and horribly as men.[4] He would be reassured to know that older gender norms would soon re-establish themselves.[5]

Observers seemed unconcerned about the historical era from which Berlin had so recently emerged. None mentioned the casual brutality that had defined German culture for so long. None reflected that Germans had been accustomed to seeing uniforms and casual violence almost inevitably linked. Why, indeed, ought a woman – nursing uniform or not – not use violence for her benefit? Was this not the way Germany had operated for half a generation? There was no time for such thoughts. Time would march on, for both those involved in the case and the city itself, to a different future.

Elisabeth Kusian herself would die in prison in 1958 of cancer, only a few years after her trial.[6] Largely but not totally forgotten, her name and case would reappear in a novel, as well as chapters in a comic book, a memoir, a forensic text, and works of history.[7] Her family, lovers, and friends would all disappear from history. The Berlin she knew would, in considerable measure, disappear, too.

Waldemar Weimann died in 1965, a respected expert in legal medicine. In the years before his death, he wrote both a significant textbook for his field and his memoir, *Diagnosis Murder*.[8] His memoir avoids the less sterling moments in his career. In 1952, shortly after the conclusion of the Kusian case, Karl D. accused Waldemar Weimann of crimes against humanity for his participation in D.'s 1934 mandatory sterilization due to schizophrenia, performed in the Third Reich. When speaking with the authorities, Weimann claimed he could not remember the incident. They chose not to pursue the matter further, accepting his argument that such procedures were not political and were in keeping with general, international norms at the time.[9] It is convenient that Weimann, a trained pathologist and psychiatrist, both claimed to have forgotten the incident while proffering a reason for why his actions were not in the least criminal. Unsurprisingly, none of the figures who determined Weimann's legal and moral culpability discussed his earlier role in determining criminal suspects' legal and moral accountability.

Arno Weimann, Waldemar Weimann's brother and Elisabeth Kusian's defence attorney, would die in 1964. Unlike his brother, history would remember his actions in the Third Reich, even as some colleagues tried to whitewash his image for posterity. To honour Arno Weimann on his death, Hermann Reuß wrote that "during the Nazi era, Dr. Weimann understood that 'integer vitae scelerisque purus' in many risky trials (for example, defending the men of 20 July, such as Dr. Goerdeler and Field Marshal von

Witzleben, in front of the People's Court). He did much worthy, blessed work, showing great navigational skill through the adversities of the regime without finding himself ready for a sacrificium intellectus."[10] Such posthumous commemorations almost constitute a genre for post-war German professionals.

Erwin Gohrbandt, the head of Moabit Hospital who took such umbrage to detectives besmirching the institution's reputation, died in 1965. Dr. Gohrbandt understood the importance of reputation and publicity; he had spent the years since the war rebuilding his own image. An obituary lauded him for pioneering work in plastic surgery and directing Moabit Hospital from 1940 to 1958.[11] Obituarists avoided referencing his activities during the Third Reich, which included studying the damage that freezing cold could do to humans. It is unclear whether Gohrbandt participated in freezing experiments on concentration camp inmates. He attended a conference at which presenters discussed the experiments. There was a great deal of overlap between the findings in his work and the work of those involved.[12] Also little remarked upon was Gohrbandt's membership in the Nazi Hochschullehrerring and his close contacts with Hermann Göring, chief of the German Air Force and Adolf Hitler's second in command.

Gohrbandt's admirers did not want to link his work to the Third Reich. One memorialist wrote that "when the fascists began the extermination of 'inferior life,' Dr. Gohrbandt did not recognize the inhumane character of this form of government and in 1934 even gave a lecture to the Berlin Surgical Society on the sterilization of men, which was published." Furthermore, "although he maintained a certain distance from the radical machinations of the Nazi regime, his military medical activities in the Second World War underscore his lack of political understanding." Like so many of its ilk, the piece quickly moved to his post-war activities, especially his work rebuilding Moabit Hospital and its reputation. It also touted his claimed adherence to democratic values.[13]

Even as the reputations of some of the trial's participants changed, Berlin, the city in which Elisabeth Kusian had perpetrated her crimes, changed too. Kantstraße 154a still stands. It is the site of a popular coffee bar.[14] Embedded in the sidewalk in front of it is a Stolperstein, a brass stumbling stone, memorializing the Behar family whom the Nazi regime sent to their death in Riga.[15] All traces of Kusian are gone. The Zoo Station, where Elisabeth Kusian met and made the fateful decision to murder Hermann Seidelmann, is still a central site in western Berlin. Rather than being remembered as a place for black markets and currency trading, though, it would enter public memory as one of the centres of the 1960s and 1970s West Berlin drug and sex work scene, both in the book *Wir Kinder vom Bahnhof Zoo*, as well as the subsequent film and television miniseries.[16]

In 1952, planning would begin to transform Knie, where Hermann Seidelmann's torso was found, into a new square. In 1953, it was renamed Ernst-Reuter-Platz in honour of the former Weimar-era German Communist who became the world-famous anti-Soviet, Social Democratic mayor of West Berlin. The soon-to-be-built square would feature a fountain at its centre, surrounded by modern, Bauhaus-inspired structures. City planners would redesign this entire locality to perfect it for a city on the verge of domination by automobile traffic. This concern for cars was yet another reminder that Elisabeth Kusian's Berlin would be wrestled and designed into a new, "modern," post-war configuration.[17]

The Karstadt department store that had become Volkspolizei headquarters in 1948 would see its reputation darken in the years after Kusian's trial. Over time, authorities would hold many East German citizens there "to clarify a matter." On 17 June 1953, demonstrators clashed with police in front of the building in the East German uprising against Sovietization and the declining standard of living. The same building housed Erich Honecker, secretary of the Central Committee of the SED for the "Sicherheitsfragen (Security Question)," as he planned the construction of the Berlin Wall.[18]

As was the case for the building, the street on which police headquarters stood was then still named Neue Königstraße. It also has a history reflecting Germany's and Berlin's. From 1966 to 1995, it was renamed Hans Beimler Straße. Beimler had been a Communist functionary who went into Soviet exile during the Third Reich, then later fought and died in the Spanish Civil War. In 1995, five years after German unification, it was renamed for Otto Braun, a Social Democrat and the last democratically elected minister-president of Prussia. Like Beimler, he also spent the years of the Third Reich in exile, in his case in Switzerland. In 2011, officials renamed the avenue yet again. Today, it is named Bernhard Weiß Straße in honour of Berlin's Weimar-era Jewish vice president of police. The Nazis tormented Weiß for years during the Weimar Republic before he emigrated to London after they assumed power.[19]

The Sandkrug Bridge, where the Volkspolizei would hand Elisabeth over to representatives of the West Berlin force, would also see its reputation develop. It was already known as a crossing point. In 1948, Wolfgang Heubner, a research scientist at the Humboldt University in East Berlin, ran across it past an armed Russian sentry, still wearing his white lab coat, when he escaped from the city's eastern sector to the West, where he would become head of the Freie Universität's Department of Pharmacology.[20] A few years later, the Western Allies would "suggest" to the Soviets that Red Army soldiers relieving those guarding the War Memorial in Tiergarten use the bridge rather than take the showier and more intimidating two-mile route along the prominent Friedrichstraße.[21] This suggestion reminded observers of the further hardening of the border between the two cities, which had been one only a little while earlier.

Stephanstraße 60, where Elisabeth had robbed Frau Sobe. in an attempt to solve her financial problems, would enter German and world history years later as the final home of Kommune 1. The plaque on the building states: "In 1968, the Kommune 1 was housed here. The 'K1' experiment aimed to break up relations based on bourgeois dependency. They rejected the claim to property in marriage and authoritarian child-rearing, destroyed the private sphere, and asked radical questions of social relations. Thus, they hit the nerve of their time. In their wake, hundreds of communes, residential and house communities, were founded; today these are part of the general cultural heritage."[22]

Behind all of this change was the sense that the growing division of Berlin would somehow become permanent. In 1952, while reflecting on Kusian's case, West Berlin's Police President Johannes Stumm wrote that "the investigation was exceptionally difficult because the horrific discoveries of body parts were made not only in the western sector of Berlin but also in the eastern sector. The division of Berlin often causes difficulties and delays in solving criminal cases."[23] The division that Stumm found problematic would only become more dramatic and concrete in the next decade with the building of the Berlin Wall in August 1961. It would stand from 1961 until 1989.

Notes

Prologue

1 "3.12.1949 – Historisches Wetter," *chroniknet*, accessed 11 May 2021. https://web.archive.org/web/20210511081219/https://chroniknet.de/extra/historisches-wetter/?wetter-datum=3.12.1949.

2 In April 1948, the Soviet Union had imposed a partial blockade on the city's western districts. On 24 June, after the United States, United Kingdom, and France unified their three occupation zones into one with a newly introduced currency reform that would tie the city closer to West Germany, the USSR cut off rail, road, and water service to the new western zone. The Soviet Union finally lifted the blockade in May 1949. See Shlaim, "Britain, the Berlin Blockade and the Cold War"; and May, "America's Berlin." More broadly, see Harrington, *Berlin on the Brink*; and Shlaim, *The United States and the Berlin Blockade 1948–1949.*

3 Treptow Park, the largest of three memorials and burial sites commissioned by the Soviet Military Authorities, is set on a site that had served as a gathering point for German revolutionary socialists at the turn of the twentieth century. Conceived and designed by a team of Russian architects and sculptors, it also served as the final burial place for up to 7,000 Red Army soldiers. As visitors enter the park, they are greeted by an arch on which is written (in both Russian and German) "1945: Eternal glory to the heroes who fell for the freedom and independence of the socialist homeland." Sixteen sarcophagi, eight on either side, engraved with scenes from the Second World War, lead visitors to a massive statue of a Soviet soldier, infant in his arms, stamping on and smashing a swastika. See Crimmins, "Reinterpreting the Soviet War Memorial in Berlin's Treptower Park after 1990," 55. At its dedication, General Alexander Kotikov, Soviet military commandant of the city, declared: "It is a symbol of the battle of the world's people, led

by the Soviet Union, for the sovereign rights of the nations, for socialism and democracy, and against slavery and the arbitrary use of power and against the arsonists of a new war" (quoted in Stangl, "The Soviet War Memorial in Treptow, Berlin," 227).

4 Orwell, "You and the Atom Bomb."

5 The passages enclosed in boxes in this book take the reader from the narrative into a deeper discussion of structures and context. I hope that they provide a deeper understanding of the tale without detracting from it. Lutz, "The German Currency Reform," 122. More generally, see the following: Tribe, "The 1948 Currency Reform," 15–55; and Reinsch, *Currency Reform.*

6 On currency in the GDR, see Zatlin, *The Currency of Socialism.* For the rest of the book, West Marks will be simplified to DM and East Marks to DM East.

7 "Schlußbericht," 27 February 1950, signed KK Menzel, in Landesarchiv Berlin, Band II Mordsache Seidelmann/Merten (Tod durch Erdrosseln) B. Rep. 058 Nr. 893, p. 190.

8 Moltke, "The Evolution of Berlin's Urban Form," 278.

9 Ribbe, "Die Anfänge Charlottenburgs."

10 Asmuss and Nachama, "Zur Geschichte der Juden in Berlin." For these figures, see 180–1.

11 Reichardt, "Violence and Community," 275–97. See especially 275–8 and 296.

12 Schütte, *Charlottenburg*, 78.

13 Schütte, 78.

14 See the photos in Hopfe, *Berlin-Charlottenburg*, 11–12.

15 Reiher, "Tendenzen der städtebaulichen Entwicklung Charlottenburgs." See especially photographs 7.1, 7.2, 10.3, 10.4, and 26.4.

16 "Verhandelt," 6 December 1949, signed Albert Granzow, countersigned Schwarz, in Landesarchiv Berlin, B. Rep. 058 Nr. 894, pp. 21–2.

17 Translations from the German archival material are by the author unless otherwise credited. For a vivid description of the march, see Knopp and Greulich, "Der große Treck," 16–85. For this particular list, see 18.

18 On the expulsion of ethnic Germans, see Service, "Reinterpreting the Expulsion of Germans from Poland, 1945–9." In 1949, the state or *Land* of Thuringia was still a new political entity, recently cobbled together from formerly Prussian and Thuringian territory. In 1946, it was the smallest *Land* of the soon-to-be DDR, with a population of 2,943,250 (16.2 per cent of the eastern population). Its capital, Erfurt, had 667,570 Eastern refugees, making Hermann Seidelmann one of many who had tumbled westward, landing in what would soon become a corner of the DDR. See Allinson, "Politics and Popular Opinion in Thuringia, 1945–1968," especially 35–8.

19 Naumann, "Prolog-der Aufsteig der NSDAP in Plauen," 277–9.
20 Schmidt, "Judisches Leben," 310.
21 Naumann, "Die Zerstörung Plauens in der Schlussphase des Zweiten Weltkriegs," 312–23.
22 Krone, "Die Nachkriegsjahre (1945–1949)," 318.
23 Krone, 323.
24 "Verhandelt," signed Gertrud Seidelmann, countersigned KK Menzel, in Landesarchiv Berlin, B. Rep. 058 Nr. 893, p. 37.
25 Salzborn, "The German Myth of a Victim Nation," 89–90. More broadly, see Moeller, "Germans as Victims?"; Schmitz, *A Nation of Victims*.
26 Victims of Nazism, those who had suffered in the camps and those who escaped that fate, formed early associations in 1945 with one simple goal: to ensure that survivors would have their basic needs of food, clothing, shoes, health care, and shelter met. By February 1947, these had coalesced into the VVN (Vereinigung der Verfolgten des Naziregimes), an official umbrella group. By 1949, the group numbered over 37,000 members, almost 6,000 of whom lived in Thuringia. On the origins, see Monteath, "A Day to Remember," especially 198. For much more detail on the organization, see Reuter and Hansel, *Das kurze Leben der VVN von 1947 bis 1953*, especially 544–5. See also März, "Zwischen Politik und Interessenvertretung."
27 Barck, "Zeugnis ablegen," 260–1.
28 For an introduction to the history of the SED, see Malycha and Winters, *Die SED*.
29 "Kaiser as a Tilemaker," *New York Times*, 20 March 1911, 4.
30 Steinweis, *Kristallnacht 1938*, 54.
31 Quoted in Meyer, Simon, and Schütz, *Jews in Nazi Berlin*, 9–10.
32 Quoted in Slevogt, "*Aufgebaut werden durch dich die Trümmer der Vergangenheit*."
33 See Bezirksamt Charlottenburg-Wilmersdorf, "Ehemalige Synagoge Fasanenstraße," accessed 7 December 2021, https://www.berlin.de/ba-charlottenburg-wilmersdorf/ueber-den-bezirk/gebaeude-und-anlagen/kirchen/artikel.111001.php; Barzilai, "S.Y. Agnon's German Consecration and the 'Miracle' of Hebrew Letters," 62–3. See also "Kaiser as a Tilemaker," 4.
34 Special Cable to the *New York Times*, "Kurt Tucholsky, Nazis' Foe, Suicide," *New York Times*, 10 January 1936.
35 Bezirksamt Charlottenburg-Wilmersdorf, "Stolpersteine Kantstr. 154a," accessed 22 June 2024, https://www.berlin.de/ba-charlottenburg-wilmersdorf/ueber-den-bezirk/geschichte/stolpersteine/artikel.179277.php; Flucht–Exil–Verfolgung, "The Behar Family," accessed 22 June 2024, https://flucht-exil-verfolgung.de/en/ort/familie-behar.
36 Photographs and scale drawings of Kusian's apartment are in PHS D 4.41 Band 24e, n.p.

37 "Vermerk," signed Weisheit and Zimmermann, dated 10 January 1950, in Landesarchiv Berlin, Band II Mordsache Seidelmann/Merten (Tod durch Erdrosseln) B. Rep. 058 Nr. 893, p. 39.
38 "Bericht," signed KS Schwarz, 9 January 1950, in Landesarchiv Berlin, Band II Mordsache Seidelmann/Merten (Tod durch Erdrosseln) B. Rep. 058 Nr. 893, p. 38.
39 "Vorführungsbericht," signed VP Rat Pohl, dated 7 January 1950, in PHS D 4.41 Band 24b, Elisabeth Kusian, p. 36.
40 "Vermerk," dated 6 January 1950, signed V Pol. Hpt. Wm. Schiller, in PHS D 4.41 Band 24b, Elisabeth Kusian, p. 20. On German nurses' strong reputation among the general public during the Third Reich, an image that would not have changed much in the ensuing few years, see the following: McFarland-Icke, *Nurses in Nazi Germany*, 26; Benedict and Shields, *Nurses and Midwives in Nazi Germany*; Steppe, "Nursing Under Totalitarian Regimes," 10–27; Steppe, "Nursing in the Third Reich"; and Lagerwey, "The Third Reich, Nursing, and AJN."
41 "Schlußbericht," 27 February 1950, signed KK Menzel, in Landesarchiv Berlin, Band II Mordsache Seidelmann/Merten (Tod durch Erdrosseln) B. Rep. 058 Nr. 893, p. 190.
42 "Verhandelt," signed KK Menzel and KK Griebsch, dated 15 February 1950, in Landesarchiv Berlin, Band II Mordsache Seidelmann/Merten (Tod durch Erdrosseln) B. Rep. 058 Nr. 893, p. 132.
43 "Schlußbericht," 27 February 1950, signed KK Menzel, pp. 190–1.
44 "Verhandelt," signed KK Menzel and KK Griebsch, dated 15 February 1950, p. 132. On RIAS, see Galle, *RIAS Berlin und Berliner Rundfunk 1945–1949*.
45 Although its central focus is on classical music, the key work is Anderton, *Rubble Music*. Some of the year's biggest hits can be found on Bear Family Records, "Die Schlager des Jahres 1949," accessed 23 May 2024, https://www.bear-family.com/various-die-schlager-des-jahres-1949-2-cd.html.
46 "Verhandelt," signed Elisabeth Kusian, co-signed KK Menzel, dated 14 February 1950, in Landesarchiv Berlin, Band II Mordsache Seidelmann /Merten (Tod durch Erdrosseln) B. Rep. 058 Nr. 893, p. 127.
47 Weimann and Niedenthal Report to the Untersuchungsrichter II beim Landgericht Berlin, in Landesarchiv Berlin B. Rep. 058 Nr. 889, pp. 5–6. Pervitin was widely used in the Third Reich and, according to Stefan Snelders and Toine Pieters, "maintained its place in everyday life, as a part of everyday life, including health care and the war effort. Historians have documented the use of Pervitin in the Third Reich as part of the Nazi effort to regiment, control and direct the German population." See Snelders and Pieters, "Speed in the Third Reich," 686.
48 "Schlußbericht," 27 February 1950, signed KK Menzel, in Landesarchiv Berlin, Band II Mordsache Seidelmann/Merten (Tod durch Erdrosseln) B. Rep. 058 Nr. 893, p. 191.

49 "Verhandelt," signed Anni Glißmann, countersigned KK Menzel, 7 January 1950, in Landesarchiv Berlin, Band II Mordsache Seidelmann /Merten (Tod durch Erdrosseln) B. Rep. 058 Nr. 893, p. 21.
50 "Schlußbericht," 27 February 1950, signed KK Menzel, p. 191.
51 "Schlußbericht," 27 February 1950, signed KK Menzel, p. 191.
52 Rigden, "The Battle of Berlin, April – May 1945," 158. The classic, book-length account of the battle is Beevor, *Berlin – The Downfall 1945*.
53 Rigden, "The Battle of Berlin, April – May 1945," 171.
54 Rigden, 174–5 and table 6 on 177.
55 The interview that Gerda Drews granted to Elinor Florence, her daughter-in-law, is at Elinor Florence, "The Battle of Berlin: An Eyewitness Account," accessed 23 May 2024, https://www.elinorflorence.com/blog/berlin-battle/.
56 "Verhandelt," signed KK Menzel and KK Griebsch, dated 15 February 1950, in Landesarchiv Berlin, Band II Mordsache Seidelmann/Merten (Tod durch Erdrosseln) B. Rep. 058 Nr. 893, p. 133.
57 "Verhandelt," signed KK Menzel and KK Griebsch, dated 15 February 1950, p. 133.
58 "Verhandelt," signed KK Menzel and KK Griebsch, dated 15 February 1950, p. 133.
59 "Schlußbericht," 27 February 1950, signed KK Menzel, in Landesarchiv Berlin, Band II Mordsache Seidelmann/Merten (Tod durch Erdrosseln) B. Rep. 058 Nr. 893, p. 191.
60 "Schlußbericht," 27 February 1950, signed KK Menzel, p. 191.
61 "Verhandelt," signed KK Menzel and KK Griebsch, dated 15 February 1950, p. 134.
62 "Verhandelt," signed KK Menzel and KK Griebsch, dated 15 February 1950, p. 134.
63 "Schlußbericht," 27 February 1950, signed KK Menzel, p. 192; and "Verhandelt," signed KK Menzel and KK Griebsch, dated 15 February 1950, p. 135.
64 "Schlußbericht," 27 February 1950, signed KK Menzel, p. 192.
65 Of course, the classic work is Freud, *The Uncanny*. More recently, see Royle, *The Uncanny*.

1. Who Was Elisabeth Kusian?

1 "Schlußbericht," 27 February 1950, signed KK Menzel, in Landesarchiv Berlin, Band II Mordsache Seidelmann/Merten (Tod durch Erdrosseln) B. Rep. 058 Nr. 893; "Verhandelt," Elisabeth Kusian presentation in U-Gefängnis, 13 February 1950, signed Elisabeth Kusian, countersigned KK Menzel, in Landesarchiv Berlin, Band II Mordsache Seidelmann/ Merten (Tod durch Erdrosseln) B. Rep. 058 Nr. 893, p. 119. On Thuringian industrialization, see Gerber, Greiling, and Swiniartzki, *Thüringen im*

Industriezeitalter. The introduction discusses how the region avoided an industrial "revolution" in favour of slow but steady industrial growth at the end of the nineteenth and beginning of the twentieth centuries.

2 Müller, "Die Schweinezucht und Schweinehaltung in Thüringen," 34, 48.
3 Gerber, Greiling, and Swiniartzki, "Einleitung," 7, 10.
4 Weimann and Niedenthal Report to the Untersuchungsrichter II beim Landgericht Berlin, in Landesarchiv Berlin B. Rep. 058 Nr. 889, 8 January 1950, p. 17.
5 "Verhandelt," Elisabeth Kusian presentation in U-Gefängnis, 13 February 1950, signed Elisabeth Kusian, countersigned KK Menzel, p. 119.
6 "Verhandelt," Elisabeth Kusian presentation in U-Gefängnis, p. 119.
7 Weimann and Niedenthal Report, p. 18.
8 "Verhandelt," Elisabeth Kusian presentation in U-Gefängnis, p. 119.
9 Weimann and Niedenthal Report, p. 18.
10 Weimann and Niedenthal Report, p. 20.
11 See Hudemann and Wittenbrock, *Stadtentwicklung im deutsch-französisch-luxemburgischen Grenzraum (19. und 20.Jh.)*, 46–7 and 64–5.
12 "Verhandelt," Elisabeth Kusian presentation in U-Gefängnis, p. 119.
13 "Bombastus – ein Name der verpflichtet," accessed 12 June 2025, https://bombastus.de/UEber-uns/. This page provides a brief history of the company.
14 Weimann and Niedenthal Report, p. 21.
15 This information is from Walter Kusian's Party Membership Card, in Bundesarchiv Berlin, BArch R 9361-IX KARTEI/24351506.
16 Weimann and Niedenthal Report, p. 22.
17 Weimann and Niedenthal Report, p. 22.
18 "Verhandelt" signed Kusian, cosigned Menzel, 7 January 1950, in Landesarchiv Berlin, Band II Mordsache Seidelmann/Merten (Tod durch Erdrosseln) B. Rep. 058 Nr. 893, pp. 26–8; and "Verhandelt," Elisabeth Kusian presentation in U-Gefängnis, p. 120.
19 Tobin, "No Time for 'Old Fighters,'" 688.
20 See Kusian's Party Membership Card, in Bundesarchiv Berlin, BArch R 9361-IX KARTEI / 24351506.
21 For Kusian's lack of dues payment and the Nazi Party's payment of his hospital fees for his injuries, see his Party record in Bundesarchiv Berlin, BArch R 9361 – II-606072.
22 Weimann and Niedenthal Report, p. 26.
23 Weimann and Niedenthal Report, p. 26
24 Weimann and Niedenthal Report, p. 26; "Schlußbericht," signed KK Menzel, 27 February 1950, in Landesarchiv Berlin, Band II Mordsache Seidelmann/Merten (Tod durch Erdrosseln) B. Rep. 058 Nr. 893, n.p.
25 "Verhandelt," signed Kusian, co-signed Menzel, 7 January 1950, in Landesarchiv Berlin, Band II Mordsache Seidelmann/Merten

(Tod durch Erdrosseln) B. Rep. 058 Nr. 893, p. 26; and "Verhandelt," Elisabeth Kusian presentation in U-Gefängnis, signed Elisabeth Kusian, countersigned KK Menzel, 13 February 1950, in Landesarchiv Berlin, Band II Mordsache Seidelmann/Merten (Tod durch Erdrosseln) B. Rep. 058 Nr. 893, p. 120.

26 "Verhandelt," Elisabeth Kusian presentation in U-Gefängnis, p. 120.
27 Weimann and Niedenthal Report, p. 30.
28 Weimann and Niedenthal Report, p. 29.
29 "Verhandelt," Elisabeth Kusian presentation in U-Gefängnis, p. 120.
30 Weimann and Niedenthal Report, p. 30.
31 This was Waldemar Weimann's conclusion in his psychiatric evaluation of Elisabeth Kusian. See Weimann and Niedenthal Report, p. 32.
32 "Schlußbericht," signed KK Menzel, 27 February 1950, in Landesarchiv Berlin, Band II Mordsache Seidelmann/Merten (Tod durch Erdrosseln) B. Rep. 058 Nr. 893, n.p.
33 "Verhandelt," Elisabeth Kusian presentation in U-Gefängnis, p. 120.
34 Weimann and Niedenthal Report, pp. 32–3.
35 "Verhandelt," Elisabeth Kusian presentation in U-Gefängnis, p. 123 (parentheses in the original).
36 "Verhandelt," Elisabeth Kusian presentation in U-Gefängnis, p. 121.
37 Moeller, "On the History of Man-Made Destruction," 107. For the memory and cultural meaning of bombing, see Crew, *Bodies and Ruins*.
38 Weimann and Niedenthal Report, pp. 33–4.
39 See Mallmann and Paul, "Omniscient, Omnipotent, Omnipresent?," 166–96; Grashoff, "Outwitting the Gestapo?," 365–86.
40 "Verhandelt," Elisabeth Kusian presentation in U-Gefängnis, p. 121.
41 "Verhandelt," Elisabeth Kusian presentation in U-Gefängnis, p. 121.
42 Interview with Waldemar Weimann, in Landesarchiv Berlin B. Rep. 058 Nr. 889, p. 41.
43 Reckewerth, "*Rein verhungern kannste*," 6, 55.
44 Interview with Waldemar Weimann, p. 42.
45 Verlohren, *Krankenhäuser in Groß-Berlin*, 314.
46 "Vermerk," signed Weisheit and Zimmermann, 10 January 1950, in Landesarchiv Berlin, Band II Mordsache Seidelmann/Merten (Tod durch Erdrosseln) B. Rep. 058. Nr. 893, p. 39.
47 Köln 1872 (n.p.) quoted in Voss, *Geschichte der höheren Mädchenschule*, 57.
48 This is according to Wolfgang Hintze, the chief medical officer on the gynaecology floor. See "Weiterverhandelt," signed Weisheit and Zimmermann, 10 January 1950, in Landesarchiv Berlin, Band II Mordsache Seidelmann/Merten (Tod durch Erdrosseln) B. Rep. 058 Nr. 893, p. 40.
49 This is according to one of her colleagues, Anna Jase. See "Bericht," signed Krim.-Ass. Zimmermann and Krim.-Sek. Skok, 17 January 1950, in

Landesarchiv Berlin, Band II Mordsache Seidelmann/Merten (Tod durch Erdrosseln) B. Rep. 058 Nr. 893, n.p.

50 No title, Gertrud Seifert declared the following to KA Grigo, 20 January 1950, in Landesarchiv Berlin, Band II Mordsache Seidelmann/Merten (Tod durch Erdrosseln) B. Rep. 058 Nr. 893, p. 103.

51 "Verhandelt," Elisabeth Kusian presentation in U-Gefängnis, signed Elisabeth Kusian, countersigned KK Menzel, 13 February 1950, in Landesarchiv Berlin, Band II Mordsache Seidelmann/Merten (Tod durch Erdrosseln) B. Rep. 058 Nr. 893, p. 121.

52 "Verhandelt," Elisabeth Kusian presentation in U-Gefängnis, p. 121 (parentheses in the original).

53 "Verhandelt," Elisabeth Kusian presentation in U-Gefängnis, p. 121. The Robert Koch Hospital was the name given to the Moabit Hospital in the Third Reich. It regained its old name after 1945.

54 "Vermerk," signed KA Weisheit, 8 January 1950, in Landesarchiv Berlin, Band II Mordsache Seidelmann/Merten (Tod durch Erdrosseln) B. Rep. 058 Nr. 893, p. 31; and "Verhandelt," signed KK Menzel, 1 February 1950, in Landesarchiv Berlin, Band II Mordsache Seidelmann/Merten (Tod durch Erdrosseln) B. Rep. 058 Nr. 893, p. 122.

55 "Verhandelt," signed KK Menzel, 1 February 1950, p. 122.

56 "Verhandelt," Elisabeth Kusian presentation in U-Gefängnis, p. 122.

57 "Verhandelt," interview with Hans Boguslawski, unsigned, 7 February 1950, in Landesarchiv Berlin, Band II Mordsache Seidelmann/Merten (Tod durch Erdrosseln) B. Rep. 058 Nr. 893, p. 110.

58 "Verhandelt," 10 January 1950, in Landesarchiv Berlin, Band II Mordsache Seidelmann/Merten (Tod durch Erdrosseln) B. Rep. 058 Nr. 893, p. 45 [the rest is missing, if there indeed was more; no signature, but this is a statement by Elise Nee.].

59 "Verhandelt," interview with Hans Boguslawski, 7 February 1950, p. 110; and "Bericht," signed Reichmuth and Sonntag, "Vermerk," signed KA Sonntag, 11 January 1950, in Landesarchiv Berlin, Band II Mordsache Seidelmann/Merten (Tod durch Erdrosseln) B. Rep. 058 Nr. 893, p. 52.

60 "Verhandelt," interview with Hans Boguslawski, 7 February 1950, p. 110.

61 "Verhandelt," interview with Hans Boguslawski, 7 February 1950, p. 110.

62 "Bericht" signed Reichmuth and Sonntag, "Vermerk," signed KA Sonntag, 11 January 1950, p. 52; and "Verhandelt,' signed Elisabeth Kusian, co-signed KK Menzel, 13 February 1950, in Landesarchiv Berlin, Band II Mordsache Seidelmann/Merten (Tod durch Erdrosseln) B. Rep. 058 Nr. 893, p. 123.

63 "Bericht," signed Reichmuth and Sonntag, "Vermerk," signed KA Sonntag, 11 January 1950, p. 52.

64 "Verhandelt," interview with Hans Boguslawski, 7 February 1950, p. 110.

65 "Verhandelt," signed Elisabeth Kusian, co-signed KK Menzel, 13 February 1950, in Landesarchiv Berlin, Band II Mordsache Seidelmann/ Merten (Tod durch Erdrosseln) B. Rep. 058 Nr. 893, p. 123.
66 "Verhandelt;" signed Johanna Dei., countersigned K.-Ass. Zimmermann and K.-Ass. Weisheit, 10 January 1950, in Landesarchiv Berlin, Band II Mordsache Seidelmann/Merten (Tod durch Erdrosseln) B. Rep. 058 Nr. 893, p. 44.
67 "Schlußbericht," signed KK Menzel, 27 February 1950, in Landesarchiv Berlin, Band II Mordsache Seidelmann/Merten (Tod durch Erdrosseln) B. Rep. 058 Nr. 893, p. 197.
68 "Verhandelt," signed Johanna Dei., countersigned K.-Ass. Zimmermann and K.-Ass. Weisheit, 10 January 1950, p. 44.
69 "Verhandelt," signed Elisabeth Kusian, co-signed KK Menzel, 13 February 1950, p. 124.
70 "Verhandelt," signed Marja Sobe., countersigned Krim.-Ass. Zimmermann, 9 January 1950, in Landesarchiv Berlin, Band II Mordsache Seidelmann/Merten (Tod durch Erdrosseln) B. Rep. 058 Nr. 893, p. 34.
71 "Verhandelt," signed Elisabeth Kusian, co-signed KK Menzel, 13 February 1950, p. 123.
72 "Verhandelt," signed Anni Glißmann, countersigned KK Menzel, 7 January 1950, in Landesarchiv Berlin, Band II Mordsache Seidelmann/ Merten (Tod durch Erdrosseln) B. Rep. 058 Nr. 893, p. 19.
73 "Verhandelt," signed Hedwig Schrö., countersigned KK Menzel, 20 January 1950, in Landesarchiv Berlin, Band II Mordsache Seidelmann/ Merten (Tod durch Erdrosseln) B. Rep. 058 Nr. 893, p. 98.
74 Interview with Walter Kusian conducted by KK Menzel, 13 January 1950, in Landesarchiv Berlin, Band II Mordsache Seidelmann/Merten (Tod durch Erdrosseln) B. Rep. 058 Nr. 893, p. 67.
75 "Verhandelt," signed Elisabeth Kusian, co-signed KK Menzel, 13 February 1950, p. 123.
76 "Durchsuchingsbericht," signed KK Menzel, 10 January 1950, in Landesarchiv Berlin, Band II Mordsache Seidelmann/Merten (Tod durch Erdrosseln) B. Rep. 058 Nr. 893, p. 47.
77 Interview with Walter Kusian conducted by KK Menzel, 13 January 1950, p. 67.
78 Timpe, *Nazi Organized Recreation and Entertainment in the Third Reich*, 39–40.
79 Timpe, *Nazi Organized Recreation and Entertainment in the Third Reich.*
80 There are many important works on the Wannsee Conference. Recent among them are Roseman, *The Wannsee Conference and the Final Solution*; Jasch and Kreutzmüller, *The Participants*.
81 "Verhandelt," signed Marja Sobe., countersigned Krim.-Ass. Zimmermann, 9 January 1950, p. 34.

82 Interview with Walter Kusian conducted by KK Menzel, 13 January 1950, p. 67.
83 "Verhandelt," signed Anni Glißmann, countersigned KK Menzel, 7 January 1950, in Landesarchiv Berlin, Band II Mordsache Seidelmann/Merten (Tod durch Erdrosseln) B. Rep. 058 Nr. 893, pp. 19–21.
84 "Verhandelt," signed Marja Sobe., countersigned Krim.-Ass. Zimmermann, 9 January 1950, p. 34.
85 "Verhandelt," signed Elisabeth Kusian, co-signed KK Menzel, 13 February 1950, p. 123.
86 "Verhandelt," signed Marja Sobe., countersigned Krim.-Ass. Zimmermann, 9 January 1950, p. 34.
87 "Verhandelt," signed Gertrud Seidelmann, countersigned KK Menzel, in Landesarchiv Berlin, B. Rep. 058 Nr. 893, p. 37; and "Verhandelt," signed Friedrich Beigang, countersigned VP Hwm Schiller, 5 January 1950, in PHS D 4.41, Band 24b, Elisabeth Kusian, p. 16.
88 "Verhandelt," signed Anni Glißmann, countersigned KK Menzel, 7 January 1950, p. 29.
89 "Verhandelt," signed Hedwig Schrö., countersigned KK Menzel, 20 January 1950, in Landesarchiv Berlin, Band II Mordsache Seidelmann/Merten (Tod durch Erdrosseln) B. Rep. 058 Nr. 893, p. 98; "Verhandelt," signed Elisabeth Kusian, co-signed KK Menzel, 13 February 1950, p. 125; "Verhandelt," signed Anni Glißmann, countersigned KK Menzel, 7 January 1950, p. 19; "Verhandelt," signed Marja Sobe., countersigned Krim.-Ass. Zimmermann, 9 January 1950, p. 34.
90 On con artists, see Frankel, *The Ponzi Scheme Puzzle*. Although Frankel concentrates on one sort of crime, she analyses how successful con artists are able to divert their victims' attention away from the obviously false parts of their activities and towards that which seems to be more likely.
91 "Vermerk," signed Weisheit and Zimmermann, dated 10 January 1950, in Landesarchiv Berlin, Band II Mordsache Seidelmann/Merten (Tod durch Erdrosseln) B. Rep. 058 Nr. 893, p. 39; "Verhandelt," interview with Hans Boguslawski, unsigned, 7 February 1950, in Landesarchiv Berlin, Band II Mordsache Seidelmann/Merten (Tod durch Erdrosseln) B. Rep. 058 Nr. 893, p. 110.
92 For a brief introduction to the history of Tegel Prison, see Slow Travel Berlin, "Tegel Prison: A History," accessed 18 June 2024, https://www.slowtravelberlin.com/tegel-prison-a-history/.
93 "Verhandelt," signed Lucie Muschan, co-signed Kriminalrat Schwarz and KK Griebsch, 12 January 1950, in Landesarchiv Berlin, Band II Mordsache Seidelmann/Merten (Tod durch Erdrosseln) B. Rep. 058 Nr. 893, p. 62.
94 "Verhandelt," signed Kurt Muschan, 10 January 1950, in Landesarchiv Berlin, Band II Mordsache Seidelmann/Merten (Tod durch Erdrosseln) B. Rep. 058 Nr. 893, p. 49.

95 "Bericht," 10 January 1950, signed Straßeng [*sic*?], in Landesarchiv Berlin, Band II Mordsache Seidelmann/Merten (Tod durch Erdrosseln) B. Rep. 058 Nr. 893, n.p. [probably p. 48].
96 "Verhandelt," signed Anni Glißmann, countersigned KK Menzel, 7 January 1950, p. 19.
97 "Verhandelt," signed Griebsch and Menzel, 17 February 1950, in Landesarchiv Berlin, Band II Mordsache Seidelmann/Merten (Tod durch Erdrosseln) B. Rep. 058 Nr. 893, p. 147.
98 "Verhandelt," signed KK Menzel and KK Griebsch, 15 February 1950, in Landesarchiv Berlin, Band II Mordsache Seidelmann/Merten (Tod durch Erdrosseln) B. Rep. 058 Nr. 893, p. 137.

2. The Seidelmann Case

1 For the story of their meeting and affair, see "Verhandelt," signed Kurt Muschan, 10 January 1950, in Landesarchiv Berlin, Band II Mordsache Seidelmann/Merten (Tod durch Erdrosseln) B. Rep. 058 Nr. 893.
2 "80-Mile Winds Lash Germany, Killing 10," *New York Times*, 5 December 1949; "Nordweststurm wütete über Berlin: Fünf Tote, vierzehn schwerverletzte durch Ruineneinstürze," *Berliner Zeitung*, 6 December 1949.
3 "Verhandelt," signed Hedwig Schrö., countersigned KK Menzel, 20 January 1950, in Landesarchiv Berlin, Band II Mordsache Seidelmann/Merten (Tod durch Erdrosseln) B. Rep. 058 Nr. 893, p. 98.
4 "Verhandelt," signed Anni Glißmann, countersigned KK Menzel, 7 January 1950, in Landesarchiv Berlin, Band II Mordsache Seidelmann/Merten (Tod durch Erdrosseln) B. Rep. 058 Nr. 893, p. 21.
5 "Verhandelt," signed Anni Glißmann, countersigned KK Menzel, 7 January 1950, pp. 19–21.
6 "Verhandelt," signed Anni Glißmann, countersigned KA Sonntag, 8 January 1950, in Landesarchiv Berlin, Band II Mordsache Seidelmann/Merten (Tod durch Erdrosseln) B. Rep. 058 Nr. 893, p. 30.
7 See untitled report, dated Berlin, 5 December 1949, signed Schwarz, in Landesarchiv Berlin, B. Rep. 058 Nr. 894, p. 5; "Eilt sehr! Leichensache!," addressed to Herrn Generalstaatsanwalt beim Landgericht Berlin, signed Pol. -Kommandeur Rockstroh, 5 December 1949, in Landesarchiv Berlin, Band a I gegen unbek. Mänl. Leiche, B. Rep. 058 Nr. 895, p. 1.
8 Anne O'Hare McCormick, "Thoughts on Visiting Hitler's Chancellery," *New York Times*, 21 March 1948.
9 Diefendorf, *In the Wake of War*, 15.
10 Hauptamt für Statistik und Wahlen, *Berlin in Zahlen, 1950*, p. 109.
11 Koerner, "Kinderalltag Ende der vierziger Jahre."
12 This original report does not contain the building address, but subsequent documents do. For example, "Vorläufiger Schlußbericht,"

12 December 1949, in Landesarchiv Berlin, B. Rep. 058 Nr. 894, p. 29. Waldemar Weimann added the detail about the ball in his memoir, Weimann, *Diagnose Mord*, 7.

13 See untitled report, dated Berlin, 5 December 1949, signed Schwarz, p. 5.

14 See untitled report, dated Berlin, 5 December 1949, signed Klein, in Landesarchiv Berlin, B. Rep. 058 Nr. 894, p. 13.

15 See "Bild 2: Aufnahme der Fundstelle vom Eingang der Ruine" and "Bild 3: Nahaufnahme der Leichenteile," in PHS D 4.41 Band 24e.

16 "In unmittelbarer Nähe der Fundstelle der Leichenteile befinden sich zahlreiche Ablagerungen von menschlichem Kot, teils neurer, teils älterer Herkunft, woraus hervorgeht, daß diese Ruine des öfterer Herkunft woraus hervorgeht, daß diese Ruine des öfteren von Personen zur Verrichtung ihrer Notdurft aufgesucht wird." See untitled report, dated Berlin, 5 December 1949, signed Schwarz, p. 5.

17 See untitled report, dated Berlin, 5 December 1949, signed Schwarz, p. 5; "An den Herrn Generalstaatsanwalt beim Landgericht Berlin," signed Kommandeur Rockstroh, 5 December 1949, in Landesarchiv Berlin, B. Rep. 058 Nr. 894, p. 4.

18 "Die Mordkommission hat die Ermittlungen aufgenommen und das Ergebnis wird nach Abschluß der Bearbeitung nachgereicht. Eilt sehr! Leichensache!" An den Herrn Generalstaatsanwalt beim Landgericht Berlin, signed Kommandeur Rockstroh, 5 December 1949, p. 4.

19 For example, see Horz and Marbach, "Economic Opportunities, Emigration Opportunities, Emigration and Exit Prisoners."

20 Geserick, Vendura, and Wirth, "University Institute of Legal Medicine in Berlin Celebrates Its 175th Anniversary."

21 Geserick, Vendura, and Wirth, *Zeitzeuge Tod*, 8; Landesinstitut für gerichtliche und soziale Medizin Berlin, "Geschichte des Landesinstitutes für gerichtliche und soziale Medizin Berlin," accessed 29 May 2024, www.berlin.de/germed/ueber-uns/geschichte/.

22 Geserick, Strauch, and Wirth, "120 Jahre Leichenschauhaus in Berlin-Mitte." See also Geserick, Vendura, and Wirth, "University Institute of Legal Medicine in Berlin Celebrates Its 175th Anniversary," 262–6.

23 Sabine Fisch, interview, "Man muss die Toten mögen," accessed 5 June 2024, https://www.sabinefisch.at/2009/04/man-muss-die-toten-mogen/.

24 Geserick, Vendura, and Wirth, "University Institute of Legal Medicine in Berlin Celebrates Its 175th Anniversary," 262.

25 Weimann's career began in 1924 when he acted as a Privatassistent at the gerichtsmedizinischen Institut der Charité, under the wing of Prof. Dr. Fritz Strassman. When Strassman and Curt Strauch retired due to age and illness in 1930 and 1931, respectively, Weimann took over the Gerichtsarztstelle, and his career continued unabated during the Third

Reich, a period about which both his biographers and his memoirs are quiet. Wirth, Strauch, and Radam, *Das Berliner Leichenschauhaus*, 33, 54.

26 Weimann, *Diagnose Mord*, 13. Much of the rest of the following section comes from Weimann's memoirs.

27 Weimann, *Diagnose Mord*, 12. "Zu Fuß braucht man etwa zehn Minuten vom Leichenschauhaus bis zum Untersuchungsgefängnis Alt-Moabit. Hier seziere ich die Körper von Toten, dort die Seelen von Tätern – oft geht es um den gleichen Fall."

28 For his Buddhas and goddesses, see Weimann, *Diagnose Mord*, 14. On Freud's collection, see Schorske, "Freud's Egyptian Dig." See also Ucko, "Unprovenanced Material Culture and Freud's Collection of Antiquities."

29 Weimann, *Diagnose Mord*, 7.

30 "Spitzenmeldung," dated Berlin, 5 December 1949, signed Schwarz, in Landesarchiv Berlin, B. Rep. 058 Nr. 894, p. 11.

31 "Bericht," dated Berlin, 6 December 1949, signed Lippert, in Landesarchiv Berlin, B. Rep. 058 Nr. 894, p. 14.

32 See "Vermerk," dated Berlin, 6 December 1949, signed Schwarz, in Landesarchiv Berlin, B. Rep. 058 Nr. 894, p. 15.

33 See "Bericht," dated Berlin, 6 December 1949, signed Hasche, in Landesarchiv Berlin, B. Rep. 058 Nr. 894, p. 16.

34 See "Bericht," dated Berlin, 7 December 1949, signed Schwarz, in Landesarchiv Berlin, B. Rep. 058 Nr. 894, p. 18. The next time Klaus appears in the records his name has changed from Sei. to Wes., but he is reported as living with the Sei. family. See "Bericht," dated Berlin, 8 December 1949, signed Lippert, in Landesarchiv Berlin, B. Rep. 058 Nr. 894, p. 22.

35 See "Bericht," dated Berlin, 7 December 1949, signed Schwarz, pp. 18–19. "Der Kopf wurde nicht vorgefunden und da in der Nähe der Fundstelle dauernd der Trümmerschutt einstürzt, wurden diese Schuttmassen beiseitegeräumt, weil angenommen warden mußte, daß der Kopf inzwischen heruntergefallen und verschüttet worden war. Trotz eingehender Suche wurde der Kopf nicht gefunden."

36 See "Bericht," dated Berlin, 7 December 7, 1949, signed Schwarz, p. 19.

37 Table, "Anzeigen bei der Kriminalpolizei," in Hauptamt für Statistik und Wahlen, *Berlin in Zahlen 1950*, 242.

38 See "Vermerk," dated Berlin, 7 December 1949, signed Blume, in Landesarchiv Berlin, B. Rep. 058 Nr. 894, p. 12.

39 Schmale, *Chausseestrasse*, 148–9.

40 See "Vermerk," dated Berlin, 7 December 1949, signed Blume, p. 15.

41 See Ernst Seidelmann's statement, dated Berlin, 7 December 1949, signed by him and Kriminal-Sekretär Blüme, who took it down, in Landesarchiv Berlin, B. Rep. 058 Nr. 894, p. 18.

42 See "Vermerk," dated Berlin, 7 December 1949, signed Blume, p. 12.

43 See "Bericht," signed Pol.-Wm. Lippert, 8 December 1949, in Landesarchiv Berlin, B. Rep. 058 Nr. 894, pp. 22–3.
44 See "Bericht," signed Pol.-Wm. Lippert, pp. 22–3.
45 Pol.-Rat (K) Schwarz, "Vorläufiger Schlußbericht," 12 December 1949, in Landesarchiv Berlin, B. Rep. 058 Nr. 894, p. 29.
46 See "Bericht," signed Pol.-Wm. Lippert, p. 23.
47 "Bericht" (Report), signed Pol.-Wm Lippert, 8 December 1949, in Landesarchiv Berlin, B. Rep. 058 Nr. 894, p. 23.
48 Ruble, "Creating Postfascist Families," 416.
49 Ruble, "Creating Postfascist Families," 426.
50 Moeller, "The 'Remasculinization' of Germany in the 1950s," 103. A number of other important works study the question of a return to tradition. See Moeller's expanded treatment in *Protecting Motherhood*. See also Carter, *How German Is She?*, and Heineman, *What Difference Does a Husband Make?*
51 Moeller, *Protecting Motherhood*, is an excellent introduction to questions of gender norms at this moment. Also of great value is Evans, *Life among the Ruins*.
52 "Bericht," signed Pol.-Wm Lippert, 9 December 1949, in Landesarchiv Berlin, B. Rep. 058 Nr. 894, p. 24.
53 "Verhandelt," signed Albert Granzow, countersigned Schwarz, 6 December 1949, in Landesarchiv Berlin, B. Rep. 058 Nr. 894, pp. 21–2.
54 This comes from a description of Wilmersdorfer Straße, less than 15 minutes away on foot, in Suwala et al., "Der Zentrumbereichskern Wilmersdorfer Straße in Berlin-Charlottenburg," 222.
55 On Knie and what would come later, see Bodenschatz, "Städtebau und Architektur des Ernst-Reuter-Platzes."
56 See "Verhandelt: Gehört wird der Polizei-Wachtmeister Klemm…," signed KS Meiser, 9 December 1949, in Berlin Landesarchiv, B. Rep. 058 Nr. 896, p. 3. The same document is in Landesarchiv Berlin, B. Rep. 058 Nr. 897, p. 2.
57 "Buntmetalldiebstähle müssen verhindert werden," *Berliner Zeitung*, 8 December 1949.
58 See "Verhandelt: Gehört wird der Polizei-Wachtmeister Klemm…," signed, KS Meiser, 9 December 1949, p. 3.
59 The description of the building is from "Schlußbericht," signed Kriminalkommisar Menzel, 27 February 1950, in PHS D 4.41, Band 24a, n.p.
60 "Bericht," signed KS Meiser, 9 December 1949, in Landesarchiv Berlin, B. Rep. 058 Nr. 897, p. 1.
61 "Bericht," signed KS Meiser, 9 December 1949, p. 1.
62 "Schlußbericht," 27 February 1950, signed KK Menzel, in Landesarchiv Berlin, Band II Mordsache Seidelmann/Merten (Tod durch Erdrosseln) B. Rep. 058 Nr. 893, p. 184.

63 Weimann, *Diagnose Mord*, 6.
64 Pross and Winau, *Nicht misshandeln: Das Krankenhaus Moabit.*
65 Weimann, *Diagnose Mord*, 6.
66 Weimann, 7.
67 Weimann, 7.
68 Fenemore, *Dismembered Policing in Postwar Berlin*, especially 40–4, 107–34.
69 Schießer interview in Hinckeldey-Stiftung, *Berliner Polizei von 1945 bis zur Gegenwart*, location 714.
70 Weimann, *Diagnose Mord*, 8.
71 Pol.-Rat Schwarz, one of the East Berlin detectives on the case, independently came to the same conclusion by 12 December at the latest and thus believed that the case would ultimately fall under West Berlin jurisdiction. For Schwarz's report, see "Vorläufiger Schlußbericht," signed Pol.-Rat Schwarz, 12 December 1949, in Landesarchiv Berlin, B. Rep. 058 Nr. 894, p. 29.
72 "Bericht," signed Pol.-Hwm. Schwalbe and Pol.-Wm. Lippert, 10 December 1949, in Landesarchiv Berlin B. Rep. 058 Nr. 894, p. 25.
73 "Unbekannter männl. Rumpftorso," signed Dr. Weimann, Dr. Springer Lehman, and Dr. Bühling, 10 December 1949, in Landesarchiv Berlin, B. Rep. 058 Nr. 896, pp. 6–7.
74 "Verhandelt," unsigned (partial document, only), 11 December 1949, in Landesarchiv Berlin, B. Rep. 058 Nr. 894, p. 26; "Leichensache! An den Herrn Generalstaatsanwalt bei dem Landgericht," Berlin, 12 December 1949, signed KK Menzel, in Landesarchiv Berlin, B. Rep. 58 Nr. 897, p. 3.
75 "Leichenteile in der Schillerstraße," *Telegraf am Abend*, 10 December 1949, in Landesarchiv Berlin, B. Rep. 058 Nr. 897, p. 29; "Männerrumpf in Kellerruine," *Der Abend*, 10 December 1949, in Landesarchiv Berlin, B. Rep. 058 Nr. 897, p. 30; "Männlicher Torso identifiziert," *Der Tag*, 11 December 1949, in Landesarchiv Berlin, B. Rep. 058 Nr. 897, p. 31.
76 "Vorläufiger Schlußbericht," signed Pol.-Rat Schwarz, 12 December 1949, p. 29.
77 Pol.-Rat (K) Schwarz, Untitled Report, 14 December 1949, in Landesarchiv Berlin, B. Rep. 058 Nr. 894, pp. 34–5.
78 "Bericht," signed Pol.-Rat Schwarz, 15 December 1949, in Landesarchiv Berlin, B. Rep. 58 Nr. 894, p. 40.
79 Pol.-Rat (K) Schwarz, Untitled Report, 14 December 1949, pp. 34–5.
80 Pol.-Rat (K) Schwarz, "Letter to the Generalstatsanwalt," 14 December 1949, in Landesarchiv Berlin, B. Rep. 058 Nr. 894, p. 38. It is important to note that he did seem to believe that the murderer was a man; at the very least, he used the male version of perpetrator (Täter) in his note, rather than opening up the possibility that the killer was a woman.

81 Pol.-Rat (K) Schwarz, "An die Pressestelle im Haus," 14 December 1949, in Landesarchiv Berlin, B. Rep. 058 Nr. 894, p. 39.

82 "zur Klärung eines Sachverhaltes." For the building's history, see the one page document, produced by the Senatsverwaltung für Bildung, Jugend und Familie, "Geschichte des Gebäudes Bernard Weiss Str 6," accessed 27 October 2021, www.berlin.de/sen/bjf/ueber-uns/historisches/geschichte_des_gebaeudes_bernhard_weiss_str_6.pdf.

83 This is also the word the Gestapo used to designate confidential agents. Hall, "An Army of Spies? The Gestapo Spy Network 1933–45," 248.

84 "Verhandelt," signed Anni Glißmann, countersigned KK Menzel, 7 January 1950, in Landesarchiv Berlin, Band II Mordsache Seidelmann/Merten (Tod durch Erdrosseln) B. Rep. 058 Nr. 893, p. 21.

85 "Schlußbericht," signed KK Menzel, 27 February 1950, in Landesarchiv Berlin, Band II Mordsache Seidelmann/Merten (Tod durch Erdrosseln) B. Rep. 058 Nr. 893, p. 192 (from the confession that Menzel stitched together from many interviews with Elisabeth Kusian); "Weiterverhandelt," signed Friedrich Beigang, countersigned KK Menzel, 16 January 1950, in Landesarchiv Berlin, Band II Mordsache Seidelmann/Merten (Tod durch Erdrosseln) B. Rep. 058 Nr. 893 [page number missing, probably p. 81].

86 "Verhandelt," signed Hedwig Ulbricht, countersigned KK Menzel, 11 January 1950, in Landesarchiv Berlin, Band II Mordsache Seidelmann/Merten (Tod durch Erdrosseln) B. Rep. 058 Nr. 893, p. 53.

87 "Schlußbericht," signed KK Menzel, 27 February 1950, p. 185.

88 Welch, "Nazi Propaganda and the *Volksgemeinschaft*."

89 Weikart, "The Role of Darwinism in Nazi Racial Thought."

90 Connelly, "Nazis and Slavs," 12.

91 Brackman, *Krisis und Aufbau in Osteuropa*, 1, quoted in (and translated by) Connelly, "Nazis and Slavs," 13.

92 Fenemore, *Dismembered Policing in Postwar Berlin*, 54.

93 "Schlußbericht," signed KK Menzel, 27 February 1950, in PHS D 4.41 Band 24a, n.p.

94 "Bericht," signed Pol.-Rat Schwarz, 17 December 1949, in Landesarchiv Berlin, B. Rep. 058 Nr. 894, p. 43.

95 "Schlußbericht," signed KK Menzel, 27 February 1950, n.p.

96 Gellately, *The Gestapo and German Society*.

97 "Schlußbericht," signed KK Menzel, 27 February 1950, n.p.

98 "Schlußbericht," signed KK Menzel, 27 February 1950, in Landesarchiv Berlin, Band II Mordsache Seidelmann/Merten (Tod durch Erdrosseln) B. Rep. 058 Nr. 893, p. 185.

99 "Bericht," signed Pol.-Obwm. Syllwasschy, 21 December 1949, in Landesarchiv Berlin, B. Rep. 058 Nr. 894, p. 49.

100 "Bericht," signed Pol.-Obwm. Syllwasschy, 21 December 1949, p. 49.

101 "Bericht," signed Pol.-Obwm. Syllwasschy, 21 December 1949, p. 49.

102 "Ermittlungen über die Aurich hatten ergeben, daß sie mit einer unbestimmten Anzahl von Männern verkehrt." "Schlußbericht," signed KK Menzel, 27 February 1950, in PHS D 4.41 Band 24a, n.p.

103 "Schlußbericht," signed KK Menzel, 27 February 1950, n.p.

104 "Schlußbericht," signed KK Menzel, 27 February 1950, n.p.

105 Loy, "Werbeflächen in Berlin: 2500 Berliner Litfaßsäulen werden abgebaut."

106 See Pol.-Rat Schwarz, Abteilung K Dezernat N2, SSB-Fernschreiben an LBdVP Brandenburg, 19 December 1949, in Landesarchiv Berlin, B. Rep. 058 Nr. 894, pp. 46–7.

107 "Verhandelt," signed Kusian, co-signed Menzel, 7 January 1950, in Landesarchiv Berlin, Band II Mordsache Seidelmann/Merten (Tod durch Erdrosseln) B. Rep. 058 Nr. 893, p. 27.

108 "Vermerk," signed KA Sonntag, 10 January 1950, in Landesarchiv Berlin, Band II Mordsache Seidelmann/Merten (Tod durch Erdrosseln) B. Rep. 058 Nr. 893, p. 50.

109 "Bericht," signed VP Komm Steffen, 9 January 1950, in PHS D 4.41 Band 24b, Band III, Kripo Ostsektor, Mordsache Seidelmann (Tod durch Erdrosseln), p. 53.

110 "Bericht," signed Reichmuth and Sonntag, "Vermerk," signed KA Sonntag, 11 January 1950, in Landesarchiv Berlin, Band II Mordsache Seidelmann/Merten (Tod durch Erdrosseln) B. Rep. 058 Nr. 893, p. 53.

111 "Verhandelt," signed Hedwig U., countersigned KK Menzel, 11 January 1950, in Landesarchiv Berlin, Band II Mordsache Seidelmann/Merten (Tod durch Erdrosseln) B. Rep. 058 Nr. 893, p. 53.

112 "Verhandelt," signed Hedwig U., countersigned KK Menzel, 11 January 1950, p. 53.

113 "Verhandelt," signed Kurt Muschan, 10 January 1950, in Landesarchiv Berlin, Band II Mordsache Seidelmann/Merten (Tod durch Erdrosseln) B. Rep. 058 Nr. 893, p. 49. Although Muschan told West Berlin detectives that the visit occurred on Christmas Eve, that date must be an error as it does not fit with Glißmann's and Hedwig U.'s testimony about the silverware and Kusian's other activities.

114 "Verhandelt," signed Hedwig U., countersigned KK Menzel, 11 January 1950, p. 53.

115 "Verhandelt" signed Anni Glißmann, countersigned KK Menzel, 7 January 1950, in Landesarchiv Berlin, Band II Mordsache Seidelmann/Merten (Tod durch Erdrosseln) B. Rep. 058 Nr. 893, pp. 30–1.

116 "Verhandelt," signed Hedwig U., countersigned KK Menzel. 11 January 1950, p. 53.

117 "Vermerk," signed Krim.-Ass. Zimmermann, 9 January 1950, in Landesarchiv Berlin, Band II Mordsache Seidelmann/Merten (Tod durch Erdrosseln) B. Rep. 058 Nr. 893, p. 37.

118 "Vermerk" signed Krim.-Ass. Zimmermann, 9 January 1950, p. 37.
119 "Verhandelt," signed Anni Glißmann, countersigned KK Menzel, 7 January 1950, pp. 19–21.
120 For a brief history of the Erika, see Museums Victoria, "Item ST 29671: Typewriter – Seidel & Naumann, Erika Model 3, Portable, 1923–1925," accessed 16 June 2024, https://collections.museumsvictoria.com.au/items/396303#. On their value, cultural and otherwise, in the East Bloc, see Bugan's memoir, *Burying the Typewriter*.
121 "Vorführungsbericht," signed VP Rat K Pohl, 7 January 1950, in PHS D 4.41 Band 24b, Band III, Kripo Ostsektor, Mordsache Seidelmann (Tod durch Erdrosseln), p. 36; "Weiterverhandelt," signed Friedrich Beigang, countersigned KK Menzel, 16 January 1950, in Landesarchiv Berlin, Band II Mordsache Seidelmann/Merten (Tod durch Erdrosseln) B. Rep. 058 Nr. 893, p. 81 [?]; "Schlußbericht," signed KK Menzel, 27 February 1950, in Landesarchiv Berlin, Band II Mordsache Seidelmann/Merten (Tod durch Erdrosseln) B. Rep. 058 Nr. 893, p. 193; "Verhandelt," signed Friedrich Beigang, countersigned VP Hwm Schiller, 5 January 1950, in PHS D 4.41 Band 24b, Elisabeth Kusian, p. 16; "Verhandelt," signed Charlotte Strach, countersigned VP Polizeirat Pohl, 5 January 1950, in PHS D 4.41 Band 24b, Elisabeth Kusian, p. 17; and "Nachtrag," signed Charlotte Strach, countersigned VP Polizeirat Pohl, 5 January 1950, in PHS D 4.41 Band 24b, Elisabeth Kusian, p. 18.
122 "Bericht," signed KA Reichmuth and KA Sonntag, 17 January 1950, in Landesarchiv Berlin, Band II Mordsache Seidelmann/Merten (Tod durch Erdrosseln) B. Rep. 058 Nr. 893, p. 89.
123 "Bericht," signed KA Reichmuth and KA Sonntag, 17 January 1950, p. 89.
124 "Verhandelt," signed Kusian, co-signed Menzel, 7 January 1950, in Landesarchiv Berlin, Band II Mordsache Seidelmann/Merten (Tod durch Erdrosseln) B. Rep. 058 Nr. 893, p. 27.
125 "Verhandelt," signed Walter Kusian, co-signed Menzel, 7 January 1950, p. 27; Interview with Walter Kusian conducted by KK Menzel, 13 January 1950, in Landesarchiv Berlin, Band II Mordsache Seidelmann/Merten (Tod durch Erdrosseln) B. Rep. 058 Nr. 893, p. 67.
126 "Verhandelt," signed Walter Kusian, co-signed Menzel, 7 January 1950, p. 27.
127 "Bericht," signed KA Reichmuth and KA Sonntag, 17 January 1950, p. 89.
128 "Verhandelt," signed Charlotte Strach, countersigned VP Polizeirat Pohl, 5 January 1950, in PHS D 4.41 Band 24b, Elisabeth Kusian, p. 17; "Weiterverhandelt," signed Friedrich Beigang, countersigned KK Menzel, 16 January 1950, in Landesarchiv Berlin, Band II Mordsache Seidelmann/Merten (Tod durch Erdrosseln) B. Rep. 058. Nr. 893, unnumbered page [probably p. 81]; "Verhandelt," signed Lucie Muschan, co-signed Kriminalrat Schwarz and KK Griebsch, 12 January 1950, in Landesarchiv Berlin, Band II Mordsache Seidelmann/Merten (Tod durch Erdrosseln) B. Rep. 058 Nr. 893, p. 63.

129 "Verhandelt," signed Ingeborg Hei., countersigned Weisheit, 16 January 1950, in Landesarchiv Berlin, Band II Mordsache Seidelmann/Merten (Tod durch Erdrosseln) B. Rep. 058 Nr. 893, p. 83; "Verhandelt," signed Coelestin He., 16 January 1950, in Landesarchiv Berlin, Band II Mordsache Seidelmann/Merten (Tod durch Erdrosseln) B. Rep. 058 Nr. 893, p. 87.

130 Interview with Walter Kusian conducted by KK Menzel, 13 January 1950, p. 67.

131 "Bericht," signed KA Reichmuth and KA Sonntag, 17 January 1950, p. 89.

3. The Murder of Doris Merten

1 See the anonymously written short articles collected under the heading "Blick auf Berlin," *Neue Zeit*, 28 December 1949.

2 For the weather, see "26.12.1949 – Historisches Wetter," *chroniknet*, accessed 18 May 2021, https://web.archive.org/web/20210518214227/https://chroniknet.de/extra/historisches-wetter/?wetter-datum=26.12.1949.

3 "Verhandelt," signed Charlotte Strach, countersigned VP Polizeirat Pohl, 5 January 1950, in PHS D 4.41 Band 24b, Elisabeth Kusian, p. 17.

4 "Bericht," signed KA Reichmuth and KA Sonntag, 17 January 1950, in Landesarchiv Berlin, Band II Mordsache Seidelmann/Merten (Tod durch Erdrosseln) B. Rep. 058 Nr. 893, p. 90.

5 "Schlußbericht," signed KK Menzel, 27 February 1950, in Landesarchiv Berlin, Band II Mordsache Seidelmann/Merten (Tod durch Erdrosseln) B. Rep. 058 Nr. 893, p. 193.

6 "Verhandelt," signed Paul Glaubitz, countersigned VP Kommandeur Rockstroh, 5 January 1950, in PHS D 4.41 Band 24b, pp. 19–20.

7 "Verhandelt," signed Charlotte Glaubitz, co-signed KA Sonntag, 8 January 1950, in Landesarchiv Berlin, Band II Mordsache Seidelmann/Merten (Tod durch Erdrosseln) B. Rep. 058 Nr. 893, pp. 29–30; "Vorführungsbericht," signed VP Polizeirat Pohl, 7 January 1950, in PHS D 4.41 Band 24b, Band III, Kripo Ostsektor, Mordsache Seidelmann (Tod durch Erdrosseln), p. 36.

8 "Verhandelt," signed Charlotte Glaubitz, co-signed KA Sonntag, 8 January 1950, pp. 29–30.

9 "Verhandelt," signed Lucie Muschan, co-signed Kriminalrat Schwarz and KK Griebsch, 12 January 1950, in Landesarchiv Berlin, Band II Mordsache Seidelmann/Merten (Tod durch Erdrosseln) B. Rep. 058 Nr. 893, p. 62.

10 "Verhandelt," signed Walter Kusian, co-signed KK Menzel, 7 January 1950, in Landesarchiv Berlin, Band II Mordsache Seidelmann/Merten (Tod durch Erdrosseln) B. Rep. 058 Nr. 893, p. 27.

11 "Schwurgerichtsanklage," signed Bechaß, 2 November 1950, in Landesarchiv Berlin, B. Rep. 058 Nr. 890, p. 19.

12 "Verhandelt," signed Walter Kusian, co-signed KK Menzel, 7 January 1950, p. 27.
13 "Schlußbericht," signed KK Menzel, 27 February 1950, in Landesarchiv Berlin, Band II Mordsache Seidelmann/Merten (Tod durch Erdrosseln) B. Rep. B058 Nr. 893, p. 193.
14 "Bericht," signed KA Reichmuth and KA Sonntag, 17 January 1950, p. 90; "Verhandelt," signed Maria Stö., 20 February1950, in Landesarchiv Berlin, Band II Mordsache Seidelmann/Merten (Tod durch Erdrosseln) B. Rep. 058 Nr. 893, p. 159.
15 "Schlußbericht," signed KK Menzel, 27 February 1950, p. 193.
16 "Vorführungsbericht," signed VP Polizeirat Pohl, 7 January 1950, in PHS D 4.41 Band 24B, Band III, Kripo Ostsektor. Mordsache Seidelmann (Tod durch Erdrosseln), p. 36.
17 "Verhandelt," signed Alfred Stu., countersigned KK Menzel, 13 January 1950, in Landesarchiv Berlin, Band II Mordsache Seidelmann/Merten (Tod durch Erdrosseln) B. Rep. 058 Nr. 893, p. 64.
18 "Schwurgerichtsanklage," signed Bechaß, 2 November 1950, p. 19.
19 "Verhandelt," signed Alfred Stu., countersigned KK Menzel, 13 January 1950, p. 64; "Vorführungsbericht," signed VP Polizeirat Pohl, 7 January 1950, p. 36; "Verhandelt," signed KK Menzel and KK Griebsch, 16 February 1950, in Landesarchiv Berlin, Band II Mordsache Seidelmann/Merten (Tod durch Erdrosseln) B. Rep. 058 Nr. 893, p. 139.
20 "Schlußbericht," signed KK Menzel, 27 February 1950, p. 194.
21 "Verhandelt," signed Charlotte Glaubitz, co-signed KA Sonntag, 8 January 1950, pp. 29–30.
22 This narrative is reconstructed from "Verhandelt," signed KK Menzel and KK Griebsch, 16 February 1950, p. 139; and "Schlußbericht," signed KK Menzel, 27 February 1950, p. 193.
23 "Schlußbericht," signed KK Menzel, 17 February 1950, p. 193; "Verhandelt," signed KK Menzel and KK Griebsch, 16 February 1950, p. 139.
24 "Verhandelt," signed KK Menzel and KK Griebsch, 16 February 1950, p. 139; "Schlußbericht," signed KK Menzel, 27 February 1950, p. 195.
25 "Schlußbericht," signed KK Menzel, 27 February 1950, p. 194.
26 "Vorführungsbericht," signed VP Polizeirat Pohl, 7 January 1950, PHS D 4.41 Band 24b, Band III, Kripo Ostsektor, Mordsache Seidelmann (Tod durch Erdrosseln), p. 37; "Verhandelt," signed KK Menzel and KK Griebsch, 16 February 1950, p. 140.
27 "Er war den ganzen Abend über etwas komisch mir gegenüber und war den ganzen Abend verstimmt." "Verhandelt," signed KK Menzel and KK Griebsch, 16 February 1950, p. 140.
28 Sigmund, *Genuss als Politikum*, 31–2, 46. Coffee would continue to be an important cultural good in both Germanies. Later, when the price of raw beans rose enough to impact the German Democratic Republic's ability

to afford them on the open market, it would forge arms for beans trade deals with Angola and Ethiopia. See Kloiber, "Brewing Relations," 62.

29 "Verhandelt," signed Maria Stö., 20 February 1950, in Landesarchiv Berlin, Band II Mordsache Seidelmann/Merten (Tod durch Erdrosseln) B. Rep. 058 Nr. 893, p. 159; "Verhandelt," signed Griebsch and Menzel, 21 February 1950, in Landesarchiv Berlin, Band II Mordsache Seidelmann/Merten (Tod durch Erdrosseln) B. Rep. 058 Nr. 893, p. 161.

30 "erstaunt und verwundert." "Verhandelt," signed KK Menzel and KK Griebsch, 16 February 1950, p. 140.

31 "Verhandelt," signed KK Menzel and KK Griebsch, 16 February 1950, p. 140.

32 "Verhandelt," signed Kurt Muschan, 10 January 1950, in Landesarchiv Berlin, Band II Mordsache Seidelmann/Merten (Tod durch Erdrosseln) B. Rep. 058 Nr. 893, p. 49.

33 "Schlußbericht," signed KK Menzel, 27 February 1950, p. 194.

34 "Verhandelt," signed Lucie Muschan, co-signed Kriminalrat Schwarz and KK Griebsch, 12 January 1950, in Landesarchiv Berlin, Band II Mordsache Seidelmann/Merten (Tod durch Erdrosseln) B. Rep. 058 Nr. 893, p. 63.

35 Walter Kusian denies that any coffee was made during his visit, but he does agree that Elisabeth might have brewed a fresh pot immediately before his arrival. See interview with Walter Kusian conducted by KK Menzel, 13 January 1950, in Landesarchiv Berlin, Band II Mordsache Seidelmann/Merten (Tod durch Erdrosseln) B. Rep. 058 Nr. 893, p. 68.

36 "Verhandelt," signed Hertha S., 10 January 1950, in Landesarchiv Berlin, Band II Mordsache Seidelmann/Merten (Tod durch Erdrosseln) B. Rep. 058 Nr. 893, p. 42; Interview with Walter Kusian conducted by KK Menzel, 13 January 1950, p. 68.

37 "Verhandelt," signed KK Menzel and KK Griebsch, 16 February 1950, p. 142.

38 "Schlußbericht," signed KK Menzel, 27 February 1950, pp. 194–5.

39 "Schlußbericht," signed KK Menzel, 27 February 1950, pp. 194–5; "Verhandelt," signed KK Menzel and KK Griebsch, 16 February 1950, pp. 141–2.

40 "Schwurgerichtsanklage," signed Bechaß, 2 November 1950, in Landesarchiv Berlin, B. Rep. 058 Nr. 890, p. 21.

41 "Schlußbericht," signed KK Menzel, 27 February 1950, p. 195.

42 Forged letters, in PHS D 4.41 Band 24b, Elisabeth Kusian, no date or page.

43 "Schlußbericht," signed KK Menzel, 27 February 1950, in PHS 4.41 Band 24a, n.p.

44 "Schlußbericht," signed KK Menzel, February 27, 1950, n.p.

45 "Vermerk," signed Weisheit and Zimmermann, 10 January 10, 1950, in Landesarchiv Berlin, Band II Mordsache Seidelmann/Merten (Tod durch Erdrosseln) B. Rep. 058 Nr. 893, p. 39.

46 "Verhandelt," signed Charlotte Strach, countersigned VP Polizeirat Pohl, 5 January 1950, in PHS D 4.41 Band 24b, Elisabeth Kusian, p. 17.
47 "Verhandelt," signed Charlotte Strach, countersigned VP Polizeirat Pohl, 5 January 1950, pp. 17–18.
48 "Verhandelt" signed Charlotte Glaubitz, co-signed KA Sonntag, 8 January 1950, in Landesarchiv Berlin, Band II Mordsache Seidelmann/Merten (Tod durch Erdrosseln) B. Rep. 058 Nr. 893, pp. 29–30.
49 "Schlußbericht," signed KK Menzel, 27 February 1950, in Landesarchiv Berlin, Band II Mordsache Seidelmann/Merten (Tod durch Erdrosseln) B. Rep. 058 Nr. 893, pp. 185–6.
50 "Verhandelt," signed KK Menzel and KK Griebsch, 16 February 1950, in Landesarchiv Berlin, Band II Mordsache Seidelmann/Merten (Tod durch Erdrosseln) B. Rep. 058 Nr. 893, p. 143.
51 Unsigned teletype, 31 December 1949, in Landesarchiv Berlin, B. Rep. 058 Nr. 894, p. 53.
52 "Verhandelt," signed Charlotte Strach, countersigned VP Polizeirat Pohl, 5 January 1950, p. 18.
53 "Verhandelt," signed Ingeborg Hei., countersigned Weisheit, 16 January 1950, in Landesarchiv Berlin, Band II Mordsache Seidelmann/Merten (Tod durch Erdrosseln) B. Rep. 058 Nr. 893, p. 83.
54 "Verhandelt," signed Kurt Muschan, in Landesarchiv Berlin, Band II Mordsache Seidelmann/Merten (Tod durch Erdrosseln) B. Rep. 058 Nr. 893, p. 82.
55 "Verhandelt," signed KK Menzel and KK Griebsch, 16 February 1950, p. 142.
56 "Vermerk," signed Zimmermann and Weisheit, 10 January 1950, in Landesarchiv Berlin, Band II Mordsache Seidelmann/Merten (Tod durch Erdrosseln) B. Rep. 058 Nr. 893, p. 43; "Verhandelt," signed Christa Bis., countersigned Weisheit, 11 January 1950, in Landesarchiv Berlin, Band II Mordsache Seidelmann/Merten (Tod durch Erdrosseln) B. Rep. 058 Nr. 893, p. 51.
57 Interview with Walter Kusian conducted by KK Menzel, 13 January 1950, in Landesarchiv Berlin, Band II Mordsache Seidelmann/Merten (Tod durch Erdrosseln) B. Rep. 058 Nr. 893, p. 68.
58 "Verhandelt," signed KK Menzel and KK Griebsch, 16 February 1950, pp. 142–3.
59 "Verhandelt," signed Ingeborg Hei., countersigned Weisheit, 16 January 1950, p. 84.
60 "Verhandelt," signed KK Menzel and KK Griebsch, 16 February 1950, p. 143.
61 "Vermerk," signed Krim.-Anw. Reichmuth, 10 February 1950, in Landesarchiv Berlin, Band II Mordsache Seidelmann/Merten (Tod durch Erdrosseln) B. Rep. 058 Nr. 893, p. 118.
62 For Walter Kusian's morning activities, see "Verhandelt," signed Ingeborg Hei., countersigned Weisheit, 16 January 1950, p. 84;

"Verhandelt," signed Coelestin He., 16 January 1950, in Landesarchiv Berlin, Band II Mordsache Seidelmann/Merten (Tod durch Erdrosseln) B. Rep. 058 Nr. 893 [probably p. 87]; Interview with Walter Kusian conducted by KK Menzel, 13 January 1950, p. 69.

63 "Verhandelt," signed Walter Kusian, co-signed Menzel, 7 January 1950, in Landesarchiv Berlin, Band II Mordsache Seidelmann/Merten (Tod durch Erdrosseln) B. Rep. 058 Nr. 893, pp. 27–8.

64 "Schlußbericht," signed KK Menzel, 27 February 1950, in Landesarchiv Berlin, Band II Mordsache Seidelmann/Merten (Tod durch Erdrosseln) B. Rep. 058 Nr. 893, p. 195.

65 "Schlußbericht," signed KK Menzel, 27 February 1950, p. 188.

66 "Weiterverhandelt," signed Lucie Hel., 10 January 1950, in Landesarchiv Berlin, Band II Mordsache Seidelmann/Merten (Tod durch Erdrosseln) B. Rep. 058 Nr. 893, p. 40.

67 "Verhandelt," signed Anni Glißmann, countersigned KK Menzel, 7 January 1950, in Landesarchiv Berlin, Band II Mordsache Seidelmann/Merten (Tod durch Erdrosseln) B. Rep. 058 Nr. 893, p. 20.

68 "Verhandelt," signed Hedwig Schrö., countersigned KK Menzel, 20 January 1950, in Landesarchiv Berlin, Band II Mordsache Seidelmann/Merten (Tod durch Erdrosseln) B. Rep. 058 Nr. 893, p. 98; "Ermittlungsbericht," signed K.-Ass. Zimmermann and K.-Ass. Sonntag, 7 January 1950, in Landesarchiv Berlin, Band II Mordsache Seidelmann/Merten (Tod durch Erdrosseln) B. Rep. 058 Nr. 893, pp. 17–18.

69 Markowski, Pol.-Obw. Polizei-Inspektion Mitte, Kriminalkommissariat, "Bericht," in PHS D 4.41 Band 24b, Elisabeth Kusian, p. 2; for 12.35, see Meldung, signed Plath, VP Oberkomm, 4 January 1950, in PHS D 4.41 Band 24b, Elisabeth Kusian, p. 2.

70 See Mankoski, Pol.-Obw., "Bericht," 4 January 1950; VP Oberkomm, Plath "Meldung," 4 January 1950, in PHS D 4.41 Band 24b, Band III, Kripo Ostsektor, Mordsache Seidelmann (Tod durch Erdrosseln), pp. 2, 4; "Ostsektorenfernschreiben, zur Kenntnisnahme," signed Schiller, VP HPTW, in Landesarchiv Berlin, Band II Mordsache Seidelmann/Merten (Tod durch Erdrosseln) B. Rep. 058 Nr. 893.

71 Hertie Stiftung, "Where We Come From: The Story of the Hertie Foundation," accessed 19 April 2021, https://www.ghst.de/fileadmin/images/02_Formulare_und_Dokumente/Geschichte_der_GHS_en-GB_.pdf.

72 CompanyHistories.com, "Hertie Waren-Und, Kaufhaus GMBH," accessed 19 April 2021, https://www.company-histories.com/HERTIE-WARENUND-KAUFHAUS-GMBH-Company-History.html.

73 CompanyHistories.com, "Hertie Waren-Und, Kaufhaus GMBH."

74 VP Komm. Steffen, "Fundortbericht," 4 January 1950, in PHS D 4.41 Band 24b, Band III, Kripo Ostsektor. Mordsache Seidelmann (Tod durch Erdrosseln), p. 5.

75 VP Polizeirat Pohl, "Leichensache!!! Eilt," 4 January 1950, in PHS D 4.41 Band 24B, Band III, Kripo Ostsektor. Mordsache Seidelmann (Tod durch Erdrosseln), p. 15.
76 For their impression of the scene, see VP Komm. Steffen, "Fundortbericht," p. 4. For the teletype, see "V. Pol.-Hptw. Schiller, "Fernschreiben," 4 January 1950, in PHS D 4.41 Band 24b, Band III, Kripo Ostsektor, Mordsache Seidelmann (Tod durch Erdrosseln), p. 3.
77 Transcribed in "Verhandelt," signed Elisabeth Kusian, co-signed KK Menzel, 14 February 1950, in Landesarchiv Berlin, Band II Mordsache Seidelmann/Merten (Tod durch Erdrosseln) B. Rep. 058 Nr. 893, p. 129.
78 "Ermittlungsbericht," signed K.-Ass. Zimmermann and K.-Ass. Sonntag, 7 January 1950, in Landesarchiv Berlin, Band II Mordsache Seidelmann/ Merten (Tod durch Erdrosseln) B. Rep. 058 Nr. 893, pp. 17–18.
79 "Verhandelt," signed KK Menzel and KK Griebsch, 16 February 1950, in Landesarchiv Berlin, Band II Mordsache Seidelmann/Merten (Tod durch Erdrosseln) B. Rep. 058 Nr. 893, p. 143; "Abschrift!," signed Blüme, 4 January 1950, in Landesarchiv Berlin, B. Rep. 058 Nr. 893, p. 6.
80 "Nachtrag," signed Kurt Muschan, 16 January 1950, in Landesarchiv Berlin, Band II Mordsache Seidelmann/Merten (Tod durch Erdrosseln) B. Rep. 058 Nr. 893, unnumbered [probably p. 82].
81 "Schlußbericht," signed KK Menzel, 27 February 1950, in PHS D 4.41 Band 24a. n.p.
82 See "Abschrift!," signed Blüme, 4 January 1950, p. 6.
83 "so dass sich die V. schon einige Gedanken machte, zumal ihr bekannt war, dass die Merten für den Inhaber sonst hinreichend vertrauenswürdig war." "Abschrift!," signed K.S. Wetzel, 5 January 1950, in Landesarchiv Berlin, B. Rep. 058 Nr. 893, p. 10.
84 See "Abschrift!," signed K.S. Wetzel, 5 January 1950, p. 10.
85 Internal report (29/30. Pol. Rev. Kriminalpolizei), signed Wetzel, 5 January 1950, in Landesarchiv Berlin, B. Rep. 058 Nr. 893, p. 10.
86 Internal report (29/30. Pol. Rev. Kriminalpolizei), signed Wetzel, 5 January 1950, p. 10.
87 For Friedrich Beigang's statement, see "Verhandelt," signed Schiller, 5 January 1950, in PHS D 4.41 Band 24b, Band III, Kripo Ostsektor, Mordsache Seidelmann (Tod durch Erdrosseln), p. 16.
88 Internal report (29/30. Pol. Rev. Kriminalpolizei), signed Wetzel, 5 January 1950, p. 10.
89 See "Verhandelt," signed VP Polizeirat Pohl, 5 January 1950, in PHS D 4.41 Band 24b Band III, Kripo Ostsektor, Mordsache Seidelmann (Tod durch Erdrosseln), p. 17.
90 Hobbs, "'Farmers on Notice,'" 266. For a general overview of the subject, see Verk, *Laubenleben*. See also Hilbrandt, *Housing in the Margins*.
91 Hauptamt für Statistik und Wahlen, *Berlin in Zahlen 1950*, 95.

92 See "Verhandelt," signed VP Polizeirat Pohl, 5 January 1950, p. 17.
93 See "Verhandelt," signed VP Polizeirat Pohl, 5 January , pp. 17–18.
94 See "Verhandelt," signed VP Polizeirat Pohl, 5 January 1950, pp. 17–18.
95 See "Nachtrag," signed VP Polizeirat Pohl, 5 January 1950, in PHS D 4.41 Band 24b Band III, Kripo Ostsektor, Mordsache Seidelmann (Tod durch Erdrosseln), p. 18.
96 "Aus der Unterhaltung heraus konnte ich entnehmen, cass sie auch nicht sehr viel von der Krankenschwester hielt. Ich sagte nämlich zu ihr, als sie den Namen der Schwester nannte, es sie dies doch ein komischer Name, worauf sie antwortete, 'ja das ist auch eine komische Frau.'" "Nachtrag," signed VP Polizeirat Pohl, 5 January 5, 1950, p. 18.
97 See "Vermerk," signed VP Hwm. K Wriedt, 5 January 1950, in PHS D 4.41 Band 24b, Band III. Kripo Ostsektor. Mordsache Seidelmann (Tod durch Erdrosseln), p. 18
98 "Bericht," signed VP Hwm K. Schiller, 6 January 1950, in PHS D 4.41 Band 24b, Band III, Kripo Ostsektor, Mordsache Seidelmann (Tod durch Erdrosseln), p. 34.
99 "Verhandelt," signed VP Hwm K. Schiller, 6 January 1950, PHS D 4.41 Band 24b, Band III, Kripo Ostsektor, Mordsache Seidelmann (Tod durch Erdrosseln), p. 34.
100 See "Verhandelt, Nochmals zur Sache befragt erklärt der Zeuge Friedrich Beigang," 5 January 1950, in PHS D 4.41 Band 24b, Band III, Kripo Ostsektor, Mordsache Seidelmann (Tod durch Erdrosseln), p. 19.
101 See Paul Glaubitz's dictated and signed statement, filed under "Verhandelt," signed VP Kommandeur Rockstroh, 5 January 1950, in PHS D 4.41 Band 24b, Band III, Kripo Ostsektor, Mordsache Seidelmann (Tod durch Erdrosseln), p. 20.
102 Dorothea Groener-Geyer to Parliamentary Council, 2 January 1949, Bundesarchiv (Koblenz) Z5/111. Translated by and quoted in Moeller, "The 'Remasculanization' of Germany in the 1950s," 102.
103 Moeller, "Reconstructing the Family in Reconstruction Germany," 140.
104 Heineman, *What Difference Does a Husband Make?*, 108.
105 For a sophisticated, extended study of this, see Evans, *Life among the Ruins*.
106 "Verhandelt," signed Hedwig Schrö., countersigned KK Menzel, 20 January 1950, in Landesarchiv Berlin, Band II Mordsache Seidelmann/Merten (Tod durch Erdrosseln) B. Rep. 058 Nr. 893, p. 99.
107 "Vermerk," signed KK Menzel, 7 January 1950, in Landesarchiv Berlin, Band II Mordsache Seidelmann/Merten (Tod durch Erdrosseln) B. Rep. 058 Nr. 893, p. 21.
108 "Inter-Office Memorandum, Snaring of Wild Rabbits" (cancelling the Kommando Order No 73 of 3 Aug 46), signed G.D. Seymour for Chief Legal Officer, 27 December 1947, in FO 1012/529, National Archives at Kew, p. 17.

109 Interview with Walter Kusian conducted by KK Menzel, 13 January 1950, in Landesarchiv Berlin, Band II Mordsache Seidelmann/Merten (Tod durch Erdrosseln) B. Rep. 058 Nr. 893, p. 70.

110 See "Abschrift!, Verhandelt!," signed Elisabeth Kusian and witnessed KS Blüme, in Landesarchiv Berlin Band II Mordsache Seidelmann/Merten (Tod durch Erdrosseln) B. Rep. 058 Nr. 893, p. 9.

111 "Vermerk," signed VP Hpt. Wm. Schiller, 6 January 1950, in PHS D 4.41 Band 24b, Band III, Kripo Ostsektor, Mordsache Seidelmann (Tod durch Erdrosseln), p. 20.

112 "Vermerk," signed VP Polizeirat Pohl, 6 January 1950, in PHS D 4.41 Band 24b, Band III, Kripo Ostsektor, Mordsache Seidelmann (Tod durch Erdrosseln), p. 26.

113 "Vermerk," signed VP Polizeirat Pohl, 6 January 1950, p. 26.

114 Interview form (Responsible Officer, VP Hwm K Schiller) for Elisabeth Kusian, 6 January 1950, signed Elisabeth Kusian, co-signed VP Hwm Wriedt and VP Hwm Schiller, in PHS D 4.41 Band 24b, Elisabeth Kusian, pp. 23–5.

115 Interview form (Responsible Officer, VP Hwm K Schiller) for Elisabeth Kusian, 6 January 1950, pp. 23–5.

116 Interview form (Responsible Officer, VP Hwm K Schiller) for Elisabeth Kusian, 6 January 1950, p. 24.

117 Interview form (Responsible Officer, VP Hwm K Schiller) for Elisabeth Kusian, 6 January 1950, p. 25.

118 For the statement as a whole, see Elisabeth Kusian's signed statement, co-signed by VP Hwm Wriedt and VP Hwm Schiller, 6 January 1950, in PHS D 4.41 Band 24b, Band III, Kripo Ostsektor, Mordsache Seidelmann (Tod durch Erdrosseln), pp. 23–5.

119 Elisabeth Kusian's signed statement, countersigned by VP Hwm Wriedt and VP Hwm Schiller, 6 January 1950, pp. 23–5.

120 Kurt Muschan's signed statement, countersigned by VP Kdr Rockstroh and VP Polizeirat Pohl, 6 January 1950, in PHS D 4.41 Band 24b, Band III, Kripo Ostsektor, Mordsache Seidelmann (Tod durch Erdrosseln), pp. 27–8.

121 Kurt Muschan's signed statement, countersigned by VP Kdr Rockstroh and VP Polizeirat Pohl, 6 January 1950, pp. 27–8.

122 Kurt Muschan's signed statement, countersigned by VP Kdr Rockstroh and VP Polizeirat Pohl, 6 January 1950, p. 27.

123 See "Vorführungsbericht," signed VP Polizeirat Pohl, 7 January 1950, in PHS D 4.41 Band 24b, Band III, Kripo Ostsektor, Mordsache Seidelmann (Tod durch Erdrosseln), p. 37.

124 VP Hwm Schiller, "Durchsuchungsbericht," 7 January 1950, in PHS D 4.41 Band 24b, Band III, Kripo Ostsektor, Mordsache Seidelmann (Tod durch Erdrosseln), p. 28.

125 See "Vermerk," typed by VP Polizeirat Pohl, 6 January 1950, in PHS D 4.41 Band 24b, Band III, Kripo Ostsektor, Mordsache Seidelmann (Tod durch Erdrosseln), p. 30; VP Hwm Wriedt and VP Hwm Schiller, "Bericht über Gegenüberstellung der Besch Kusian mit dem Zeugen Muschan," 6 January 1950, in PHS D 4.41 Band 24b, Band III, Kripo Ostsektor, Mordsache Seidelmann (Tod durch Erdrosseln), p. 31.

126 VP Hwm Wriedt and VP Hwm Schiller, "Bericht über Gegenüberstellung der Besch Kusian mit dem Zeugen Muschan," 6 January 1950, p. 31.

127 VP Hwm Wriedt and VP Hwm Schiller, "Bericht über Gegenüberstellung der Besch Kusian mit dem Zeugen Muschan," p. 31.

128 VP Hwm Wriedt and VP Hwm Schiller, "Bericht über Gegenüberstellung der Besch Kusian mit dem Zeugen Muschan," p. 31.

129 See "Vermerk," signed VP Hwm Wriedt and VP Hwm Schiller, 6 January 1950, in PHS D 4.41 Band 24b, Band III, Kripo Ostsektor, Mordsache Seidelmann (Tod durch Erdrosseln), p. 30; VP Hwm Wriedt and VP Hwm Schiller, "Bericht über Gegenüberstellung der Besch Kusian mit dem Zeugen Muschan," p. 31.

4. Building the Case: Berlin's Police Departments Investigate Elisabeth Kusian

1 For the weather, see Weather Spark, "January 7, 1951, Weather History at Berlin Tempelhof Airport," accessed 2 June 2024, https://weatherspark.com/h/d/148297/1951/1/7/Historical-Weather-on-Sunday-January-7–1951-at-Berlin-Tempelhof-Airport-Germany#Figures-Temperature.

2 There is a slight disagreement about the chronology of this. In a report submitted by KA Reichmuth and KA Sonntag, it happened the following day and slightly differently. In their telling, Kusian saw that the room was sealed. When he saw the coal in the bathroom, he asked what it was all about. The two women had no answer but said it must be something "frightful" and advised him to go to the police department. See "Bericht," signed KA Reichmuth and KA Sonntag, 17 January 1950, in Landesarchiv Berlin, Band II Mordsache Seidelmann/Merten (Tod durch Erdrosseln) B. Rep. 058 Nr. 893, p. 89.

3 Interview with Walter Kusian conducted by KK Menzel, 13 January 1950, in Landesarchiv Berlin, Band II Mordsache Seidelmann/Merten (Tod durch Erdrosseln) B. Rep. 058 Nr. 893, p. 70.

4 "Urschriftlich dem Herrn Vernemungsrichter im Polizeipräsidium," signed VP Kommandeur Rockstroh, 7 January1950, in PHS D 4.41 Band 24b, Band III, Kripo Ostsektor, Mordsache Seidelmann (Tod durch Erdrosseln), p. 37; "Einlieferungsanzeige," signed VP Kommandeur Rockstroh, 6 January 1950, in PHS D 4.41 Band 24b, Band III, Kripo Ostsektor, Mordsache Seidelmann (Tod durch Erdrosseln), p. 38.

5 See her signed form, dated 7 January 1950, to this effect, in PHS D 4.41 Band 24b, Band III, Kripo Ostsektor, Mordsache Seidelmann (Tod durch Erdrosseln), p. 40.

6 For a list of the articles of clothing, see "Ermittlungsbericht," signed K.-Ass. Zimmermann and K.-Ass. Sonntag, 7 January 1950, in Landesarchiv Berlin, Band II Mordsache Seidelmann/Merten (Tod durch Erdrosseln) B. Rep. 058 Nr. 893, p. 17.

7 See "Bericht," signed KK Menzel, 7 January 1950, in Landesarchiv Berlin, Band II Mordsache Seidelmann/Merten (Tod durch Erdrosseln) B. Rep. 058 Nr. 893, p. 12. The use of benzidine to determine the presence of blood was common at the time. See Grodsky, Wright, and Kirk, "Simplified Preliminary Blood Testing."

8 See "Bericht," signed KK Menzel, 7 January 1950, p. 12.

9 Bartels, "Berlin's Tiergarten," 143–74. See especially pages 143 and 172. See also Schmiedecke, *Berlin Tiergarten*, 7–10.

10 See "Bericht," signed KK Menzel, 7 January 1950, p. 12.

11 "Bericht," signed VP Komm. K Steffen, 7 January 1950, in PHS D 4.41 Band 24b, Band III, Kripo Ostsektor, Mordsache Seidelmann (Tod durch Erdrosseln), p. 42.

12 "Vermerk," signed VP Hwm Wriedt and VP Hwm Schiller, 7 January 1950, in PHS D 4.41 Band 24b, Band III, Kripo Ostsektor, Mordsache Seidelmann (Tod durch Erdrosseln), p. 45.

13 See "Bericht," signed KK Menzel, 7 January 1950, p. 12,

14 "Vermerk," signed K.-Ass. Sonntag, 7 January 1950, in Landesarchiv Berlin, Band II Mordsache Seidelmann/Merten (Tod durch Erdrosseln) B. Rep. 058 Nr. 893, p. 17.

15 "Ermittlungsbericht," signed K.-Ass. Zimmermann and K.-Ass. Sonntag, 7 January 1950, pp. 17–18.

16 "Verhandelt," signed Anni Glißmann, countersigned KK Menzel, 7 January 1950, in Landesarchiv Berlin, Band II Mordsache Seidelmann/Merten (Tod durch Erdrosseln) B. Rep. 058 Nr. 893, pp. 19–21.

17 "Vermerk," signed KK Menzel, 7 January 1950, in Landesarchiv Berlin, Band II Mordsache Seidelmann/Merten (Tod durch Erdrosseln) B. Rep. 058 Nr. 893, p. 22.

18 "Bericht," signed KK Menzel, 7 January 1950, p 24.

19 Unsigned, undated story, "Krankenschwester als Doppelmörderin verhaftet," *Der Abend*, in Landesarchiv Berlin, B. Rep. 058 Nr. 892, n.p.; Unsigned, undated story, "Opfer mit der Wäscheleine erdrosselt … und mit dem Brotmesser zerstückelt – Doppelmörderin gestand," [newspaper name cut from clipping], in Landesarchiv Berlin, B. Rep. 058 Nr. 892,. n.p.

20 "Wetter in Deutschland am 8.1.1950," *chroniknet*, accessed 5 June 2025, https://chroniknet.de/historisches-wetter/deutschland/8.1.1950.

21 Bericht," signed KK Menzel, 8 January 1950, in Landesarchiv Berlin, Band II Mordsache Seidelmann/Merten (Tod durch Erdrosseln) B. Rep. 058 Nr. 893, p. 25.

22 "Vermerk," signed KK Menzel, 8 January 1950, in Landesarchiv Berlin, Band II Mordsache Seidelmann/Merten (Tod durch Erdrosseln) B. Rep. 058 Nr. 893, p. 26.

23 "Verhandelt," signed Walter Kusian, countersigned KK Menzel, 8 January 1950, in Landesarchiv Berlin, Band II Mordsache Seidelmann/Merten (Tod durch Erdrosseln) B. Rep. 058 Nr. 893, pp. 26–8.

24 Beddies and Schmiedebach, "'Euthanasie.'"

25 "Verhandelt," signed Walter Kusian, countersigned by KK Menzel, 8 January 1950, p. 28.

26 "Verhandelt," signed Charlotte Glaubitz, co-signed K.A. Sonntag, 8 January 1950, in Landesarchiv Berlin, Band II Mordsache Seidelmann/Merten (Tod durch Erdrosseln) B. Rep. 058 Nr. 893, pp. 29–30.

27 "Verhandelt," signed Anni Glißmann, co-signed K.A. Sonntag, 8 January 1950, in Landesarchiv Berlin, Band II Mordsache Seidelmann/Merten (Tod durch Erdrosseln) B. Rep. 058 Nr. 893, p. 31.

28 "Vermerk," signed Krim.-Ass. Sonntag and Krim-Ass. Zimmermann, 9 January 1950, in Landesarchiv Berlin, Band II Mordsache Seidelmann/Merten (Tod durch Erdrosseln) B. Rep. 058 Nr. 893, p. 32.

29 "Bericht," signed Krim.-Ass. Sonntag and Krim-Ass. Zimmermann, 9 January 1950, in Landesarchiv Berlin, Band II Mordsache Seidelmann/Merten (Tod durch Erdrosseln) B. Rep. 058 Nr. 893, p. 32.

30 "Vermerk," signed K.A. Sonntag, 8 January 1950, in Landesarchiv Berlin, Band II Mordsache Seidelmann/Merten (Tod durch Erdrosseln) B. Rep. 058 Nr. 893, p. 31.

31 "Vermerk," signed K.A. Sonntag, 8 January 1950, p. 31.

32 See "Teufelsberg," Berlin.de, accessed 20 June 2024, https://www.berlin.de/en/attractions-and-sights/3560349-3104052-teufelsberg.en.html.

33 Anderson, *Buried City, Unearthing Teufelsberg*, 3.

34 "Vermerk," signed Krim.-Anw. Reichmuth and K.-Ass. Weisheit, 8 January 1950, in Landesarchiv Berlin, Band II Mordsache Seidelmann/Merten (Tod durch Erdrosseln) B. Rep. 058 Nr. 893, p. 25.

35 "Vermerk," signed KK Griebsch, 9 January 1950, in Landesarchiv Berlin, Band II Mordsache Seidelmann/Merten (Tod durch Erdrosseln) B. Rep. 058 Nr. 893, p. 36.

36 For the weather, see "Wetter in Deutschland am 6.1.1950," *chroniknet*, accessed 5 June 2025, https://chroniknet.de/historisches-wetter/deutschland/6.1.1950#google_vignette.

37 "Durchsuchingsbericht," signed KK Menzel, 10 January 1950, in Landesarchiv Berlin, Band II Mordsache Seidelmann/Merten (Tod durch Erdrosseln) B. Rep. 058 Nr. 893, pp. 46–7.

38 "Durchsuchingsbericht," signed KK Menzel, 10 January 1950, p. 46–7.
39 "Durchsuchingsbericht," signed KK Menzel, 10 January 1950, p. 47.
40 "Verhandelt," signed Gertrud Seidelmann, countersigned Krim. Komm. Menzel, 9 January 1950, in Landesarchiv Berlin, Band II Mordsache Seidelmann/Merten (Tod durch Erdrosseln) B. Rep. 058 Nr. 893, p. 37.
41 "Vermerk," signed KK Griebsch, 9 January 1950, in Landesarchiv Berlin, Band II Mordsache Seidelmann/Merten (Tod durch Erdrosseln) B. Rep. 058 Nr. 893, p. 36.
42 "Eilt sehr! Haftsache!," written to Herrn Generalstaatsanwalt be idem Landgericht Berlin, signed KK Menzel, 9 January 1950, in Landesarchiv Berlin, Band II Mordsache Seidelmann/Merten (Tod durch Erdrosseln) B. Rep. 058 Nr. 896, p. 15.
43 "Vermerk," signed Krim.-Ass. Weisheit, 9 January 1950, in Landesarchiv Berlin, Band II Mordsache Seidelmann/Merten (Tod durch Erdrosseln) B. Rep. 058 Nr. 893, p. 32.
44 "Bericht," signed VP Komm Steffen, 9 January 1950, in PHS D 4.41 Band 24b, Band III, Kripo Ostsektor, Mordsache Seidelmann (Tod durch Erdrosseln), p. 53.
45 "Vermerk," signed Krim.-Ass. Weisheit, 9 January 1950, p. 32.
46 "Vermerk," signed VP Rat Schwarz, 9 January 1950, in PHS D 4.41 Band 24b, Band III, Kripo Ostsektor, Mordsache Seidelmann (Tod durch Erdrosseln), p. 45.
47 "Vermerk," signed Krim. Komm. Menzel, 9 January 1950, in Landesarchiv Berlin, Band II Mordsache Seidelmann/Merten (Tod durch Erdrosseln) B. Rep. 058 Nr. 893, p. 32.
48 "Verhandelt," signed Marja Sobe., countersigned Krim.-Ass. Zimmermann, 9 January 1950, in Landesarchiv Berlin, Band II Mordsache Seidelmann/Merten (Tod durch Erdrosseln) B. Rep. 058 Nr. 893, p. 34.
49 Donath and Schulz, *Denkmale in Berlin*, 16–18, 71.
50 "Nachtrag," signed Marja Sobe., countersigned Krim.-Ass. Zimmermann, 9 January 1950, in Landesarchiv Berlin, Band II Mordsache Seidelmann/Merten (Tod durch Erdrosseln) B. Rep. 058 Nr. 893, p. 34.
51 "Vermerk," signed Krim.-Ass. Zimmermann, 9 January 1950, in Landesarchiv Berlin, Band II Mordsache Seidelmann/Merten (Tod durch Erdrosseln) B. Rep. 058 Nr. 893, p. 37.
52 "Vermerk," signed Krim.-Ass. Zimmermann, 9 January 1950, p. 37.
53 "Vermerk," signed Krim.-Ass. Weisheit, 9 January 1950, in Landesarchiv Berlin, Band II Mordsache Seidelmann/Merten (Tod durch Erdrosseln) B. Rep. 058 Nr. 893, p. 32.
54 Freyaldenhoven's denazification file is at the Landesarchiv Berlin, C. Rep. 031–01–04, Nr. 475.
55 "Bericht," signed KS Schwarz, 9 January 1950, in Landesarchiv Berlin, Band II Mordsache Seidelmann/Merten (Tod durch Erdrosseln) B. Rep. 058 Nr. 893, p. 38.

56 "Vermerk," signed Krim.-Ass. Weisheit, 9 January 1950, p. 32.
57 "Bericht," signed VP Komm Steffen, 9 January 1950, p. 53.
58 "Vermerk," signed Krim. Komm. Menzel, 9 January 1950, p. 32.
59 "Verhandelt," signed Charlotte Strach, countersigned Krim. Komm. Menzel, 9 January 1950, in Landesarchiv Berlin, Band II Mordsache Seidelmann/Merten (Tod durch Erdrosseln) B. Rep. 058 Nr. 893, p. 33; "Nachtrag," signed Charlotte Strach, countersigned Krim. Komm. Menzel, 9 January 1950, in Landesarchiv Berlin, Band II Mordsache Seidelmann/Merten (Tod durch Erdrosseln) B. Rep. 058 Nr. 893, p. 33. Also in PHS D 4.41 Band 24b, Band III, Kripo Ostsektor, Mordsache Seidelmann (Tod durch Erdrosseln), p. 46.
60 "Verhandelt," signed Gertrud Seidelmann, countersigned Krim. Komm. Menzel, 9 January 1950, in Landesarchiv Berlin, Band II Mordsache Seidelmann/Merten (Tod durch Erdrosseln) B. Rep. 058 Nr. 893, p. 37.
61 "Haftsache," signed KK Menzel, 9 January 1950, in Landesarchiv Berlin, Band II Mordsache Seidelmann/Merten (Tod durch Erdrosseln) B. Rep. 058 Nr. 893, pp. 35–6. For Griebsch's note on his conversation with KK Rockstroh, see "Vermerk," signed KK Griebsch, 9 January 1950 in Landesarchiv Berlin, Band II Mordsache Seidelmann/Merten (Tod durch Erdrosseln) B. Rep. 058 Nr. 893, p. 36.
62 "Verhandelt," signed VP Hwm Wriedt, VP Rat Pohl, and VP Rat Schwarz, 9 January 1950, in PHS D 4.41 Band 24b, Band III, Kripo Ostsektor, Mordsache Seidelmann (Tod durch Erdrosseln), p. 47. The report said that Merten gave this answer. It was obviously a typo. Indeed, somebody pencilled in a question mark beside the name.
63 "Verhandelt," signed VP Hwm Wriedt, VP Rat Pohl, and VP Rat Schwarz, 9 January 1950, p. 47.
64 "Verhandelt: Aus dem Fraungefängnis Barnimstraße vorgeführt erscheint die Besch. Elisabeth Kusian," 9 January 1950. She spoke with VP Kommandeur Rockstroh, VP Hwm Schiller, and VP Rat Schwarz. The stenographer was VP Hwm Wriedt. In PHS D 4.41 Band 24b, Band III, Kripo Ostsektor, Mordsache Seidelmann (Tod durch Erdrosseln), pp. 49–52.
65 The statement took four double-sided sheets of paper to record. See "Verhandelt: Aus dem Fraungefängnis Barnimstraße vorgeführt erscheint die Besch. Elisabeth Kusian," 9 January 1950, pp. 49–52.
66 Dempsey, "Berlin's Hackescher Markt," 257–9.
67 It is also possible that she was referring to the Alte Ballhaus on Joachimstrasse. See "History: Ballhaus Berlin," Ballhaus Berlin, accessed 9 June 2024, www.ballhausberlinhostel.de/en/historie/; "The Alte Ballhaus at Joachimstrasse 20 in Berlin," alamy, https://www.alamy.com/the-alte-ballhaus-at-joachimstrasse-20-in-berlin-operated-by-hahn-und-rittershaus-gmbh-later-became-carl-kellers-festsaelen-the-photograph-was-taken-around-1920-image385780754.html.

68 Quoted in Schmale, *Chausseestrasse*, 161–2.
69 "Verhandelt: Aus dem Fraungefängnis Barnimstraße vorgeführt erscheint die Besch. Elisabeth Kusian," 9 January 1950, p. 52.
70 "Verhandelt," signed Coelestin He., 16 January 1950, in Landesarchiv Berlin, Band II Mordsache Seidelmann/Merten (Tod durch Erdrosseln) B. Rep. 058 Nr. 893, n.p. [probably p. 87].

5. Finalizing the Case: Berlin's Police Departments Finish with Elisabeth Kusian

1 For the weather, see "10.1.1950 – Historisches Wetter," *chroniknet*, accessed 19 April 2021, https://web.archive.org/web/20210419035058/https://chroniknet.de/extra/historisches-wetter/?wetter-datum=10.1.1950.
2 "Verhandelt," signed VP Owm Rudat, 10 January 1950, in PHS D 4.41 Band 24b, Band III, Kripo Ostsektor, Mordsache Seidelmann (Tod durch Erdrosseln), p. 57.
3 "Bericht," signed VP Rat Schwarz, 10 January 1950, in PHS D 4.41 Band 24B, Band III, Kripo Ostsektor, Mordsache Seidelmann (Tod durch Erdrosseln), p. 48.
4 "Bericht," Signed VP Rat Schwarz, 10 January 1950, p. 48.
5 For Helmut Hiller's statement, see the untitled four-sided interview entered into the Volkspolizei's files, in PHS D 4.41 Band 24b, Band III, Kripo Ostsektor, Mordsache Seidelmann (Tod durch Erdrosseln), pp. 54–5.
6 For Rolf Hiller's statement, see the untitled three-sided interview entered into the Volkspolizei's files, in PHS D 4.41 Band 24B, Band III, Kripo Ostsektor, Mordsache Seidelmann (Tod durch Erdrosseln), pp. 56–7.
7 "Gegenüberstellung," signed Rolf Hiller and Elisabeth Kusian, countersigned VP Schwarz, 10 January 1950, in PHS D 4.41 Band 24b, Band III, Kripo Ostsektor, Mordsache Seidelmann (Tod durch Erdrosseln), p. 57.
8 "Gegenüberstellung," signed Rolf Hiller and Elisabeth Kusian, countersigned VP Schwarz, p. 57.
9 "Verhandelt," signed Elisabeth Kusian, countersigned VP Rat Schwarz, VP Rat Pohl, and VP Komm. Steffen, 10 January 1950, in PHS D 4.41 Band 24b, Band III, Kripo Ostsektor, Mordsache Seidelmann (Tod durch Erdrosseln), pp. 58–61.
10 She would tell the East Germans the broad truth but invent details that the West Berlin squad would later prove false. For example, she would claim that her trips to dispose of Hermann Seidelmann had taken place over several nights. The West Berlin squad believed that they all took place on one busy night.
11 "Verhandelt," signed Elisabeth Kusian, countersigned VP Rat Schwarz, VP Rat Pohl, and VP Komm. Steffen, 10 January 1950, p. 60.

12 The statement is in "Verhandelt," signed Elisabeth Kusian, countersigned VP Rat Schwarz, VP Rat Pohl, and VP Komm. Steffen, 10 January 1950, pp. 58–61.
13 Kellenbach, *The Mark of Cain*, 37.
14 Kellenbach, 41.
15 For an intelligent survey of the literature, see Clark, "West Germany Confronts the Nazi Past."
16 She did this with no problem at the first site but had trouble remembering the details of the second. The third presented no difficulties. "Vermerk," signed VP Rat Pohl, 10 January 1950, in PHS D 4.41 Band 24b, Band III, Kripo Ostsektor, Mordsache Seidelmann (Tod durch Erdrosseln), p. 61.
17 "Vermerk," signed VP Rat Pohl, 10 January 1950, p. 62.
18 "Bericht," signed VP Kommandeur Rockstroh, 10 January 1950, in PHS D 4.41 Band 24b, Band III, Kripo Ostsektor, Mordsache Seidelmann (Tod durch Erdrosseln), p. 63.
19 "Verhandelt," signed Joachim Kü., 10 January 1950, in Landesarchiv Berlin, Band II Mordsache Seidelmann/Merten (Tod durch Erdrosseln) B. Rep. 058 Nr. 893, p. 39.
20 "Weiterverhandelt," signed Wolfgang Hintze, 10 January 1950, in Landesarchiv Berlin, Band II Mordsache Seidelmann/Merten (Tod durch Erdrosseln) B. Rep. 058 Nr. 893, p. 40.
21 "Weiterverhandelt," signed Lucie Hel., 10 January 1950, in Landesarchiv Berlin, Band II Mordsache Seidelmann/Merten (Tod durch Erdrosseln) B. Rep. 058 Nr. 893, p. 40.
22 "Weiterverhandelt," signed Martha Kc., 10 January 1950, in Landesarchiv Berlin, Band II Mordsache Seidelmann/Merten (Tod durch Erdrosseln) B. Rep. 058 Nr. 893, p. 41.
23 "Weiterverhandelt," signed Magdalene Brey., 10 January 1950, in Landesarchiv Berlin, Band II Mordsache Seidelmann/Merten (Tod durch Erdrosseln) B. Rep. 058 Nr. 893, p. 41.
24 "Weiterverhandelt," signed Magdalene Brey., 10 January 1950, p. 41; "Verhandelt," signed Hertha Schö., 10 January 1950, in Landesarchiv Berlin, Band II Mordsache Seidelmann/Merten (Tod durch Erdrosseln) B. Rep. 058 Nr. 893, pp. 42–3; "Weiterverhandelt," signed Erna Stabenow, 10 January 1950, in Landesarchiv Berlin, Band II Mordsache Seidelmann/Merten (Tod durch Erdrosseln) B. Rep. 058 Nr. 893, p. 43; "Vermerk," signed K.-Ass. Zimmermann and K.-Ass. Weisheit, 10 January 1950, in Landesarchiv Berlin, Band II Mordsache Seidelmann/Merten (Tod durch Erdrosseln) B. Rep. 058 Nr. 893, p. 43; and "Verhandelt," signed Johanna Dei., countersigned K.-Ass. Zimmermann and K.-Ass. Weisheit, 10 January 1950, in Landesarchiv Berlin, Band II Mordsache Seidelmann/Merten (Tod durch Erdrosseln) B. Rep. 058 Nr. 893, p. 44.

25 "Vermerk," signed Weisheit and Zimmerman, 10 January 1950, in Landesarchiv Berlin, Band II Mordsache Seidelmann/Merten (Tod durch Erdrosseln) B. Rep. 058 Nr. 893, p. 42.
26 "Verhandelt," signed Olga Maus, countersigned KK Menzel, 10 January 1950, in Landesarchiv Berlin, Band II Mordsache Seidelmann/Merten (Tod durch Erdrosseln) B. Rep. 058 Nr. 893, page obscured [probably p. 46].
27 "Verhandelt," signed Kurt Muschan, 10 January 1950, in Landesarchiv Berlin, Band II Mordsache Seidelmann/Merten (Tod durch Erdrosseln) B. Rep. 058 Nr. 893, p. 49.
28 "Vermerk," signed KK Menzel, 10 January 1950, in Landesarchiv Berlin, Band II Mordsache Seidelmann/Merten (Tod durch Erdrosseln) B. Rep. 058 Nr. 893, p. 50. See also "Vermerk," signed KA Sonntag, 10 January 1950, in Landesarchiv Berlin, Band II Mordsache Seidelmann/Merten (Tod durch Erdrosseln) B. Rep. 058 Nr. 893, p. 51.
29 "Verhandelt," signed Lucie Muschan, co-signed Kriminalrat Schwarz and KK Griebsch, 12 January 1950, in Landesarchiv Berlin, Band II Mordsache Seidelmann/Merten (Tod durch Erdrosseln) B. Rep. 058 Nr. 893, p. 62.
30 "Verhandelt," signed Kurt Muschan, 10 January 1950, p. 49.
31 Mouton, "Missing, Lost, and Displaced Children in Postwar Germany," 63, 67.
32 Quoted in Zahra, *Reconstructing Europe's Families After World War II*, 9.
33 Zahra, 6.
34 Quoted in Case, "Innocents Lost."
35 "Bericht," signed KA Sonntag, 10 January 1950, in Landesarchiv Berlin, Band II Mordsache Seidelmann/Merten (Tod durch Erdrosseln) B. Rep. 058 Nr. 893, page obscured [probably p. 48].
36 "Weiterverhandelt," signed Helene Weis., 16 January 1950, in Landesarchiv Berlin, Band II Mordsache Seidelmann/Merten (Tod durch Erdrosseln) B. Rep. 058 Nr. 893, n.p.
37 "Vermerk," signed KA Sonntag, 10 January 1950, in Landesarchiv Berlin, Band II Mordsache Seidelmann/Merten (Tod durch Erdrosseln) B. Rep. 058 Nr. 893, p. 50.
38 "Krankenschwestern eigentlich doch gute Menschen sein müßten." "Verhandelt," signed Lucie Muschan, co-signed Kriminalrat Schwarz and KK Griebsch, 12 January 1950, p. 62.
39 "Bericht," signed Krim.-Anw. Reichmuth and Krim.-Ass. Sonntag, 11 January 1950, in Landesarchiv Berlin, Band II Mordsache Seidelmann/Merten (Tod durch Erdrosseln) B. Rep. 058 Nr. 893, p. 53.
40 "Verhandelt," signed Hedwig U., countersigned KK Menzel, 11 January 1950, in Landesarchiv Berlin, Band II Mordsache Seidelmann/Merten (Tod durch Erdrosseln) B. Rep. 058 Nr. 893, p. 53.
41 "Vermerk," signed VP Rat Pohl, 11 January 1950, in PHS D 4.41 Band 24b, Band III, Kripo Ostsektor, Mordsache Seidelmann (Tod durch Erdrosseln) [probably p. 63].

42 "Verhandelt," (Übertragung aus dem Stenogram) signed Pohl, Schwarz, and Eick, 12 January 1950, in PHS D 4.41, Band 24b, Elisabeth Kusian, p. 64.
43 "Schlußbericht," signed KK Menzel, 27 February 1950, in Landesarchiv Berlin, Band II Mordsache Seidelmann/Merten (Tod durch Erdrosseln) B. Rep. 058 Nr. 893, p. 189.
44 For the interview, see "Interview with Walter Kusian conducted by KK Menzel," 13 January 1950, in Landesarchiv Berlin, Band II Mordsache Seidelmann/Merten (Tod durch Erdrosseln) B. Rep. 058 Nr. 893, pp. 66–71. For the arrest, see "Vorführungsbericht," unsigned, 14 January 1950, in Landesarchiv Berlin, Band II Mordsache Seidelmann/Merten (Tod durch Erdrosseln) B. Rep. 058 Nr. 893, p. 72.
45 "Bericht," signed VP Komm Steffen, 13 January 1950, in PHS D 4.41 Band 24b, Elisabeth Kusian, p. 65.
46 "Vermerk," signed VP Komm Steffen, 14 January 1950, in PHS D 4.41 Band 24b, Elisabeth Kusian, p. 65.
47 "Vorführungsbericht," unsigned, 14 January 1950, in Landesarchiv Berlin, Band II Mordsache Seidelmann/Merten (Tod durch Erdrosseln) B. Rep. 058 Nr. 893, pp. 72–3.
48 "Vermerk," signed Menzel, 16 January 1950, in Landesarchiv Berlin, Band II Mordsache Seidelmann/Merten (Tod durch Erdrosseln) B. Rep. 058 Nr. 893, p. 74.
49 "Verhandelt," signed Marie Schü. [no countersignature], 16 January 1950, Landesarchiv Berlin, Band II Mordsache Seidelmann/Merten (Tod durch Erdrosseln) B. Rep. 058 Nr. 893, p. 80.
50 "Vermerk," signed Menzel, 16 January 1950, p. 74.
51 See the note from Rockstroh to Polizeikrankenhaus, 16 January 1950, in PHS D 4.41 Band 24b, Elisabeth Kusian, p. 70; "Bericht," signed Krim.-Ass. Zimmermann and Krim.-Sek. Skok, 17 January 1950, in Landesarchiv Berlin, Band II Mordsache Seidelmann/Merten (Tod durch Erdrosseln) B. Rep. 058 Nr. 893 [probably p. 91]; "Durchsuchungsbericht," signed K.-Anw. Reichmuth and Krim.-Ass. Zimmermann, 16 January 1950, in Landesarchiv Berlin, Band II Mordsache Seidelmann/Merten (Tod durch Erdrosseln) B. Rep. 058 Nr. 893, p. 83; "Weiterverhandelt," signed Friedrich Beigang, countersigned KK Menzel, 16 January 1950 in Landesarchiv Berlin, Band II Mordsache Seidelmann/Merten (Tod durch Erdrosseln) B. Rep. 058 Nr. 893, p. 81.
52 "Bericht," signed Krim.-Ass. Zimmermann and Krim.-Sek. Skok, 17 January 1950 [probably p. 91].
53 "Verhandelt," signed Schwarz, Wriedt, Pohl, and Rockstroh, 17 January 1950, in PHS D 4.41 Band 24b, Elisabeth Kusian, pp. 71–2.
54 "Verhandelt," signed Schwarz, Wriedt, Pohl, and Rockstroh, 17 January 1950, p. 72.
55 "Verhandelt," signed Schwarz, Wriedt, Pohl, and Rockstroh, 17 January 1950, p. 72.

56 "Verhandelt," signed Schwarz, Wriedt, Pohl, and Rockstroh, 17 January 1950, p. 72.
57 "Verhandelt," signed Schwarz, Wriedt, Pohl, and Rockstroh, 17 January 1950, p. 73.
58 "Verhandelt," signed Schwarz, Wriedt, Pohl, and Rockstroh, 17 January 1950, p. 73
59 "Verhandelt," signed Schwarz, Wriedt, Pohl, and Rockstroh, 17 January 1950, pp. 73–4.
60 "Schlußbericht," signed Kommandeur Rockstroh, 23 January 1950, in PHS D 4.41 Band 24b, Elisabeth Kusian, p. 91.
61 "Bericht," signature illegible, 18 January 1950, in Landesarchiv Berlin, Band II Mordsache Seidelmann/Merten (Tod durch Erdrosseln) B. Rep. 058 Nr. 893 [probably p. 92].
62 "Verhandelt," signed Dr. Wolfgang Hintze, co-signed KK Menzel, 18 January 1950, in Landesarchiv Berlin, Band II Mordsache Seidelmann/Merten (Tod durch Erdrosseln) B. Rep. 058 Nr. 893, n.p.
63 "Haftbefehl," signed Ruppender (Assessor), 21 January 1950, in Landesarchiv Berlin, Band II Mordsache Seidelmann/Merten (Tod durch Erdrosseln) B. Rep. 058 Nr. 893, n.p. [probably p. 101].
64 "Bericht," signed Menzel, 8 February 1950, in Landesarchiv Berlin, Band II Mordsache Seidelmann/Merten (Tod durch Erdrosseln) B. Rep. 058 Nr. 893 [probably p. 117]; and "Schlußbericht," signed KK Menzel, 27 February 1950, in Landesarchiv Berlin, Band II Mordsache Seidelmann/Merten (Tod durch Erdrosseln) B. Rep. B058 Nr. 893, p. 189.
65 Illegible signature, request dated 21 February 1950, in Landesarchiv Berlin, Band II Mordsache Seidelmann/Merten (Tod durch Erdrosseln) B. Rep. 058 Nr. 893, p. 169.
66 "Tierquälereien kamen für mich nicht in Frage." "Verhandelt," signed Elisabeth Kusian, co-signed KK Menzel, 13 February 1950, in Landesarchiv Berlin, Band II Mordsache Seidelmann/Merten (Tod durch Erdrosseln) B. Rep. 058 Nr. 893, p. 119.
67 "Verhandelt," signed Elisabeth Kusian, co-signed KK Menzel, 13 February 1950, p. 121.
68 "Verhandelt," signed Elisabeth Kusian, co-signed KK Menzel, 13 February 1950, p. 122.
69 "Verhandelt," signed Elisabeth Kusian, co-signed KK Menzel, 13 February 1950, p. 124.
70 "Verhandelt," signed Elisabeth Kusian, co-signed KK Menzel, 14 February 1950, in Landesarchiv Berlin, Band II Mordsache Seidelmann/Merten (Tod durch Erdrosseln) B. Rep. 058 Nr. 893, p. 124.
71 "Verhandelt," signed Elisabeth Kusian, co-signed KK Menzel, 14 February 1950, p. 124.
72 "Verhandelt," signed Elisabeth Kusian, co-signed KK Menzel, 14 February 1950, p. 125.

73 "Verhandelt," signed Elisabeth Kusian, co-signed KK Menzel, 14 February 1950, pp. 126–7.
74 "Verhandelt," signed Elisabeth Kusian, co-signed KK Menzel, 14 February 1950, p. 127.
75 "Verhandelt," signed Elisabeth Kusian, co-signed KK Menzel, 14 February 1950, p. 127.
76 "Verhandelt," signed Elisabeth Kusian, co-signed KK Menzel, 14 February 1950, p. 128.
77 "Verhandelt," signed Elisabeth Kusian, co-signed KK Menzel, 14 February 1950, p. 128.
78 "Verhandelt," signed Elisabeth Kusian, co-signed KK Menzel, 14 February 1950, pp. 128–9.
79 "Verhandelt," signed Elisabeth Kusian, co-signed KK Menzel, 14 February 1950, p. 129.
80 "Verhandelt," signed Elisabeth Kusian, co-signed KK Menzel, 14 February 1950, p. 129.
81 "Verhandelt," signed Elisabeth Kusian, co-signed KK Menzel, 14 February 1950, pp. 130–1.
82 "Vermerk, "signed KK Menzel, 15 February 1950, in Landesarchiv Berlin, Band II Mordsache Seidelmann/Merten (Tod durch Erdrosseln) B. Rep. 058 Nr. 893, p. 131.
83 "Verhandelt," signed KK Menzel and KK Griebsch, 15 February 1950, in Landesarchiv Berlin, Band II Mordsache Seidelmann/Merten (Tod durch Erdrosseln) B. Rep. 058 Nr. 893, p. 131.
84 "Verhandelt," signed KK Menzel and KK Griebsch, 15 February 1950, p. 132.
85 "Verhandelt," signed KK Menzel and KK Griebsch, 15 February 1950, p. 133.
86 "Vermerk," signed KK Menzel, 15 February 1950, p. 137.
87 "Vermerk," signed KK Menzel, 15 February 1950, p. 137.
88 "Verhandelt," signed KK Menzel and KK Griebsch, 16 February 1950, in Landesarchiv Berlin, Band II Mordsache Seidelmann/Merten (Tod durch Erdrosseln) B. Rep. 058 Nr. 893, p. 138.
89 "Verhandelt," signed KK Menzel and KK Griebsch, 16 February 1950, pp. 138–9.
90 "Verhandelt," signed KK Menzel and KK Griebsch, 16 February 1950, p. 142.
91 "Verhandelt," signed KK Menzel and KK Griebsch, 16 February 1950, p. 142.
92 "Verhandelt," signed KK Menzel and KK Griebsch, 17 February 1950, in Landesarchiv Berlin, Band II Mordsache Seidelmann/Merten (Tod durch Erdrosseln) B. Rep. 058 Nr. 893, p. 145.
93 "Verhandelt," signed KK Menzel and KK Griebsch, 17 February 1950, pp. 96, 149. For his rejection of the claims, see "Interview with Dr. Med. Freyaldenhoven, Wilhelm Gottfried Hubert," 30 March 1950, signed Freyaldenhoven, in Landesarchiv Berlin, B. Rep. 058 Nr. 896, p. 108.

94 "Bericht," signed KK Menzel, 18 February 1950, in Landesarchiv Berlin, Band II Mordsache Seidelmann/Merten (Tod durch Erdrosseln) B. Rep. 058 Nr. 893, n.p.; "Bfg. Beschluss," signed Ruppender (Assessor), 20 January 1950, in Landesarchiv Berlin, Band II Mordsache Seidelmann/Merten (Tod durch Erdrosseln) B. Rep. 058 Nr. 893, p. 154.

95 "Verhandelt," signed KK Griebsch and KK Menzel, 21 February 1950, in Landesarchiv Berlin, Band II Mordsache Seidelmann/Merten (Tod durch Erdrosseln) B. Rep. 058 Nr. 893, p. 162.

96 "Verhandelt," signed KK Griebsch and KK Menzel, 21 February 1950, p. 163.

97 "Verhandelt," signed KK Griebsch and KK Menzel, 21 February 1950, pp. 163–4.

98 "Verhandelt," signed KK Griebsch and KK Menzel, 21 February 1950, pp. 163–4.

99 "Vermerk," signed KA Weisheit and KA Zimmermann, 22 February 1950, in Landesarchiv Berlin, Band II Mordsache Seidelmann/Merten (Tod durch Erdrosseln) B. Rep. 058 Nr. 893, n.p. [probably p. 173]. On the radio, see B-F-G "An die Staatsanwaltschaft beim Landgericht Berlin," 21 March 1950, in Landesarchiv Berlin, B. Rep. 058 Nr. 896, n.p.; and "Untersuhungsrichter II to Berliner Finanzierungs-Ges.m.b.H," signed Dr. Otto (Landgerichtsrat), 6 April 1950, in Landesarchiv Berlin, B. Rep. 058 Nr. 896, p. 58.

100 "Vermerk," signed KK Menzel, 23 February 1950, in Landesarchiv Berlin, Band II Mordsache Seidelmann/Merten (Tod durch Erdrosseln) B. Rep. 058 Nr. 893, p. 174.

101 "Verhandelt," signed Kurt Muschan, countersigned KK Menzel, 24 February 1950, in Landesarchiv Berlin, Band II Mordsache Seidelmann/Merten (Tod durch Erdrosseln) B. Rep. 058 Nr. 893, p. 181.

102 Letter from the Generalstaatsanwalt bei dem Landgericht to the Untersuchungsrichter bei dem Landgericht Berlin, 11 March 1950, signature illegible, in Landesarchiv Berlin, B. Rep. 058 Nr. 896, p. 47.

6. The Trial of Elisabeth Kusian

1 R., "'Die Schöne Frau vom Zoo…' stand auf der Zigarettenschachtel des ermordeten Seidelmann," *Der Abend*, 11 January 1951; and Kr., "Treppenhaus in der Dämmerung," *Der Abend*, 13 January 1951. For a description of *Vom Teufel Gejagt*, see "Chased by the Devil (Vom Teufel gejagt)," Harvard Film Archive, accessed 29 May 2023, https://harvardfilmarchive.org/calendar/chased-by-the-devil-2018-11.

2 Procontra, "Sensation und Hintergrunde," *Der Kurier*, 13 January 1951.

3 H.H., "Doppelmörderin vor Gericht: Zum morgigen Beginn des Prozesses Kusian – Die psychologischen Hintergründe der beiden Morde," *Telegraf*, 14 January 1951.

4 For the weather, see "Berlin Weather in 1951," Extreme Weather Watch, accessed 30 May 2023, www.extremeweatherwatch.com/cities/berlin/year-1951.
5 "Neun Kinder starben für McCloy: Kohlennot in Westberlin ist die Ursache," *Neues Deutschland*, 14 January 1951; "Streiflichter aus Berlin," *Neues Deutschland*, 14 January 1951.
6 "Auftakt zum Fünfjahrplan: 'Leuna-Werk Walter Ulbricht': Feierliche Umbennung des ehemaligen IG-Farben Werkes in Anwesenheit des Initiators des Fünfjahrplanes, Walter Ulbricht"; "Umfassungsoperationen der Volksarmee: Durchbruch östlich von Wonjy/125 Kilomater vor Taigu/Interventen eingekesselt"; and "Erfolgreiche Streiks in Westberlin: Ij Neukölln und bei AEG-Turbine /UGO-Führung will Lohnkampf abwürgen," all in *Neues Deutschland*, 14 January 1951.
7 "Vor dem Kusian Prozeß: Die Erfolge der Berliner Volkspolizei lassen sich nicht vertuschen," *Neues Deutschland*, 14 January 1951.
8 Schertz, "100 Jahre Prozesse in Moabit," 30.
9 Zuckmayer, *Der Hauptmann von Köpenick*.
10 Schertz, "100 Jahre Prozesse in Moabit," 32–6.
11 Haase and Borgas, "Bau- und andere Geschichten aus dem Kriminalgericht Moabit," 24.
12 Schertz, "100 Jahre Prozesse in Moabit," 39.
13 Haase and Borgas, "Bau- und andere Geschichten aus dem Kriminalgericht Moabit, 11–14.
14 Hett, *Death in the Tiergarten*, 48.
15 The only novel-length, fictional treatment of her case is Bosetzky, *Der kalte Engel*, translated into English as *Cold Angel: Murder in Berlin 1949*.
16 The description of the Moabit complex is drawn from Hett's brilliant *Death in the Tiergarten*, 17.
17 For the weather, see "Berlin Weather in 1951," Extreme Weather Watch, accessed 30 May 2023, www.extremeweatherwatch.com/cities/berlin/year-1951. The scene is described in "Elisabeth Kusian 'Ich verweigere die Aussage,'" *Die Neue Zeitung*, 15 January 1951.
18 Reuß, "Kleinere Beiträge," 173.
19 König, *Vom Dienst am Recht*, 243.
20 König, 243.
21 König, 242.
22 Bohlander, *Principles of German Criminal Procedure*, 49–50.
23 Yorck von Wartenburg, *The Power of Solitude*, 78.
24 Yorck von Wartenburg, 48 and passim.
25 The description comes from "Vor dem Kusian Prozeß: Die Erfolge der Berliner Volkspolizei lassen sich nicht vertuschen," *Neues Deutschland*, 14 January 1951. See also "Lügen, Morphium, Liebe, Mord…: Das

Leben der Elisabeth Kusian – Über ihre Verbrechen schweigt sie – Erste Zeugenaussagen," *Telegraf*, 15 January 1951.

26 Bohlander, *Principles of German Criminal Procedure*, 7.

27 "Lügen, Morphium, Liebe, Mord…: Das Leben der Elisabeth Kusian – Über ihre Verbrechen schweigt sie – Erste Zeugenaussagen," *Telegraf*, 15 January 1951; "Sensation im Kusian-Prozeß," *Der Abend*, 15 January 1951.

28 "Lügen, Morphium, Liebe, Mord…: Das Leben der Elisabeth Kusian."

29 Eig. Ber., "Ein für die Stumm-Polizei peinlicher Prozeß," *Tägliche Rundschau*, 16 January 1951.

30 Eig. Ber., "Ein für die Stumm-Polizei peinlicher Prozeß."

31 Eig. Ber., "Ein für die Stumm-Polizei peinlicher Prozeß."

32 Eig. Ber., "Ein für die Stumm-Polizei peinlicher Prozeß."

33 J.D., "Indizien und Gutsachten gegen die Kusian: 'Schwarze Unbekannte' gesucht / Sachverständiger: Voll zurechtnungsfähig / Freitag Fortsetzung," *Der Tag*, 16 January 1951.

34 J.D., "Indizien und Gutsachten gegen die Kusian."

35 J.D., "Indizien und Gutsachten gegen die Kusian."

36 H.H., "Frau Kusian beschuldigt ihren Mann: Zwischenfall im Doppelmordprozeß – Zeuge im Gerichtssaal festgenommen," *Telegraf*, 17 January 1951; "Mein Mann hat die Morde begangen: Sensationelle Wendung im Prozeß Kusian. – Festnahme des Zeugen Walter Kusian im Gerichtssaal," *Die Neue Zeitung*, 17 January 1951.

37 Rudolf Hirsch, "Die Westjustiz wird mit dem Fall Kusian nicht Fertig," *Tägliche Rundschau*, 17 January 1951.

38 H.H., "Frau Kusian beschuldigt ihren Mann."

39 "Mein Mann hat die Morde begangen: Sensationelle Wendung im Prozeß Kusian. – Festnahme des Zeugen Walter Kusian im Gerichtssaal," *Die Neue Zeitung*, 17 January 1951. The following story of the exchange and accusation is pieced together from a series of articles from different newspapers. Each reporter emphasized a different statement or statements.

40 The description of her as if bitten comes from Carl Corvus, "'Mein Mann war der Mörder': Sensationelle Wendung im Kusian Prozeß – Im Scdhwurgerichtssaal festgenommen," *Der Tagesspiegel*, 17 January 1951. The rest is from Hirsch, "Die Westjustiz wird mit dem Fall Kusian nicht Fertig."

41 H.H., "Frau Kusian beschuldigt ihren Mann."

42 Corvus, "'Mein Mann war der Mörder.'"

43 H.H., "Frau Kusian beschuldigt ihren Mann."

44 Corvus, "'Mein Mann war der Mörder.'"

45 "Volkspolizei hat vorbildlich gearbeitet: Der zweite Tag des Kusian-Prozesses / Neue 'Geständnisse,'" *Neues Deutschland*, 17 January 1951.

46 "Mein Mann hat die Morde begangen."
47 Kh/-e, "Dramatische Wendung im Kusian-Prozeß: Angeklagte belastet ihren Mann/Walter Kusian verhaftet/Couch als Beweisstück vor Gericht," *Der Tag*, 17 January 1951.
48 H.H., "Frau Kusian beschuldigt ihren Mann."
49 Eigenbericht "Der Abend," "Walter Kusian streitet die Morde ab: Taxi fahrer gesucht. Wer führ in der Mordnacht Mann mit schwerem Gepäck?" *Der Abend*, 17 January 1951.
50 Procontra, "Frau Kusian gebärdet sich als Märtyrerin," *Der Kurier*, 17 January 1951.
51 Eigenbericht "Der Abend," "Walter Kusian streitet die Morde ab."
52 Eigenbericht "Der Abend," "Walter Kusian streitet die Morde ab."
53 J.D., "Indizien und Gutsachten gegen die Kusian: 'Schwarze Unbekannte' gesucht/ Sachverständiger: Voll zurechtnungsfähig/ Freitag Fortsetzung," *Der Tag*, 16 January 1951.
54 Cobra, "Mordprozeß Elisabeth Kusian: Sensation um jeden Preis/Herrn M. Macht von sich reden," *Berliner Zeitung*, 16 January 1951.
55 "Veränderte Situation im Kusianprozeß," *Der Kurier*, 16 January 1951.
56 "Lüge oder Wahrheit?" *Der Tagesspiegel*, 17 January 1951.
57 Moeller, "War Stories," 1013.
58 Moeller, 1026.
59 Potter, *Art of Suppression*, 103.
60 Heineman, "The Hour of the Woman," 355.
61 Heineman, 360.
62 Eig. Ber., "Ein für die Stumm-Polizei peinlicher Prozeß."
63 Hirsch, "Die Westjustiz wird mit dem Fall Kusian nicht Fertig."
64 Cobra, "Mordprozeß Elisabeth Kusian: Sensation um jeden Preis"; "Rummel um den Kusian-Prozeß: Ablenkung von der Remilitarisierung/Welche Rolle spielte Kurt M.?" *Neues Deutschland*, 16 January 1951.
65 Spilker, *The East German Leadership and the Division of Germany*, 212–15. The quotation is from 214.
66 For the views of a historian who thinks it might have, but it collapsed under the exigencies of the Cold War, see Lemke, "Eine deutsche Chance?," 25–40.
67 Grotewohl, "Für eine ungeteilte deutsche Republik," 247–80.
68 Grotewohl, "Die westlichen Besatungsmächte zerreißen," 281–7.
69 Cobra, "Mordprozeß Elisabeth Kusian: Vorbildliche Arbeit der Volkspolizei – einzig verläßliche Unterlage," *Berliner Zeitung*, 18 January 1951.
70 Dix, "Frau Kusians Couch vor dem Richtertisch: Die Angeklagte wird zur Blutprobe geführt – Der geheimnisvolle Taxichauffeur," *Die Neue Zeitung*, 18 January 1951.

71 Rudolf Hirsch, "Kusian-Prozeß auf dem toten Punkt," *Tägliche Rundschau*, 18 January 1951.
72 Carl Corvus, "Elisabeth Kusian erneut belastet: Die Couch im Gerichtssaal – Gutachten der medizinischen Sachverständigen," *Der Tagesspiegel*, 18 January 1951.
73 Dix, "Frau Kusians Couch vor dem Richtertisch."
74 Corvus, "Elisabeth Kusian erneut belastet."
75 H.H., "Die Geheimnisvolle 'dunkle Dame': Mißfallenskundgebungen gegen die Angeklagte Kusian – Verteidiger unter der Mord-Couch," *Telegraf*, 18 January 1951.
76 H.H., "Die Geheimnisvolle 'dunkle Dame.'"
77 H.H., "Die Geheimnisvolle 'dunkle Dame.'"
78 H.H., "Die Geheimnisvolle 'dunkle Dame.'"
79 Corvus, "Elisabeth Kusian erneut belastet."
80 Dix, "Frau Kusians Couch vor dem Richtertisch."
81 Dix, "Frau Kusians Couch vor dem Richtertisch."
82 H.H., "Die Geheimnisvolle 'dunkle Dame.'"
83 Cobra, "Mordprozeß Elisabeth Kusian: Vorbildliche Arbeit der Volkspolizei."
84 Procontra, "Ein Alibi, aus Papierschnitzeln zusammengesetzt: Bandaufnahme enthüllt den Widerspruch im Kusian Monolog," *Der Kurier*, 20 January 1951; "Kusian-Urteil nicht vor Mittwoch," *Telegraf*, 19 January 1951.
85 Procontra, "Ein Alibi, aus Papierschnitzeln zusammengesetzt."
86 "Staatsanwalt sucht Taxifahrer," *Telegraf*, 19 January 1951.
87 J.D., "Fall Kusian wird immer undurchsichtiger: Auch die Astrologin half nichts/War doch ein Mann dabei? 'Das ist er!' Fortsetzung Dienstag," *Der Tag*, 20 January 1951.
88 J.D., "Fall Kusian wird immer undurchsichtiger."
89 Procontra, "Ein Alibi, aus Papierschnitzeln zusammengesetzt."
90 J.D., "Fall Kusian wird immer undurchsichtiger."
91 Procontra, "Ein Alibi, aus Papierschnitzeln zusammengesetzt."
92 Procontra, "Ein Alibi, aus Papierschnitzeln zusammengesetzt"; "Hatte die Angeklagte Helfer? Widersprechende Zeugenaussagen – Lautsprecherübertragung des Geständnisses," *Der Tagesspiegel*, 20 January 1951.
93 "Hatte die Angeklagte Helfer?"
94 "Hatte die Angeklagte Helfer?"
95 J.D., "Fall Kusian wird immer undurchsichtiger"; Cobra, "Mordprozeß Elisabeth Kusian: Walter Kusian haftentlassen/Fauler Astrologen-Zauber," *Berliner Zeitung*, 20 January 1951; H.H., "Die Kusian erneut schwer belastet: Verhandlung bis Dienstag ausgesetzt – Der geschiedene Man aus der Haft entlassen," *Telegraf*, 20 January 1951.

96 Fricke, "'Zur Botschaft des Widerstandes im Deutschland der Diktaturen,'" 73.
97 Procontra, "Ist Frau Kusian soviel Aufhebens wert?" *Der Kurier*, 22 January 1951.
98 Belgum, *Popularizing the Nation*.
99 H.H., "'Das Gemeinste Weib, das ich kenne' Was eine Untersuchingsgefangene über die Kusian sagte – Das Gerichtspsychiater als Zeuge," *Telegraf*, 24 January 1951.
100 H.H., "'Das Gemeinste Weib, das ich kenne.'"
101 H.H., "'Das Gemeinste Weib, das ich kenne.'"
102 "Kusian-Prozeß; Weimann sagt aus," *Der Kurier*, 23 January 1951.
103 Dix, "'Ich allein habe die beiden getötet': Abschluß der Beweisaufnahme im Kusian Prozeß – Heute Pläydoyers," *Neue Zeitung*, 24 January 1951; Carl Corvus, "'Sie stellen Fragen, Herr Staatsanwalt' Elisabeth Kusian bleibt bei letztem Geständnis – Schluß der Beweissaufnahme," *Der Tagesspiegel*, 24 January 1951.
104 Corvus, "'Sie stellen Fragen, Herr Staatsanwalt'"; R.H., "Jetzt had der Staatsanwalt das Wort," *Der Abend*, 24 January 1951.
105 Rudolf Hirsch, "Korsch findet einmal ein hartes Wort," *Tägliche Rundschau*, 24 January 1951.
106 H.H., "'Das Gemeinste Weib, das ich kenne.'"
107 Corvus, "'Sie stellen Fragen, Herr Staatsanwalt.'"
108 Procontra, "Haß und Furcht beschworen die Katastrophe. Frau Kusian: 'Ich hatte meinen Mann ermordet…!'" *Der Kurier*, 24 January 1951.
109 Jochen Harringa, "Die Verstrickung der drei Liebenden," *Der Tagesspiegel*, 24 January 1951.
110 Cobra, "Mordprozeß Elisabeth Kusian. Abschluß der Beweisaufnahme/ 'Diese Trauben sind zu sauer…,'" *Berliner Zeitung*, 24 January 1951.
111 R.H., "Jetzt had der Staatsanwalt das Wort," *Der Abend*, 24 January 1951.
112 H.H., "'Das Gemeinste Weib, das ich kenne'"; R.H., "Jetzt had der Staatsanwalt das Wort."
113 H.H., "'Kein Mitleid mit der Mörderin!': Staatsanwalt Kuntze halt sein Plädoyer – Die Verteidiger haben das Wort," *Telegraf*, 25 January 1951.
114 H.H., "'Kein Mitleid mit der Mörderin!'"; and Carl Corvus, "Lebenslänglich Zuchthaus für Elisabeth Kusian: Urteilsverkündung nach einstündiger Beratung – Die Plädoyers des Staatsanwalts und der Verteidigung," *Der Tagesspiegel*, 25 January 1951.
115 H.H., "'Kein Mitleid mit der Mörderin!'"
116 H.H., "'Kein Mitleid mit der Mörderin!'"
117 "Lebenslänglich für Elisabeth Kusian," *Die Neue Zeitung*, 25 January 1951.
118 J.D., "Höchststrafe nach kurzer Beratung: Die Begrundung des Kusian-Urteils/Ehemann entlastet/Stärkstes Indiz: die Aussage-Protokolle," *Der Tag*, 25 January 1951.

119 Procontra, "Höchststrafe für Frau Kusian: Es blieben Rätsel – aber keine Zweifel," *Der Kurier*, 25 January 1951.

120 Procontra, "Höfchststrafe für Frau Kusian."

121 Maria Sack, "Und was wird aus den Kindern? Elisabeth Kusians Töchter und ihr Sohn kennen das Schicksal ihrer Mutter," *Der Tagesspiegel*, 26 January 1951.

122 "Fruchtbares Grauen," *Der Abend*, no date [probably 25 January 1951].

123 H. Schad, "Das Urteil ist gesprochen: Elisabeth Kusian wurde zu lebenslänglicher Zuchthausstrafe verurteilt," *Die Welt am Sonntag*, 28 January 1951.

After

1 Cobra, "Justitia tanzte Boogie-Woogie: Hinter den Kulissen des Kusian – Theaters in Moabit," *Die Berliner Zeitung*, 26 January 1951.

2 "Zweimal lebenslänglich für Kusian: 'Sensationsprozeß' konnte das Westberliner Elend nicht verschleiern," *Neues Deutschland*, 25 January 1951.

3 Geerling, Magee, and Smyth, "Occupation, Reparations, and Rebellion."

4 Dr. Friedrich Karl Fromm, "Hat Frau Kusian 'Fair Trial' gehabt?," *Die Neue Zeitung*, 3 February 1951.

5 See, for example, Moeller, *Protecting Motherhood*.

6 Pollak, *Tatort Sektorengrenze*, 91.

7 The novel is Bosetzky, *Der kalte Engel*. The Kusian comic is in Kleist, *Berliner Mythen*. The memoir is Weimann, *Diagnose Mord*. The work of forensic science is Geserick, Vendura, and Wirth, *Zeitzeuge Tod*. The work of history is Fenemore, *Dismembered Policing in Postwar Berlin*.

8 Weimann, *Diagnose Mord*.

9 The case file including accusation, Weimann's rebuttal, and the resolution can be found in Landesarchiv Berlin, B. Rep. 058 Nr. 10121.

10 Reuß, "Kleinere Beiträge."

11 Jaeger and Gabka, "In Memoriam Erwin Gohrbandt."

12 Nebe and Kleinmanns, "Wenn der Paladin krank wurde," 173fn38.

13 Luther, "Zum Wirken des Chirurgen Erwin Gohrbandt (1890–1965)," 1005–8. "Selbst als die Faschisten mit der Vernichtung 'minderertigen Lebens' begannen, erkannte Gohrbandt nicht den inhumanen Charakter dieser Staatsform und hielt 1934 vor der Berliner Chirurgischen Gesellschaft sogar einen Vortrag über die Sterilisation des Mannes, der veröffentlicht wurde." And "Trotzdem er zu den radikalen Machenschaften des Nazi-Regimes eine gewissen Distanz bewahrte, unterstreichen seine militärärztlichen Aktivitäten im zweiten Weltkrieg sein mangelndes politisches Verständnis." Both quotations are from 1006.

14 Bagco Coffee Bar, "What's the Vibe?," accessed 10 August 2024, https://www.yelp.com/biz/bagco-coffee-bar-berlin.

15 Traces of War, "Stumbling Stones Kantstraße 154a," accessed 10 August 2024, https://www.tracesofwar.com/sights/31503/Stumbling-Stones-Kantstraße-154a.htm.

16 Christiane, *Wir Kinder von Bahnhof Zoo.*

17 On Knie and what would come later, see Bodenschatz, "Städtebau und Architektur des Ernst-Reuter-Platzes."

18 "zur Klärung eines Sachverhaltes." For the building's history, see the one page document, produced by the Senatsverwaltung für Bildung, Jugend und Familie, "Geschichte des Gebäudes Bernard Weiss Str. 6," accessed 27 October 2021, https://www.berlin.de/sen/bjf/ueber-uns/historisches/geschichte_des_gebaeudes_bernhard_weiss_str_6.pdf.

19 Senatsverwaltung für Bildung, Jugend und Familie, "Historisches: Das Haus in der Bernhard-Weiß-Straße 6," accessed 27 October 2021, https://www.berlin.de/sen/bjf/ueber-uns/historisches/. On Weiß, see Rott, *"Ich gehe meinen Weg ungehindert geradeaus": Dr. Bernhard Weiß (1880–1951).*

20 Heubner, "Education in the Shadow of the Iron Curtain."

21 Spencer, "Berlin: One Year of the Wall."

22 A photo of the plaque can be seen at Wikipedia, "Kommune 1," accessed 20 June 2024, https://en.wikipedia.org/wiki/Kommune_1. For a personal history of Kommune I, see Enzensberger, *Die Jahre der Kommune I, Berlin 1967–1969.*

23 Quoted in Pollak, *Tatort Sektorengrenze,* 90.

Bibliography

Archives

Bundesarchiv Berlin

BArch R 9361 – II-606072 (Walter Kusian's Nazi Party File)
BArch R 9361 – IX-KARTEI/24351506 (Walter Kusian's Nazi Party Card)

Landesarchiv Berlin

A. Rep. 001–06, Nr. 32459 (Postwar Personnel Files on Waldemar Weimann)
A. Rep. 001–06, Nr. 33880 (Postwar Personnel Files on Waldemar Weimann)
B. Rep. 008–10 Nr. 1379 (Nazi Era Personnel Files on Waldemar Weimann)
B. Rep. 058 Nr. 889 (Official Psychiatric Evaluation of Elisabeth Kusian)
B. Rep. 058 Nr. 890 (Prosecutorial Files)
B. Rep. 058 Nr. 891 (Conviction Records and Death Notice)
B. Rep. 058 Nr. 892 (Diagram and Photograph of Elisabeth Kusian's Apartment)
B. Rep. 058 Nr. 893 (Police Investigation Records, Including Witness Reports, Statements, and Final Police Report with Police Narrative of the Events)
B. Rep. 058 Nr. 894 (Internal Police Reports and Interdepartmental Correspondence)
B. Rep. 058 Nr. 895 (Internal Police Reports)
B. Rep. 058 Nr. 896 (Internal Police Reports)
B. Rep. 058 Nr. 897 (Internal Police Reports)
B. Rep. 058 Nr. 898 (Elisabeth Kusian's Handwritten Diary)
B. Rep. 058 Nr. 899 (Press Clippings Related to the Case and to the Subsequent Trial)
B. Rep. 058 Nr. 10121 (The Case and Trial of Waldemar Weimann for Crimes against Humanity)
C. Rep. 031–01–04 Nr. 475 (Denazification File for Wilhelm Freyaldenhoven)

Polizeihistorische Sammlung Berlin

PHS D 4.41 Band 24a (Volkspolizei Files on the Kusian Case)
PHS D 4.41 Band 24b (Volkspolizei Files on the Kusian Case)
PHS D 4.41 Band 24c (Volkspolizei Files on the Kusian Case)
PHS D 4.41 Band 24d (Volkspolizei Files on the Kusian Case)
PHS D 4.41 Band 24e (Volkspolizei Files on the Kusian Case)

The National Archives at Kew

FO 1012/209 (German Prisons)
FO 1012/328 (Consumer Goods)
FO 1012/337 (Berlin Magistrate)
FO 1012/505 (Confiscated Goods)
FO 1012/529 (Public Safety, General)
FO 1012/530 (German Courts, Jurisdiction)
FO 1012/590 (Morale)
FO 1012/671 (Complaints and Enquiries: Criminal)
FO 1012/741 (Conditions of Service in Berlin Police: Statutes)
FO 1012/751 (Reorganisation of Police)
FO 1012/757 (Berlin Police Federation)

Newspapers

Der Abend
Berliner Zeitung
Der Kurier
Der Morgen
Neues Deutschland
Neue Zeit
Die Neue Zeitung
Der Tag
Der Tagesspiegel
Tägliche Rundschau
Telegraf
Die Welt am Sonntag

Published Primary Sources

Andreas-Friedrich, Ruth. *Battleground Berlin: Diaries, 1938–1949.* Translated by Anna Boerresen. New York: Paragon House, 1990.

Anonymous. *A Woman in Berlin: Eight Weeks in the Conquered City, A Diary.* Translated by Philip Boehm. New York: Virago Press, 2000.

Bach, Julian. *America's Germany: An Account of the Occupation*. New York: Random House, 1946.

Bader, Karl Siegfried. *Soziologie der deutschen Nachkriegskriminalität*. Tübingen: J.C.B. Mohr, 1949.

Barthel, Johanna. *Berlin nach dem Krieg – wie ich es erlebt habe*. Berlin: Berliner Forum, 1977.

Bundesministerium für Vertriebene, ed. *Berlin. Kriegs- und Nachkriegsschicksal der Reichshauptstadt. Dokumente deutscher Kriegsschäden, Bd. IV 2*. Bonn: Bundesministerium für Vertriebene, 1967.

Byford-Jones, W. *Berlin Twilight*. London: Hutchinson, 1947.

Deutscher, Isaac. *Reportagen Aus Nachkriegsdeutschland*. Translated by Tamara Deutscher. Hamburg: Junius, 1980.

Frederiksen, Oliver J. *The American Military Occupation of Germany, 1945–1953*. Historical Division Headquarters, United States Army, Europe, 1953.

Hauptamt für Statistik und Wahlen. *Berlin in Zahlen 1950*. Berlin: Hauptamt für Statistik, 1950.

Howley, Frank. *Berlin Command*. New York: Putnam, 1950.

Kruse, Peter, ed. *Bomben, Trümmer, Lucky Strikes: Die Stunde Null in bisher unbekannten Manuskripten*. Berlin: WJS, 2004.

Maginnis, John J. *Military Government Journal: Normandy to Berlin*. Amherst: University of Massachusetts Press, 1971.

Malzahn, Manfred. *Germany 1945–1949*. London: Routledge, 1991.

Rürup, Reinhard, ed. *Berlin 1945: Eine Dokumentation*. Berlin: W. Arenhövel, 1995.

Settel, Arthur, ed. *This Is Germany: A Report on Post War Germany by 21 Newspaper Correspondents*. New York: William Sloane, 1950.

Weimann, Waldemar. *Diagnose Mord: Die Memoiren eines Gerichtsmediziners*. Bayreuth: Hestia, 1964.

Yorck von Wartenburg, Marion. *The Power of Solitude: My Life in the German Resistance*. Translated by Julie M. Winter. Lincoln: University of Nebraska Press, 2000.

Published Secondary Sources

Abenstein, Edelgard, and Jeannine Fiedler. *Berlin: Kunst und Architecture*. Potsdam: Ullmann Publishing, 2009.

Allinson, Mark Andrew. "Faith, Hope and Apathy: Politics and Popular Opinion in Thuringia, 1945–1968." PhD diss., University of London, University College, 1997.

Asmuss, Burkhard, and Andreas Nachama. "Zur Geschichte der Juden in Berlin und das Jüdische Gemeindezentrum in Charlottenburg." In Ribbe, *Von der Residenz zur City*, 165–228.

Anderson, Benedict. *Buried City, Unearthing Teufelsberg: Berlin and Its Geography of Forgetting*. Oxford: Taylor & Francis, 2017. https://doi.org/10.4324/9781315570556.

Anderton, Abby. *Rubble Music: Occupying the Ruins of Postwar Berlin 1945–1950*. Bloomington: Indiana University Press, 2019. https://doi.org/10.2307/j.ctvm202n8.

Ankum, Katharina von, ed. *Women in the Metropolis: Gender and Modernity in Weimar Culture*. Berkeley: University of California Press, 1997. https://doi.org/10.1525/9780520917606.

Badstübner, Rolf, and Heinz Heitzer, eds. *Die DDR in der Übergangsperiode: Studien zur Vorgeschichte und Geschichte der DDR 1945 bis 1961*. Berlin: Akademie Verlag, 1982.

Barck, Simone. "Zeugnis ablegen. Zum frühen Antifaschismus-Diskurs am Beispiel des VVN-Verlags." In *Verwaltete Vergangenheit: Geschichtskultur und Herrschaftslegitimation in der DDR*, edited by Martin Sabrow, 252–91. Leipzig: Akademische Verlangsanstalt, 1997.

Bartels, E.H. "Berlin's Tiergarten: Evolution of an Urban Park." *The Journal of Garden History* 2, no. 2 (1982): 143–74. https://doi.org/10.1080/01445170.1982.10412400.

Barz, Jürgen, Johann Bösche, Hans Joachim, Rosemarie Käppner, Rainer Mattern, and Harald Frohberg, eds. *Fortschritte der Rechtsmedizin: Festschrift für Georg Schmidt*. Berlin: Springer Verlag, 1983. https://doi.org/10.1007/978-3-642-68930-7.

Barzilai, Maya. "S.Y. Agnon's German Consecration and the 'Miracle' of Hebrew Letters." *Prooftexts* 33, no. 1 (Winter 2013): 48–75. https://doi.org/10.2979/prooftexts.33.1.48.

Beddies, Thomas, and Heinz-Peter Schmiedebach. "‚Euthanasie'-Opfer Und Versuchsobjekte. Kranke Und Behinderte Kinder in Berlin Während Des Zweiten Weltkriegs/'Euthanasia'-Victims and Test Objects. The Fate of Diseased, Disabled and Mentally Retarded Children in Berlin during World War II." *Medizinhistorisches Journal* 9, nos. 2/3 (2004): 165–96. https://www.jstor.org/stable/25805369.

Beevor, Antony. *Berlin: The Downfall 1945*. London: Penguin Books, 2003.

Belgum, Kirsten. *Popularizing the Nation: Audience, Representation, and the Production of Identity in Die Gartenlaube, 1853–1900*. Lincoln: University Nebraska Press, 1998.

Benedict, Susan, and Linda Shields, eds. *Nurses and Midwives in Nazi Germany: The Euthanasia Programs*. New York: Routledge, 2014. https://doi.org/10.4324/9781315832616.

Ben Hounet, Yazid, and Deborah Puccio-Den, eds. *Truth, Intentionality and Evidence: Anthropological Approaches to Crime*. London: Routledge, 2017. https://doi.org/10.4324/9781315627748.

Bessel, Richard. "Establishing Order in Post-War Eastern Germany." *Past and Present* 210, Supplement 6 (2011): 139–57. https://doi.org/10.1093/pastj/gt4.

Bessel, Richard, and Dirk Schumann, eds. *Life after Death: Approaches to a Cultural and Social History of Europe During the 1940s and 1950s.* Cambridge: Cambridge University Press, 2003. https://doi.org/10.1017/CBO9781139052344.

Betts, Paul. "Manners, Morality, and Civilization: Reflections on Postwar German Etiquette Books." In Biess and Moeller, *Histories of the Aftermath*, 196–214. https://doi.org/10.1515/9781845459987-013.

Biess, Frank. "Feelings in the Aftermath: Toward a History of Postwar Emotions." In Biess and Moeller, *Histories of the Aftermath*, 30–48. https://doi.org/10.1515/9781845459987-004.

Biess, Frank, and Robert Moeller, eds. *Histories of the Aftermath: The Legacies of the Second World War in Europe.* New York: Berghahn Books, 2010. https://doi.org/10.3167/9781845457327.

Black, Monica. "Death and the Making of West Berlin, 1948–1951." *German History* 27, no. 1 (2009): 6–31. https://doi.org/10.1093/gerhis/ghn075.

– *Death in Berlin from Weimar to Divided Germany.* Cambridge: Cambridge University Press, 2010.

Bodenschatz, Harald. "Städtebau und Architektur des Ernst-Reuter-Platzes." Vortrag im Rahmen der Ersten Standortkonferenz Ernst-Reuter-Platz im Architekturgebäude der TU Berlin am 30.11.2011 (Veranstalter: Regionalmanagement City West). https://www.bauhaus-reuse.de/index.php/content/bau_und_architektur_des_erp/.

Bohlander, Michael. *Principles of German Criminal Procedure.* London: Bloomsbury, 2012. ProQuest Ebook Central.

Bosetzky, Horst. *Cold Angel: Murder in Berlin 1949.* Translated by Catherine Dop Miller. New York: Enigma Books, 2012.

– *Der kalte Engel.* Berlin: Jaron Verlag, 2002.

Botting, Douglas. *From the Ruins of the Reich: Germany 1945–1949.* New York: Random House, 1985.

Boyle, Kevin. *Arc of Justice: A Saga of Race, Civil Rights, and Murder in the Jazz Age.* New York: Henry Holt, 2007.

Brett-Smith, Richard. *Berlin '45: The Grey* City. London: St. Martin's Press, 1967.

Bugan, Carmen. *Burying the Typewriter: A Memoir.* St. Paul: Graywolf Press, 2012.

Caldwell, Peter C., and Karrin Hanshew. *Germany Since 1945: Politics, Culture, and Society.* London: Bloomsbury, 2018.

Carter, Erica. *How German Is She? Postwar West German Reconstruction and the Consuming Woman.* Ann Arbor: University of Michigan Press, 1997.

Case, Holly. "Innocents Lost: On Postwar Orphans." *The Nation*, 31 October 2011. https://www.thenation.com/article/archive/innocents-lost-postwar-orphans/.

Certeau, Michel de. *The Practice of Everyday Life*. Berkeley: University of California Press, 1984.

Chan, Janet. "Changing Police Culture." *British Journal of Criminology* 36, no. 1 (Winter 1996): 109–34. https://doi.org/10.1093/oxfordjournals.bjc.a014061.

Christiane, F. *Wir Kinder von Bahnhof Zoo*. Hamburg: Gruner und Jahr, 1979.

Clark, C.M. "West Germany Confronts the Nazi Past: Some Recent Debates on the Early Postwar Era, 1945–1960." *The European Legacy* 4, no. 1 (1999): 113–30. https://doi.org/10.1080/10848779908579949.

Clarke, David, and Ute Wölfel, eds. *Remembering the German Democratic Republic: Divided Memory in a United Germany*. London: Palgrave Macmillan, 2011. https://doi.org/10.1057/9780230349698.

Collier, Irwin, Jr., and David H. Papell. "About Two Marks: Refugees and the Exchange Rate Before the Berlin Wall." *The American Economic Review* 78, no. 3 (June 1988): 531–42. https://www.jstor.org/stable/1809150.

Connelly, John. "Nazis and Slavs: From Racial Theory to Racist Practice." *Central European History* 32, no. 1 (March 1999): 1–33. https://doi.org/10.1017/S0008938900020628.

Crew, David F. *Bodies and Ruins: Imagining the Bombing of Germany, 1945 to the Present*. Ann Arbor: University of Michigan Press, 2017. https://doi.org/10.3998/mpub.340367.

–, ed. *Nazism and German Society, 1933–1945*. London: Routledge, 1994.

Crimmins, Courtney Glore. "Reinterpreting the Soviet War Memorial in Berlin's Treptower Park after 1990." In *Remembering the German Democratic Republic*, edited by David Clarke and Ute Wölfe, 54–64. London: Palgrave Macmillan, 2011. https://doi.org/10.1057/9780230349698_4.

D'Cruze, Shani, and Louise A. Jackson. *Women, Crime and Justice in England Since 1660*. London: Palgrave Macmillan, 2009. https://doi.org/10.1007/978-1-137-05720-4.

Delhi, Martin. "Shaping History: Alexander Mitscherlich and German Psychoanalysis after 1945." *Psychoanalysis and History* 11, no. 1 (January 2009): 57–74. https://doi.org/10.3366/E1460823508000287.

Demps, Laurenz, Klaus Hübner, and Georg Schertz. *Berliner Polizei: Von 1945 bis zur Gegenwart*. Berlin: Förderkreis PHS Berlin, 2020.

Dempsey, Anna M. "Berlin's Hackescher Markt: Gentrification, Cultural Memory and the New Public Square." In *Local/Global Narratives*, edited by Renate Rechtien and Karoline von Oppen, 255–79. Amsterdam: Brill, 2007. https://doi.org/10.1163/9789042032132_014.

Diefendorf, Jeffrey M. *In the Wake of War: The Reconstruction of German Cities After World War II*. New York: Oxford University Press, 1993. https://doi.org/10.1093/oso/9780195072198.001.0001.

Dinter, Andreas. *Berlin in Trümmern: Ernährungslage und medizinische Versorgung der Bevölkerung Berlins nach dem II. Weltkrieg*. Berlin: Wünsche, 1999.

Donath, Matthias, and Gabriele Schulz, eds. *Denkmale in Berlin: Bezirk Mitte. Ortsteile Wedding und Gesundbrunnen*. Petersberg: Michael Imhof Verlag, 2004.

Dörr, Margarete. *Wer die Zeit nicht miterlebt hat – Frauenerfahrungen im Zweiten Weltkrieg und in den Jahren danach*. Frankfurt: Campus Verlag, 1998.

Edensor, Tim. *Industrial Ruins: Space, Aesthetics, and Materiality*. New York: Bloomsbury, 2005. https://doi.org/10.5040/9781474214940.

Eghigian, Greg. "The Psychologization of the Socialist Self: East German Forensic Psychology and Its Deviants, 1945–1975." *German History* 22, no. 2 (April 2004): 181–205. https://doi.org/10.1191/0266355404gh305oa.

Elder, Sace. *Murder Scenes: Normality, Deviance, and Criminal Violence in Weimar Berlin*. Ann Arbor: University of Michigan Press, 2010. https://doi.org/10.3998/mpub.1177008.

Enzensberger, Ulrich. *Die Jahre der Kommune I, Berlin 1967–1969*. Cologne: Kiepenheuer & Witsch, 2004.

Etzel, Matthias. *Die Aufhebung von nationalsozialistischen Gesetzen durch den Alliierten Kontrollrat (1945–48)*. Tübingen: Mohr Siebeck, 1992.

Evans, Jennifer V. *Life Among the Ruins: Cityscape and Sexuality in Cold War Berlin*. New York: Palgrave Macmillan, 2011. https://doi.org/10.1057/9780230316652.

Evans, Richard J. *Tales from the German Underworld*. New Haven: Yale University Press, 1998.

Fenemore, Mark. *Dismembered Policing in Postwar Berlin: The Limits of Four-Power Government*. New York: Bloomsbury, 2023. https://doi.org/10.5040/9781350334205.

Fest, Joachim. *Plotting Hitler's Death: The Story of the German Resistance*. Translated by Bruce Little. New York: Henry Holt, 1994.

Fichter, Tilman, and Siegward Lönnendonker. *Kleine Geschichte des SDS*. Essen: Klartext, 2007.

50 Jahre Rudolf-Virchow-Krankenhaus. Berlin: Verwahltung des Rudolf Virchow-Krankenhauses, 1956.

Fischer, Wolfram, Klaus Hierholzer, Michael Hubenstorf, Peter Th. Walther, and Rolf Winau, eds. *Exodus von Wissenschaften aus Berlin: Fragestellungen – Ergebnisse – Desiderate. Entwicklungen vor und nach 1933*. Berlin: Walter de Gruyter, 1994. https://doi.org/10.1515/9783110883725.

Förderkreis Polizeihistorische Sammlung Berlin E.V., ed. *Berliner Kriminalpolizei von 1945 bis zur Gegenwart*. Berlin: Förderkreis PHS Berlin, 2019.

Frankel, Tamar. *The Ponzi Scheme Puzzle: A History and Analysis of Con Artists and Victims*. Oxford: Oxford University Press, 2012. https://doi.org/10.1093/acprof:osobl/9780199926619.001.0001.

Freud, Sigmund. *The Uncanny*. Translated by David McLintock. New York: Penguin Books, 2003.

Fricke, Karl Wilhelm. *Politik und Justiz in der DDR: Zur Geschichte der politischen Verfolgung 1945–1968*. Cologne: Verlag Wissenschaft und Politik, 1979.

– "'Zur Botschaft des Widerstandes im Deutschland der Diktaturen': Vortrag zur Ehrenpromotion im Rahmen der Diplom-Abschlußfeier des Fachbereichs Politische Wissenschaft der Freien Universität Berlin am. 12. Juli 1996." *Zeitschrift des Forschungsverbundes SED-Staat* 2, no. 2 (1996): 71–5.

Fülberth, Johannes. *Das Gefängnis Spandau 1918–1947*. Berlin: BeBra Wissenschaft Verlag, 2014.

Fulbrook, Mary. *Anatomy of a Dictatorship: Inside the GDR 1949–1989*. Oxford: Oxford University Press, 1995. https://doi.org/10.1093/oso/9780198203124.001.0001.

Galle, Petra. *RIAS Berlin und Berliner Rundfunk 1945–1949: Die Entwicklung ihrer Profile in Programm, Personal und Organisation vor dem Hintergrund des beginnenden Kalten Krieges*. Munster: Lit Verlag, 2003.

Geerling, Wayne, Gary B. Magee, and Russell Smyth. "Occupation, Reparations, and Rebellion: The Soviets and the East German Uprising of 1953." *The Journal of Interdisciplinary History* 52, no. 2 (Autumn 2021): 225–50. https://doi.org/10.1162/jinh_a_01698.

Gélieu, Claudia von, *Barnimstraße 10: Das Berliner Frauengefängnis 1868–1974*. Berlin: Metropol Verlag, 2014.

Gellately, Robert. *The Gestapo and German Society: Enforcing Racial Policy 1933–1945*. Oxford: Oxford University Press, 1990. https://doi.org/10.1093/acprof:oso/9780198228691.001.0001.

Gerber, Stefan, Werner Greiling, and Marco Swiniartzki. "Einleitung." In Gerber, Greiling, and Swiniartzki, *Thüringen im Industriezeitalter*, 7–24.

–, eds. *Thüringen im Industriezeitalter: Konzepte, Fallbeispiele und regionale Verläufe vom 18. Bis zum 20. Jahrhundert*. Vienna: Böhlau Verlag, 2019. https://doi.org/10.7788/9783412513313.

Geserick, Günther, H. Strauch, and Ingo Wirth. "120 Jahre Leichenschauhaus in Berlin-Mitte: Das älteste Institut für gerichtliche Medizin/Rechtsmedizin in Deutschland soll geschlossen werden." *Rechtsmedizin* 17, no. 2 (April 2007): 77–82. https://doi.org/10.1007/s00194-007-0428-0.

Geserick, Gunther, Klaus Vendura, and Ingo Wirth. "University Institute of Legal Medicine in Berlin Celebrates its 175th Anniversary." *Forensic Science, Medicine and Pathology* 4 (December 2008): 262–6. https://doi.org/10.1007/s12024-008-9051-y.

– *Zeitzeuge Tod: Spektakuläre Fälle der Gerichtsmedizin*. Leipzig: Militzke, 2001.

Ginzberg, Carlo. *The Cheese and the Worms: The Cosmos of a Sixteenth-Century Miller*. Translated by John Tedeschi. Baltimore: Johns Hopkins University Press, 1980.

Glaser, Hermann. *The Rubble Years: The Cultural Roots of Postwar Germany 1945–1949.* New York: Paragon House, 1968.

Graham-Dixon, Francis. *The Allied Occupation of Germany: The Refugee Crisis, Denazification and the Path to Reconstruction*. London: I.B. Taurus, 2013. https://doi.org/10.5040/9780755621392.

Grashoff, Udo. "Outwitting the Gestapo? German Communist Resistance Between Loyalty and Betrayal." *Journal of Contemporary History* 57, no. 2 (April 2022): 365–86. https://doi.org/10.1177/0022009421997906.

Greenberg, David F., ed. *Crime and Capitalism: Readings in Marxist Criminology.* Philadelphia: Temple University Press, 1993.

Greenblatt, Stephen. *Shakespearean Negotiations: The Circulation of Social Energy in Renaissance England*. Berkeley: University of California Press, 1988. https://doi.org/10.1525/9780520908529.

Grodsky, Morris, Keith Wright, and Paul L. Kirk. "Simplified Preliminary Blood Testing: An Improved Technique and a Comparative Study of Methods." *Journal of Criminal Law, Criminology, and Police Science* 42, no. 15 (1951): 95–104. https://doi.org/10.2307/1140307.

Grossman, Atina. "Grams, Calories, and Food: Languages of Victimization, Entitlement and Human Rights in Occupied Germany, 1945–1949." *Central European History* 44, no. 1 (March 2011): 118–48. https://doi.org/10.1017/S0008938910001202.

Grotewohl, Otto. "Für eine ungeteilte deutsche Republik: 'Entwurf einer Verfassung für die Deutsche Demokratische Republik.' Rede auf der 5. Sitzung des Deutschen Volksrates 22. Oktober 1948." In *Im Kampf Um Die Einige Deutsche Demokratische Republik: Reden Und Aufsätze*, 247–80.

– *Im Kampf um die Einige Deutsche Demokratische Republik: Reden und Aufsätze. Band I Auswahl aus den Jahren 1945–1949.* Berlin: Dietz Verlag, 1954.

– "Die westlichen Besatzungsmächte zerreißen Berlin (1 November 1948)." In *Im Kampf Um Die Einige Deutsche Demokratische Republik: Reden Und Aufsätze*, 281–7.

– *Über Politik, Geschichte und Kultur – Ausgewählte Reden und Schriften 1945 bis 1961.* Berlin: Dietz Verlag, 1979.

Guenther, Irene. "Out of the Ruins: Fashioning Berlin, 1945-1952." *Fashion Theory* 21, no. 4 (2017): 391–421. https://doi.org/10.1080/1362704X.2016.1272780.

Haase, Norbert, and Hans-Michael Borgas. "Bau- und andere Geschichten aus dem Kriminalgericht Moabit (eine Führung durch das 'Neue' Kriminalgericht)." In *Das Neue Kriminalgericht in Moabit: Festschrift zum 100. Geburtstag am 17 April 2006*, edited by Alois Wosnitzka. Berlin: BWV Berliner Wissenschafts-Verlag, 2006.

Hall, Claire M. "An Army of Spies? The Gestapo Spy Network 1933–45." *Journal of Contemporary History* 44, no. 2 (April 2009): 247–65. https://doi.org/10.1177/0022009408101250.

Harenberg, Helmut. *Die Chronik Berlins*. Dortmund: Chronik Verlag, 1986.

Harrington, Daniel F. *Berlin on the Brink: The Blockade, the Airlift, and the Early Cold War*. Lexington: University of Kentucky Press, 2012.

Heineman, Elizabeth. "The Hour of the Woman: Memories of Germany's 'Crisis Years' and West German National Identity." *American Historical Review* 101, no. 2 (April 1996): 354–95. https://doi.org/10.1086/ahr/101.2.354.

– *What Difference Does a Husband Make?: Women and Marital Status in Nazi and Postwar Germany*. Berkeley: University of California Press, 1999. https://doi.org/10.1525/9780520937314.

Herber, Friedrich. *Gerichtsmedizin unterm Hakenkreuz*. Leipzig: Militzke Verlag, 2002.

Herzog, Dagmar. "Desperately Seeking Normality: Sex and Marriage in the Wake of War." In *Life After Death: Approaches to a Cultural and Social History of Europe During the 1940s and 1950s*, edited by Richard Bessel and Dirk Schumann, 161–92. Cambridge: Cambridge University Press, 2003. https://doi.org/10.1017/CBO9781139052344.008.

Hett, Benjamin Carter. *Death in the Tiergarten: Murder and Criminal Justice in the Kaiser's Berlin*. Cambridge, MA: Harvard University Press, 2004. https://doi.org/10.4159/9780674038615.

Heubner, Wolfgang O.L. "Education in the Shadow of the Iron Curtain." *Science* 118, no. 3057 (1953): 121–4. https://doi.org/10.1126/science.118.3057.121.

Hilbrandt, Hanna. *Housing in the Margins: Negotiating Urban Formalities in Berlin's Allotment Gardens*. Oxford: Wiley, 2021. https://doi.org/10.1002/9781119540946.

Hilton, Laura J. "The Black Market in History and Memory: German Perceptions of Victimhood from 1945 to 1948." *German History* 28, no. 4 (December 2010): 479–97. https://doi.org/10.1093/gerhis/gh1.

Hinckeldey-Stiftung, ed. *Berliner Polizei von 1945 bis zur Gegenwart*. Introduction by Laurenz Demps. Berlin: SAGA Egmont, 2019. Ebook.

Hinds, Lynn Boyd, and Theodore Windt. *The Cold War as Rhetoric: The Beginnings 1945–1950*. New York: Praeger, 1991.

Hobbs, Mark. "'Farmers on Notice': The Threat Faced by Weimar Berlin's Garden Colonies in the Face of the City's *Neues Bauen* Housing Programme." *Urban History* 39, no. 2 (May 2012): 263–84. https://doi.org/10.1017/S0963926812000053.

Hopfe, Christian. *Berlin-Charlottenburg: Handel, Handwerk und Gewerbe in alten Bildern*. Erfurt: Sutton Verlag, 2017.

Horz, Carlo M., and Moritz Marbach, "Economic Opportunities, Emigration Opportunities, Emigration and Exit Prisoners." *British Journal of Political Science* 52, no. 1 (2022): 21–40. https://doi.org/10.1017/S0007123420000216.

Hudemann, Rainer, and Rolf Wittenbrock. *Stadtentwicklung im deutsch-französisch-luxemburgischen Grenzraum (19. und 20.Jh.), Développement *urbain dans la région frontalière France-Allemagne-Luxemburg (XIXe-XX$_{e}$ s.).* Saarbrücken: SDV Saarbrücker Druckerei und Verlag, 1991.

Inglis, Fred. *The Cruel Peace: Everyday Life in the Cold War.* New York: Basic Books, 1991.

Jaeger, Felix, and Joachim Gabka, "In Memoriam Erwin Gohrbandt." In *Handbuch der plastischen Chirurgie,* edited by Erwin Gohrbandt, Joachim Gabka, and Alfred Berndorfer, ix. Berlin: Walter de Gruyter, 1972.

Jähner, Harald. *Aftermath: Life in the Fallout of the Third Reich, 1945–1955.* Translated by Shaun Whiteside. New York: Vintage Books, 2021.

Jarausch, Konrad, and Hannes Siegrist, eds. *Amerikanisierung und Sowjetisierung in Deutschland 1945–1970.* Frankfurt, a.M.: Campus Verlag, 1997.

Jasch, Hans-Christian, and Christoph Kreutzmüller, eds. *The Participants: The Men of the Wannsee Conference.* Translated by Charlotte Kreutzmüller-Hughes and Jane Paulick. New York: Berghahn, 2017.

Johnson, Eric. *Urbanization and Crime: Germany 1871–1914.* Cambridge: Cambridge University Press, 1995. https://doi.org/10.1017/CBO9780511572524.

Johnson, Eric, and Eric Monkkonen, eds. *The Civilization of Crime: Violence in Town and Country Since the Middle Ages.* Champaign: University of Illinois Press, 1996.

"Kaiser as a Tilemaker." *New York Times,* 20 March 1911, 4.

Kellenbach, Katharina von. *The Mark of Cain: Guilt and Denial in the Post-War Lives of Nazi Perpetrators.* New York: Oxford University Press, 2013. https://doi.org/10.1093/acprof:oso/9780199937455.001.0001.

Kleist, Reinhard. *Berliner Mythen.* Hamburg: Carlsen Verlag, 2016.

Kloiber, Andrew. "Brewing Relations: Coffee, East Germany, and Laos." *Gastronomica* 17, no. 4 (Winter 2017): 61–74. https://doi.org/10.1525/gfc.2017.17.4.61.

Knopp, Guido, ed. *Die große Flucht: Das Schicksal der Vertriebenen.* Munich: Econ Ullstein List Verlag GmbH & Co., 2001.

Knopp, Guido, and Anja Greulich. "Der große Treck." In Knopp, *Die große Flucht,* 16–8.

Koerner, Silvia. "Kinderalltag Ende der vierziger Jahre." LeMO-Zeitzeugen, Lebendiges Museum Online, Stiftung Haus der Geschichte der Bundesrepublik Deutschland. Accessed 6 July 2021. https://www.hdg.de/lemo/zeitzeugen/silvia-koerner-kinderalltag-ende-der-vierziger-jahre.html.

König, Stefan. *Vom Dienst am Recht: Rechtsanwälte als Strafverteidiger im Nationalsozialismus.* Berlin: Walter de Gruyter, 1987. https://doi.org/10.1515/9783110894325.

Krone, Andreas. "Die Nachkriegsjahre (1945–1949)." In Stadt Plauen and Der Oberbürgermeister, *Plauen 900,* 318.

Kunze, Gerhard. *Grenzerfahrungen: Kontakte und Verhandlungen zwischen dem Land Berlin und der DDR 1949–1989.* Berlin: Walter de Gruyter, 1999.

Lachmund, Jens. "Exploring the City of Rubble: Botanical Fieldwork in Bombed Cities in Germany after World War II." *Osiris* 18, no. 1 (2003): 234–54. https://doi.org/10.1086/649386.

Ladd, Brian. *The Ghosts of Berlin: Confronting German History in the Urban Landscape.* Chicago: University of Chicago Press, 1997. https://doi.org/10.7208/chicago/9780226467603.001.0001.

Lagerwey, Mary Deane. "The Third Reich, Nursing, and AJN." *AJN The American Journal of Nursing* 109, no. 8 (August 2009): 44–9. https://doi.org/10.1097/01.NAJ.0000358496.14549.d9.

Large, David Clay. *Berlin*. New York: Basic Books, 2000.

Lemke, Michael. "Eine deutsche Chance? Die innerdeutsche Diskussion um den Grotewohl-Brief vom November 1950 auf der Entscheidungsebene." *Zeitschrift fur Geschichtswissenschaft* 44, no. 2 (1996): 25–40.

Liang, His-Huey. *The Berlin Police Force in the Weimar Republic.* Berkeley: University of California Press, 1970. https://doi.org/10.1525/9780520318762.

Loy, Thomas. "Werbeflächen in Berlin: 2500 Berliner Litfaßsäulen werden abgebaut." *Der Tagesspiegel*, 30 January 2019. https://www.tagesspiegel.de/berlin/2500-berliner-litfasssaulen-werden-abgebaut-5542054.html.

Luther, Bernd. "Zum Wirken des Chirurgen Erwin Gohrbandt (1890–1965) für die Berliner Universität, den Magistrat der Stadt und die Berliner Chirurgische Gesellschaft." *Zeitschrift für ärztliche Fortbildung* 84, no. 19 (1990): 1005–8. PMID: 2270698.

Lutz, Friedrich August. "The German Currency Reform and the Revival of the German Economy." *Economica* 16, no. 62 (May 1949): 122–42. https://doi.org/10.2307/2549853.

Major, Patrick. *Behind the Berlin Wall: East Germany and the Frontiers of Power.* Oxford: Oxford University Press, 2009. https://doi.org/10.1093/acprof:oso/9780199243280.001.0001.

Mallach, Hans Joachim, ed. *Geschichte der Gerichtlichen Medizin im deutschsprachigen Raum*. Lübeck: Schmidt-Römhild, 1996.

Mallmann, Klaus-Michael, and Gerhard Paul. "Omniscient, Omnipotent, Omnipresent? Gestapo, Society and Resistance." In *Nazism and German Society, 1933–1945*, edited by David Crew, 166–96. London: Routledge, 2013.

Malycha, Andreas, and Peter Jochen Winters. *Die SED: Geschichte einer deutschen Partei.* Munich: Verlag C.H. Beck, 2009.

März, Jascha. "Zwischen Politik und Interessenvertretung: Die Verbände der politischen Opfer des Nationalsozialismus in der Bundesrepublik Deutschland von 1947 bis 1990." PhD diss., Universität zu Köln, 2016.

May, Ernest R. "America's Berlin: Heart of the Cold War." *Foreign Affairs* 77, no. 4 (July–August 1998): 148–60. https://doi.org/10.2307/20049037.

McFarland-Icke, Bronwyn Rebekah. *Nurses in Nazi Germany: Moral Choice in History*. Princeton: Princeton University Press, 1999. https://doi.org/10.1515/9780691221403.

Medhurst, Martin J., Robert L. Ivie, Philip Wander, and Robert L. Scott. *Cold War Rhetoric: Strategy, Metaphor, and Ideology*. New York: Greenwood Publishing Group, 1990.

Meyer, Beate, Hermann Simon, and Chana Schütz, eds. *Jews in Nazi Berlin: From Kristallnacht to Liberation*. Chicago: University of Chicago Press, 2009.

Meyer, Sibylle, and Eva Schulze. *Von Liebe sprach damals keiner: Familienalltag in der Nachkriegszeit*. Munich: Beck, 1985.

Millington, Richard. "'Crime Has No Chance': The Discourse of Everyday Criminality in the East German Press, 1961–1989." *Central European History* 50, no. 1 (March 2017): 59–85. https://doi.org/10.1017/S0008938917000036.

Miltenberger, Sonja. *Jüdisches Leben am Kurfürstendamm*. Berlin: Text-Verlag, 2011.

Mittmann, Wolfgang. *Gladow-Bande: Die Revolverhelden von Berlin*. Berlin: Das Neue Berlin, 2003.

Moeller, Robert G. "Germans as Victims? Thoughts on a Post–Cold War History of World War II's Legacies." *History and Memory* 17, nos. 1–2 (Spring–Winter 2005): 145–94. https://doi.org/10.2979/his.2005.17.1-2.145.

– "On the History of Man-Made Destruction: Loss, Death, Memory, and Germany in the Bombing War." *History Workshop Journal* 61, no. 1 (Spring 2006): 103–34. https://doi.org/10.1093/hwj/dbi057.

– *Protecting Motherhood: Women and the Family in the Politics of Postwar West Germany*. Berkeley: University of California Press, 1993. https://doi.org/10.1525/9780520311190.

– "Reconstructing the Family in Reconstruction Germany: Women and Social Policy in the Federal Republic, 1949–1955." *Feminist Studies* 15, no. 1 (Spring 1989): 137–69. https://doi.org/10.2307/3177825.

– "The 'Remasculinization' of Germany in the 1950s: Introduction." *Signs: Journal of Women in Culture and Society* 24, no. 1 (Autumn 1998): 101–6. https://doi.org/10.1086/495319.

– "War Stories: The Search for a Usable Past in the Federal Republic of Germany." *The American Historical Review* 101, no. 4 (October 1996): 1008–48. https://doi.org/10.2307/2169632.

Möhr, Bodo. *Rudolf-Virchow-Krankenhaus: 1906–1981*. Berlin: Rudolf-Virchow-Krankenhaus, 1981.

Moltke, Wilhelm von. "The Evolution of Berlin's Urban Form Through History, Illustrated by Selected Examples." In *Views of Berlin: From a Boston Symposium*, edited by Gerhard Kirchhoff, 277–97. Boston: Birkhäuser Boston, 1989. https://doi.org/10.1007/978-1-4899-6715-2_23.

Monkkonen, Eric. *Crime, Justice, History*. Columbus: Ohio State University Press, 2002.

Monteath, Peter. "A Day to Remember: East Germany's Day of Remembrance for the Victims of Fascism." *German History* 26, no. 2 (April 2008): 195–218. https://doi.org/10.1093/gerhis/ghn003.

Moorhouse, Robert. *Berlin at War*. New York: Basic Books, 2010.

Mouton, Michelle. "Missing, Lost, and Displaced Children in Postwar Germany: The Great Struggle to Provide for the War's Youngest Victims." *Central European History* 48, no. 1 (March 2015): 53–78. https://doi.org/10.1017/S0008938915000035.

Müller, Fritz. "Die Schweinezucht und Schweinehaltung in Thüringen: Eine Geschichtliche, Statistische und Züchterische Abhandlung." PhD diss., Thüringischen Landesuniversität zu Jena, 1929.

Naimark, Norman. *The Russians in Germany: A History of the Soviet Zone of Occupation, 1945–1949*. Cambridge, MA: Harvard University Press, 1997.

Naumann, Gerd. "Die Zerstörung Plauens in der Schlussphase des Zweiten Weltkriegs." In Stadt Plauen and Der Oberbürgermeister, *Plauen 900*, 312–23.

– "Prolog-der Aufsteig der NSDAP in Plauen." In Stadt Plauen and Der Oberbürgermeister, *Plauen 900*, 270–9.

Nebe, Julia, and Jan Kleinmanns. "Wenn der Paladin krank wurde – Hermann Görings Leibarzt Ramon von Ondarza." In *Die Ärzte der Nazi-Führer: Karrieren und Netzwerke*, edited by Mathias Schmidt, Dominik Groß, and Jens Westemeier, 167–89. Berlin: Lit Verlag Dr. W. Hopf, 2018.

Orwell, George. "You and the Atom Bomb." *Tribune*, 19 October 1945. https://www.orwellfoundation.com/the-orwell-foundation/orwell/essays-and-other-works/you-and-the-atom-bomb/.

Pike, David. *The Politics of Culture in Soviet Occupied Germany, 1945–1949*. Stanford: Stanford University Press, 1992.

Pollak, Hans. *Tatort Sektorengrenze: Berliner Kriminalfälle der Nachkriegszeit*. Berlin: Verlag Neues Leben, 1994.

Potter, Pamela M. *Art of Suppression: Confronting the Nazi Past in Histories of the Visual and Performing Arts*. Berkeley: University of California Press, 2016. https://doi.org/10.1525/california/9780520282346.001.0001.

Pross, Christian, and Rolf Winau, eds. *Nicht misshandeln: Das Krankenhaus Moabit. 1920–1933. Ein Zentrum jüdischer Ärzte in Berlin; 1933–1945, Verfolgung-Widerstand-Zerstörung*. West Berlin: Edition Hentrich, 1984.

Ranft, Andreas, and Stefan Selzer, eds. *Städte aus Trümmern. Katastrophenbewältigung zwischen Antike und Moderne*. Göttingen: Vandenhoeck & Ruprecht, 2004.

Rechtien, Renate, and Karoline von Oppen, eds. *Local/Global Narratives*. Amsterdam: Brill, 2007. https://doi.org/10.1163/9789042032132.

Reckewerth, Ulf. "Rein verhungern kannste: Zur frühen Geschichte des Rudolf Virchow-Krankenhauses – Konzept und Realisierung des letzten Städtischen Krankenhauses Berlin." PhD diss., Universität Berlin, 1999.

Reichardt, Sven. "Violence and Community: A Micro-Study on Nazi Storm Troopers." *Central European History* 46, no. 2 (June 2013): 275–97. https://doi.org/10.1017/S0008938913000617.

Reiher, Monika. "Tendenzen der städtebaulichen Entwicklung Charlottenburgs seit 1945." In Ribbe, *Von der Residenz zur City*, 497–629.

Reinsch, Ruth Helene. *Currency Reform and Reconstruction of the West-German Economy, 1948–1949*. Lexington: University Press of Kentucky, 1997.

Reuß, Ernst. *Berliner Justizgeschichte*. Berlin: Berlin Verlag, 2000.

Reuß, Hermann. "Kleinere Beiträge: Rechtsanwalt Dr. Arno Weimann." *Juristische Rundschau* 1964, no. 5 (1964): 173. https://doi.org/10.1515/juru.1964.1964.5.173.

Reuter, Elke, and Detlef Hansel. *Das kurze Leben der VVN von 1947 bis 1953: Die Geschichte der Vereinigung der Verfolgten des Naziregimes in der sowjetischen Besatzungszone und in der DDR*. Berlin: Edition Ost, 1997.

Ribbe, Wolfgang. "Die Anfänge Charlottenburgs in der Residenzlandschaft um Berlin." In Ribbe, *Von der Residenz zur City*, 11–38.

–, ed. *Von der Residenz zur City: 275 Jahre Charlottenburg*. Berlin: Colloquium Verlag, 1980.

Richie, Alexandra. *Faust's Metropolis: A History of Berlin*. New York: Carroll and Graf, 1998.

Rigden, Ian. "The Battle of Berlin, April – May 1945." In *A History of Modern Urban Operations*, edited by Gregory Fremont-Barnes, 151–83. Camberley, Cham: Palgrave Macmillan, 2020. https://doi.org/10.1007/978-3-030-27088-9_6.

Roseman, Mark. *The Wannsee Conference and the Final Solution*. New York: Picador, 2002.

Rott, Joachim. *"Ich gehe meinen Weg ungehindert geradeaus": Dr. Bernhard Weiß (1880–1951) Polizeivizepräsident in Berlin. Leben und Wirken*. Berlin: Frank & Timme GmbH, 2010.

Royle, Nicholas. *The Uncanny*. Manchester: Manchester University Press, 2003.

Rubenhold, Hallie. *The Five: The Untold Lives of the Women Killed by Jack the Ripper*. Boston: Mariner Books, 2019.

Ruble, Alexandria N. "Creating Postfascist Families: Reforming Family Law and Gender Roles in Postwar East and West Germany." *Central European History* 53, no. 2 (June 2020): 414–31. https://doi.org/10.1017/S0008938920000175.

Rurüp, Reinhard. "'Parvenue Polis' and 'Human Workshop': Reflections on the History of the City of Berlin." *German History* 6, no. 3 (1988): 233–49. https://doi.org/10.1093/gh/6.3.233.

Sabrow, Martin, ed. *Verwaltete Vergangenheit: Geschichtskultur und Herrschaftslegitimation in der DDR*. Leipzig: Akademische Verlangsanstalt, 1997.

Salzborn, Samuel. "The German Myth of a Victim Nation: (Re-)presenting Germans as Victims in the New Debate on their Flight and Expulsion from Eastern Europe." In *A Nation of Victims? Representations of German Wartime Suffering from 1945 to the Present*, edited by Helmut Schmitz, 87–104. Amsterdam: Brill, 2007. https://doi.org/10.1163/9789401204453_006.

Schaefer, Sagi. "Growing Apart: Farmers and the Division of Germany, 1945–1965." *Central European History* 50, no. 4 (December 2017): 493–513. https://doi.org/10.1017/S0008938917000929.

Schertz, Georg. "100 Jahre Prozesse in Moabit auch ein Spiegel ihrer Zeit." In *Das Neue Kriminalgericht in Moabit: Festschrift zum 100. Geburtstag am 17 April 2006*, edited by Alois Wosnitzka, 30–9. Berlin: Berliner Wissenschafts-Verlag, 2006.

Schilling, Willy. *Hitlers Trutzgau: Thüringen im Dritten Reich*. Jena: Verlag Dr. Bussert & Stadeler, 2005.

Schivelbusch, Wolfgang. *In a Cold Crater: Cultural and Intellectual Life in Berlin 1945–1948*. Translated by Kelly Barry. Berkeley: University of California Press, 1998. https://doi.org/10.1525/9780520377868.

Schlosser, Nicholas J. "Creating an 'Atmosphere of Objectivity': Radio in the American Sector, Objectivity and the United States' Propaganda Campaign Against the German Democratic Republic, 1945–1961." *German History* 29, no. 4 (December 2011): 610–27. https://doi.org/10.1093/gerhis/ghr067.

Schmale, Holger. *Chausseestrasse: Berliner Geschichte in Brennglas*. Berlin: Ch. Links Verlag, 2022.

Schmidt, Waltraud. "Judisches Leben." In Stadt Plauen and Der Oberbürgermeister, *Plauen 900*, 310.

Schmiedecke, Ralf. *Berlin-Tiergarten*. Erfurt: Sutton Verlag, 2011.

Schmitz, Helmut. *A Nation of Victims? Representations of German Wartime Suffering from 1945 to the Present*. Amsterdam: Brill, 2007. ProQuest Ebook Central.

Schorske, Carl. "Freud's Egyptian Dig." *New York Review of Books*, 27 May 1993. https://www.nybooks.com/articles/1993/05/27/freuds-egyptian-dig/.

Schütte, Dieter. *Charlottenburg*. Berlin: Colloquium Verlag, 1988.

Sennet, Richard. *Flesh and Stone: The Body and the City in Western Civilization*. New York: W.W. Norton, 1994.

Service, Hugo. "Reinterpreting the Expulsion of Germans from Poland, 1945–9." *Journal of Contemporary History* 47, no. 3 (July 2012): 528–50. https://doi.org/10.1177/0022009412441652.

Shlaim, Avi. "Britain, the Berlin Blockade and the Cold War." *International Affairs* 60, no. 1 (Winter 1983): 1–14. https://doi.org/10.2307/2618926.

– *The United States and the Berlin Blockade 1948–1949: A Study in Crisis Decision-Making*. Vol. 2 of *International Crisis Behavior*. Berkeley: University of California Press, 2022.

Sigmund, Monika. *Genuss als Politikum: Kaffeekonsum in beiden deutschen Staaten*. Oldenburg: De Gruyter, 2015. https://doi.org/10.1515/9783110348736.

Slevogt, Esther. *"Aufgebaut werden durch dich die Trümmer der Vergangenheit" (Jes. 58,12): Das jüdische Gemeindehaus in der Fasanenstrasse*. Berlin: Hentrich & Hentrich, 2009.

Smith, Helmut Walser. *The Butcher's Tale: Murder and Anti-Semitism in a German Town*. New York: W.W. Norton, 2003.

Snelders, Stefan, and Toine Pieters. "Speed in the Third Reich: Metamphetamine (Pervitin) Use and a Drug History from Below." *Social History of Medicine* 24, no. 3 (December 2011): 686–99. https://doi.org/10.1093/shm/hk1.

Spencer, Robert. "Berlin: One Year of the Wall." *International Journal* 17, no. 4 (December 1962): 420–25. https://doi.org/10.1177/002070206201700406.

Spilker, Dirk. *The East German Leadership and the Division of Germany: Patriotism and Propaganda 1945–1953*. Oxford: Oxford University Press, 2006. ProQuest Ebook Central. https://doi.org/10.1093/acprof:oso/9780199284122.001.0001.

Stadt Plauen and Der Oberbürgermeister, eds. *Plauen 900. Von den Anfängen bis in die Gegenwart. Zum 900-jährigen Jubiläum der ersten urkundlichen Erwähnung Plauens*. Dresden: Sandstein Verlag, 2021.

Stangl, Paul. "The Soviet War Memorial in Treptow, Berlin." *Geographical Review* 93, no. 2 (2003): 213–36. https://doi.org/10.1111/j.1931-0846.2003.tb00030.x.

Steege, Paul. "Holding on in Berlin: March 1948 and SED Efforts to Control the Soviet Zone." *Central European History* 38, no. 3 (September 2005): 417–49. https://doi.org/10.1163/156916105775563580.

– *Black Market, Cold War: Everyday Life in Berlin, 1946–1949*. Cambridge: Cambridge University Press, 2007.

Steinweis, Alan E. *Kristallnacht 1938*. Cambridge, MA: Harvard University Press, 2009. https://doi.org/10.4159/9780674054653.

Steppe, Hilde. "Nursing in the Third Reich." *History of Nursing Society Journal* 3, no. 4 (1991): 21–37.

– "Nursing Under Totalitarian Regimes: The Case of National Socialism." In *Nursing History and the Politics of Welfare*, edited by Ann Marie Rafferty, Jane Robinson, and Ruth Elkan, 10–27. New York: Routledge, 1997.

Suwala, Lech, Nina Pfeil, Max Lange, Linus Pfeiffer, and Hans-Hermann Albers. "Der Zentrumbereichskern Wilmersdorfer Straße in Berlin-Charlottenburg in Zeiten multipler Krisen – gestärkt durch Nutzungsmischung, Kiezcharakter und Kuration?" *Standort* 47, no. 3 (September 2023): 220–8. https://doi.org/10.1007/s00548-023-00866-x.

Tatar, Maria. *Lustmord: Sexual Murder in Weimar Germany*. Princeton: Princeton University Press, 1995. https://doi.org/10.1515/9780691216218.

Teo, Hsu-Ming. "The Continuum of Sexual Violence in Occupied Germany, 1945–49." *Women's History Review* 5, no. 2 (2006): 191–218. https://doi.org/10.1080/09612029600200204.

Timpe, Julia. *Nazi-Organized Recreation and Entertainment in the Third Reich.* London: Palgrave Macmillan, 2017. https://doi.org/10.1057/978-1-137-53193-3.

Tobin, Patrick. "No Time for 'Old Fighters': Postwar West Germany and the Origins of the 1958 Ulm *Einsatzkommando* Trial." *Central European History* 44, no. 4 (December 2011): 684–710. https://doi.org/10.1017/S0008938911000690.

Tribe, Keith. "The 1948 Currency Reform: Structure and Purpose." In *50 Years of the German Mark: Essays in Honour of Stephen F. Frowen*, edited by Jens Hölscher, 15–55. London: Palgrave Macmillan, 2001.

Ucko, Peter. "Unprovenanced Material Culture and Freud's Collection of Antiquities." *Journal of Material Culture* 6, no. 3 (November 2001): 269–322. https://doi.org/10.1177/135918350100600302.

Verk, Sabine. *Laubenleben: Eine Untersuchung zum Gestaltungs-, Gemeinschafts- und Umweltverhalten von Kleingärtnern*. Münster: Waxmann Verlag, 1994.

Verlohren, Urte. *Krankenhäuser in Groß-Berlin: Die Entwicklung der Berliner Krankenhauslandschaft zwischen 1920 und 1939.* Berlin: BeBra Wissenschaft Verlag, 2019.

Voss, Ludwig. *Geschichte der höheren Mädchenschule: Allgemeine Schulentwicklung in Deutschland und Geschichte der höheren Mädchenschulen Kölns*. Opladen: Verlag Stocky & Co., 1952.

Wagner, Patrick. *Hitlers Kriminalisten*. München: Verlag C.H. Beck, 2002.

Walkowitz, Judith. *City of Dreadful Delight: Narratives of Sexual Danger in Late-Victorian London*. Chicago: University of Chicago Press, 1992. https://doi.org/10.7208/chicago/9780226081014.001.0001.

Weikart, Richard. "The Role of Darwinism in Nazi Racial Thought." *German Studies Review* 36, no. 3 (October 2013): 537–56. https://www.jstor.org/stable/43555141.

Weinmann, Sarah, ed. *Unspeakable Acts: True Tales of Crime, Murder, Deceit, and Obsession*. New York: Ecco, 2020.

Welch, David. "Nazi Propaganda and the *Volksgemeinschaft*: Constructing a People's Community." *Journal of Contemporary History* 39, no. 2 (April 2004): 213–38. https://www.jstor.org/stable/3180722.

Wirth, Ingo, Hansjürg Strauch, and Georg Radam. *Das Berliner Leichenschauhaus und das Institut für Gerichtliche Medizin 1886–1986*. Berlin: Humboldt-Universität zu Berlin, 1986.

Wosnitzka, Alois, ed. *Das Neue Kriminalgericht in Moabit: Festschrift zum 100 Geburtstag am 17. April 2006*. Berlin: Berliner Wissenschafts-Verlag, 2006.

Zahra, Tara. *Reconstructing Europe's Families After World War II.* Cambridge, MA: Harvard University Press, 2011.

Zatlin, Jonathan R. *The Currency of Socialism – Money and Political Culture in East Germany*. Cambridge: Cambridge University Press, 2007.
Zierenberg, Malte. *Berlin's Black Market: 1939–1950*. Washington, DC: Palgrave MacMillan, 2015. https://doi.org/10.1007/978-1-137-01775-8.
Zuckmayer Carl. *Der Hauptmann von Köpenick. Ein deutsches Märchen in drei Akten*. Frankfurt a.M.: Fischer Verlag, 1931.

Index

Note: Figures are indicated by an *f* appended to the page number and maps are indicated by an *m*.

GERMAN AND EUROPEAN STUDIES

General Editor: James Retallack

1 Emanuel Adler, Beverly Crawford, Federica Bicchi, and Rafaella Del Sarto, *The Convergence of Civilizations: Constructing a Mediterranean Region*
2 James Retallack, *The German Right, 1860–1920: Political Limits of the Authoritarian Imagination*
3 Silvija Jestrovic, *Theatre of Estrangement: Theory, Practice, Ideology*
4 Susan Gross Solomon, ed., *Doing Medicine Together: Germany and Russia between the Wars*
5 Laurence McFalls, ed., *Max Weber's 'Objectivity' Revisited*
6 Robin Ostow, ed., *(Re)Visualizing National History: Museums and National Identities in Europe in the New Millennium*
7 David Blackbourn and James Retallack, eds., *Localism, Landscape, and the Ambiguities of Place: German-Speaking Central Europe, 1860–1930*
8 John Zilcosky, ed., *Writing Travel: The Poetics and Politics of the Modern Journey*
9 Angelica Fenner, *Race under Reconstruction in German Cinema: Robert Stemmle's Toxi*
10 Martina Kessel and Patrick Merziger, eds., *The Politics of Humour: Laughter, Inclusion, and Exclusion in the Twentieth Century*
11 Jeffrey K. Wilson, *The German Forest: Nature, Identity, and the Contestation of a National Symbol, 1871–1914*
12 David G. John, *Bennewitz, Goethe, Faust: German and Intercultural Stagings*
13 Jennifer Ruth Hosek, *Sun, Sex, and Socialism: Cuba in the German Imaginary*
14 Steven M. Schroeder, *To Forget It All and Begin Again: Reconciliation in Occupied Germany, 1944–1954*
15 Kenneth S. Calhoon, *Affecting Grace: Theatre, Subject, and the Shakespearean Paradox in German Literature from Lessing to Kleist*
16 Martina Kolb, *Nietzsche, Freud, Benn, and the Azure Spell of Liguria*
17 Hoi-eun Kim, *Doctors of Empire: Medical and Cultural Encounters between Imperial Germany and Meiji Japan*
18 J. Laurence Hare, *Excavating Nations: Archaeology, Museums, and the German-Danish Borderlands*
19 Jacques Kornberg, *The Pope's Dilemma: Pius XII Faces Atrocities and Genocide in the Second World War*
20 Patrick O'Neill, *Transforming Kafka: Translation Effects*
21 John K. Noyes, *Herder: Aesthetics against Imperialism*
22 James Retallack, *Germany's Second Reich: Portraits and Pathways*
23 Laurie Marhoefer, *Sex and the Weimar Republic: German Homosexual Emancipation and the Rise of the Nazis*

24 Bettina Brandt and Daniel L. Purdy, eds., *China in the German Enlightenment*
25 Michael Hau, *Performance Anxiety: Sport and Work in Germany from the Empire to Nazism*
26 Celia Applegate, *The Necessity of Music: Variations on a German Theme*
27 Richard J. Golsan and Sarah M. Misemer, eds., *The Trial That Never Ends: Hannah Arendt's* Eichmann in Jerusalem *in Retrospect*
28 Lynne Taylor, *In the Children's Best Interests: Unaccompanied Children in American-Occupied Germany, 1945–1952*
29 Jennifer A. Miller, *Turkish Guest Workers in Germany: Hidden Lives and Contested Borders, 1960s to 1980s*
30 Amy Carney, *Marriage and Fatherhood in the Nazi SS*
31 Michael E. O'Sullivan, *Disruptive Power: Catholic Women, Miracles, and Politics in Modern Germany, 1918–1965*
32 Gabriel N. Finder and Alexander V. Prusin, *Justice behind the Iron Curtain: Nazis on Trial in Communist Poland*
33 Parker Daly Everett, *Urban Transformations: From Liberalism to Corporatism in Greater Berlin, 1871–1933*
34 Melissa Kravetz, *Women Doctors in Weimar and Nazi Germany: Maternalism, Eugenics, and Professional Identity*
35 Javier Samper Vendrell, *The Seduction of Youth: Print Culture and Homosexual Rights in the Weimar Republic*
36 Sebastian Voigt, ed., *Since the Boom: Continuity and Change in the Western Industrialized World after 1970*
37 Olivia Landry, *Theatre of Anger: Radical Transnational Performance in Contemporary Berlin*
38 Jeremy Best, *Heavenly Fatherland: German Missionary Culture and Globalization in the Age of Empire*
39 Svenja Bethke, *Dance on the Razor's Edge: Crime and Punishment in the Nazi Ghettos*
40 Kenneth S. Calhoon, *The Long Century's Long Shadow: Weimar Cinema and the Romantic Modern*
41 Randall Hansen, Achim Saupe, Andreas Wirsching, and Daqing Yang, eds., *Authenticity and Victimhood after the Second World War: Narratives from Europe and East Asia*
42 Rebecca Wittmann, ed., *The Eichmann Trial Reconsidered*
43 Sebastian Huebel, *Fighter, Worker, and Family Man: German-Jewish Men and Their Gendered Experiences in Nazi Germany, 1933–1941*
44 Samuel Clowes Huneke, *States of Liberation: Gay Men between Dictatorship and Democracy in Cold War Germany*
45 Tuska Benes, *The Rebirth of Revelation: German Theology in an Age of Reason and History, 1750–1850*
46 Skye Doney, *The Persistence of the Sacred: German Catholic Pilgrimage, 1832–1937*

47 Matthew Unangst, *Colonial Geography: Race and Space in German East Africa, 1884–1905*
48 Deborah Barton, *Writing and Rewriting the Reich: Women Journalists in the Nazi and Post-war Press*
49 Martin Wagner, *A Stage for Debate: The Political Significance of Vienna's Burgtheater, 1814–1867*
50 Andrea Rottmann, *Queer Lives across the Wall: Desire and Danger in Divided Berlin, 1945–1970*
51 Jeffrey Schneider, *Uniform Fantasies: Soldiers, Sex, and Queer Emancipation in Imperial Germany*
52 Alexandria N. Ruble, *Entangled Emancipation: Women's Rights in Cold War Germany*
53 Johanna Schuster-Craig, *One Word Shapes a Nation: Integration Politics in Germany*
54 Kiran Klaus Patel, ed., *Tangled Transformations: Unifying Germany and Integrating Europe, 1985–1995*
55 Abraham Rubin, *Conversion and Catastrophe in German-Jewish Émigré Autobiography*
56 Ulf Brunnbauer, Philipp Ther, Piotr Filipkowski, Andrew Hodges, Stefano Petrungaro, and Peter Wegenschimmel, *In the Storms of Transformation: Two Shipyards between Socialism and the EU*
57 Alexandra Birch, *Hitler's Twilight of the Gods: Music and the Orchestration of War and Genocide in Europe*
58 Jeffrey Champlin, *Born Again: Romanticism and Fundamentalism*
59 Priscilla Layne, Michelle James, and Lisabeth Hock, eds., *Afrika and Alemania: German-Speaking Women, Africa, and the African Diaspora*
60 Douglas McKnight, *Echoes of the Past: Carinthian Slovene Memories of the Second World War*
61 James McSpadden, *A Continent of Colleagues: Backroom Politics and Interwar Democracy*
62 Katharina Clausius and Claudia Clausius, eds., *(Re)Centring the Weimar Republic*
63 Richard Bodek, *Death in the Rubble: The Female Killer Who Stalked Cold War Berlin*